Becoming Strength

By

Sharon Trammell

E-book ISBN: 979-8-9912848-103

Paperback ISBN: 979-8-9912848-0-6

Hardcover ISBN: 979-8-9912848-2-0

Acknowledgments

I want to take this opportunity to thank Hand in Hand Farms for all of their support. The individuals affiliated with this organization have supported my family immensely throughout our story. I also want to thank Organic Photography for the contribution of capturing the front cover photo of me. The pictures turned out amazing! I want to thank my teacher, spiritualist Cynthia Greer, for her support during this journey as well. She saw the vision of this book before I had even started it. Her own writing has also helped me evolve. Finally, I want to say a thank you to the entire Ford Family Foundation. The support I received from this foundation during my educational journey, changed my life.

Dedication

I am dedicating this book to my son Luke and my daughter Carroll. You guys are my ride-or-die adventure buddies. You two have pushed me to better myself constantly. I love you more than you will ever know! I also want to dedicate this book to Cynthia, my teacher. Your love and patience have helped me transform my life as I have experienced soul healing. Finally, to my best friend. You believed in me when no one did, "Wifey".

Forward

I always knew that writing a book was part of my soul's mission. As a little girl, I often wrote novels, folding papers in half and putting my ideas into words with a ballpoint pen. I knew from the beginning that writing would be part of my life. This is my story. All of it is true. I have changed the names and descriptions of the characters, to protect their identities.

My conscious, human self, never planned to live through so much pain or heartbreak. I didn't know that I would have to go through a living hell to get to where I could look back and realize that this all shaped me. My hope, in writing this, is to encourage others. If I did it, and survived, you can too. As one of my favorite people told me many times, "if I can do it, you can do it better!" What I have gone through, I would never wish on anyone. However, the experiences have taught me that anything I set my mind to, I can, and will achieve. Freedom is possible if we choose our own wellbeing over the judgments of others. If we allow the light to enter our lives and choose to not feed our fears, we can be free from any circumstance or situation, no matter how ugly and dark. Everything is in the mind. Change and healing is always an option, no matter what one has been through. May this book touch you at a soul level and may you feel the warmth of divine love touch your own life through my story.

With Love, Sharon

Contents

Chapter One

I woke up, trying to remember my dreams. I knew I had dreamed about my mom and it was her birthday. But we weren't celebrating because she didn't expect anything from any of us. She just smiled and asked if anyone needed anything. I tried to think hard. "Maybe it's because it's almost Christmas," I thought. As I lay there waking up, a memory drifted to me. So long ago, such a different lifetime.

The year was 2019. It was two days before Christmas. The pickup was running and we were getting ready to go to my parents'. The kids were already loaded in their car seats in the back. My mom's birthday was two days after Christmas and we always celebrated both at the same time. But I had been crying all afternoon, again. I had told Mac that I wasn't going. I didn't deserve to get yelled at, to be told that I was a bad mom because my house wasn't perfectly clean. I had told him it definitely wasn't fair that I wasn't allowed to go to the gym before going to my parents! I knew I needed to submit to him, but it made me so angry that I couldn't get in a workout before going. But getting into the truck was how we would work through the problem. We would drive for two hours and talk it out. It would be okay and by the time we got to my parents', it would all be swept under the rug. For tonight anyway. We would work it out, like regular couples did. I would submit and if I didn't then Mac would remind me how I wasn't being a good wife. He would remind me that biblical wives would never defy their husbands. He would remind me how disappointed my father would be, that my father hadn't raised a rebellious woman and that none of my family knew who I was anymore since I had started disobeying his orders. I knew all this. I still refused to go. Besides, he was so angry I didn't feel safe letting him drive us. I told him to go by himself. He threatened to call my dad. My dad always talked me down; this was his job as my father, to make sure I submitted to my husband, my current authority.

Tonight, this wasn't going to do it. As expected, he called my dad. I wanted to be liked by my dad, so I listened. To the same speech it always was. About how Mac wasn't perfect but he was trying to do his best to be the leader in the family. "I'm not taking a side here, Sharon. I am trying to help you guys work through your issues but I will listen to your side too," my dad was saying. I explained how I had wanted to go to the gym before coming so I could keep to my regular lifting schedule. I explained how I was trying really hard to keep the baby weight off, to keep myself healthy, so that I could take care of my kids. I left out the part about how much crying I had done recently. I left out how I felt insignificant and ignored, how we had been fighting constantly and going to the gym was the only way I knew to clear my head. My dad took a deep breath, chuckling. After a moment,

"Well, you know what I think…gyms really are pointless. All these people lifting weights when there are miles of hiking trails, roads you could be riding or you could even go on a run right from your house if you have to! Women wandering around in little shorts that let their butts hang out, while the men struggle to control themselves with all that temptation, it's just not a great environment for any married woman. The only men who should see that stuff is their husbands. Clothes like that are for the bedroom! It's no wonder men look. You know, one time there was a woman at my work who dressed like that, and I started having thoughts about her. I had to go and apologize to your mother afterwards for even thinking like that. But I wouldn't have, if that woman had kept her body covered like she should have!"

He was going on a tangent now. I had heard this all before. I knew how it went. But I still continued explaining myself. My father patiently explained that, if my husband didn't want me to go to the gym, he must have a good reason. He must be trying to protect me, because he really was a good man. I started crying again.

Why did no one understand me? I knew they all loved me, but it was so frustrating that they wouldn't actually listen to me. I gave the phone back to my husband. My dad kept talking, not knowing I wasn't listening. I went inside the house. Mac put the phone down and came in to retrieve me. We were in the living room. I was across from him. "I am not going", I repeated, glaring at him. I knew how angry it made him when I defied him.

But I was finished. I couldn't do two hours of arguing. I couldn't do more lectures from my father and I certainly wasn't in the mood to watch my husband flirt with my sister again, as he had so many times before when our extended family was together. Mac lunged at me suddenly, grabbing me by the hair, dragging me angrily towards the door.

I fought to get free, pushing his hands off me, running outside towards the truck, which was still running. The kids were both still in their car seats in the back, unsure what was going on. Luke, my five-year-old, looked scared. His big brown eyes were open wide and he was looking around frantically, trying to see what the commotion was. He looked so small back there, wearing a brown hoody, his tiny legs, clad in jeans, hanging down from the booster seat. His nut-brown hair, which I had just cut into a mohawk, was standing straight up even more than normal.

Carroll, my blonde haired, blue eyed two-year-old, was still too young to know what was going on, so she just sat there in wide eyed silence, looking at her brother. She held tightly to her pink polka dot blanket that never left her side. It was tucked tightly around her, covering the unicorn pajamas she wore. I reassured them both. I got in, backing out before Mac had a chance to follow me out of the house. I didn't know where I was going. I drove for about fifteen minutes, pulling over then and reaching for my phone. I shakily dialed a number to a friend, unsure what to do. I explained to Bethany what had happened. Without hesitation, she told me to call the police.

I sighed, blinking back tears. "I really don't want to get the law involved, he didn't actually hurt me or leave any marks" I explained. "He's just angry again and I need a break to let him cool down. I'll go home tomorrow." "No," she said, "you need to document this". She said I needed to call and let them know what happened. She said I could do it without pressing any charges, but that it was important in the case that it happened again. I hadn't known where I was going, but as I hung up the phone, I had an idea. Ten minutes later, I pulled the truck in to Dex's yard, turning around to see if any headlights had followed me.

Dex lived far out in the woods at the very end of a long gravel drive, at the foothills of two mountains. I sat in my truck for a moment, taking in a deep breath, still shaking. I had never run away from Mac before. As I sat there, I felt bad for him, worried how he was probably lonely at home, probably already afraid that I was leaving him or about to spend the night with another man. I knew about his fears and I didn't want to make them worse. He was probably on the phone with my dad again, explaining how he didn't know what to do next. Or maybe he was in his truck, racking his brain to figure out where I had gone. He would have no reason to check here, at Dex's house.

Dex was an old school hippie, with flowing gray hair and beard. He was in his early sixties. He looked a little like Jesus probably had, minus the robe and sandals. He did, however, wear loose fitting cotton pants, and T-shirts from bands that played in the seventies and eighties when he had been a younger man. He loved music, having played some sort of tropical sounding flute when he had lived in a hut in South America during his younger years. He sometimes brought his flutes out at hippie gatherings, even now. He believed in Zen and connecting with nature through long meditations in the grass, smoking too much weed, and lighting incense.

He lived by extending peace and light to everyone, including flies, ants, and mice. They all had an equal right to be here, he believed, even if they were in his house. What if some bigger force tried to kill me because I was in his territory? He had asked me once when I noted sugar ants crawling on his countertop. Dex had always been a family friend. In one way, it made sense to me that I had ended up here in his little oasis from the world. Surrounded by tall trees, with a house built by his own hands, a safe haven from the storm that was brewing at home.

When I had unloaded both children, I walked quickly across the lawn and up the little path towards the door. While I had been driving, dusk had set in. It was now almost completely dark and there was a sliver of a moon in the sky, shrouded by clouds. It had rained most of the day, but the veil of clouds was thin enough now that they had drifted aside, as if to give me a glimpse of the moon to light my walk to the door. From the outside, especially under the night sky, Dex's house looked like a forest hut that had been built with scraps of wood. Though somewhat dilapidated, it always felt welcoming.

I didn't take time to look around. I pushed open the door, knocking as I peeked my head into the little living room. Dex was sitting on his straight-backed leather and wood chair, watching a bike race on his double screen computer. I didn't waste time. I blurted out everything, biting my lip in shame as I felt slightly helpless explaining that Mac had hurt me.

When I was finished, Dex just nodded. He didn't look surprised. I had never opened up to anyone except my parents, but he simply told me I could stay as long as I needed to. "I do think you should call the police though," he told me. I was still afraid, so he reached for his landline phone and dialed the sheriff's non-emergency line. He explained that he was concerned for my safety and didn't know if Mac would try to follow me here.

When the sheriff arrived a half an hour later, he let me know he was recording so that he could document the conversation. He asked me what happened. Dex explained how I had gotten there and didn't want to call, but that he had called anyway. I told them the story. I stressed to them, how I didn't want to press charges. "I don't want anything on his record," I explained. "I am trying to be fair; I know he didn't actually mean to hurt me or anything, but I was scared for my safety. That's the only reason I left". They told me that they wouldn't say anything to Mac about it, but that, if there were any marks on me, they would be forced to press charges. I assured them there weren't. I was completely fine. The sheriff who had done the talking gave me a business card and then they left.

I set up the kid's beds on the wood floor, which was covered by a large oriental rug that had lost too many threads, long ago. I spread blankets with couch cushions to make it comfortable. I tucked Luke in with the bunchy down comforter Dex had handed me. Dex had set another larger comforter on the coffee table, piling two pillows on top. I turned to the old couch to set up my bed. It was propped up on cement blocks, with two-by-fours supporting the cement blocks to keep it off the wood floor, which looked as though it had been made from left over lumber scraps and then painted to touch it up.

This couch was a deep velvet red and had probably originated sometime during the '80's. It had collected dust which just added to the look. Running my hands along it, I felt how scratchy and uncomfortable it was. It would do, though. I was thankful to have a place to stay at all, especially in this weather, which had turned to freezing fog by now. I tucked myself onto the couch, picking up little Carroll and tucking her in next to me. This couch wasn't big enough for two, but she had never done anything except sleep with me. At home, we were working on getting her to sleep in her own bed, but I usually let her come in and tuck in next to me when she got scared. I kissed her little forehead, brushing the fine curls out of her eyes. I pulled the thick comforter up to her chin, turning on my side to make more room on the narrow couch.

The lights were off and the place smelled of incense and lingering marijuana smoke, with a hint of wood smoke. It was toasty warm, thanks to the wood stove that sat on cement blocks in the opposite corner of the room. Dunagen, the black Pitbull, had finally settled in his dog bed next to the computer. The children were still talking. They were asking why we were here. "When are we gonna' go back to dad?" Luke asked.

Carroll was clinging to me, as she had been the entire time since we got there. I assured them we would go back; Dad would be in a better mood tomorrow. I told them I was sorry for messing up their night, for not taking them to their grandparents'. The guilt was settling in hard now. I knew my dad would be calling me in the morning, questioning as to why I had thought running away was the answer. I sighed, looking at the door. It was locked.

I knew Mac didn't know where I was; surely, he wouldn't follow me even if he figured it out. He wouldn't go to those extremes. He was safe for me, he just made mistakes when he got angry. He would never purposely hurt me or the children, I told myself. I told Luke to try to go to sleep. I kissed Carroll again, pulling her little body against mine. Tomorrow would be a new day and we would make things right with dad. We would make it up to him for ruining his plans.

Chapter Two

We went home the next morning. It was Christmas Eve. Walking into the quiet house, on this special day, not seeing Mac anywhere, felt weird. I knew he normally was given Christmas Eve off from his work, so I wasn't sure where he was. The guilt of the day before hung heavily in my energy. I felt bad for leaving him. I had ruined the holiday for him and my parents. I hadn't had a choice though. I cleaned the house, tidying up everything that had been left yesterday during the chaos. I washed laundry and took Kitten, our brown and white hound pup, on a short walk, trying to hold the leash in one hand while holding Carroll's tiny hand in the other, reminding Luke to not run ahead too far.

The neighborhood was silent; I could feel the energy of families coming together, many staying from out of town, all feeling the anticipation of Christmas day looming in the air. It was a time of peace and celebration for many. Ironic, I thought, how the most peaceful and joyous time of the year had turned so chaotic in our home. At lunch, I made the kids a special meal with their favorite foods, hot dogs and mac n cheese. I decided to skip the gym for the day; the childcare wouldn't be open anyway. Also, I didn't want to ruffle feathers. I would go again in a couple days, after Mac and I had talked everything out.

As the day drew on, my anxiety began to grow. He still wasn't home and it was almost dusk. Darkness always came so fast in the winter. The sky, which was clear, began to turn a deep pink as the winter sunlight disappeared behind the hills in the distance to the west. Looking over the grass field across from our home, I saw the winter fog begin to roll in, lying low across the field, soon to rise and shroud the night sky from the stars that looked down on the quiet world. It didn't feel like Christmas Eve. Normally, we would be making an effort to spend time with the kids, gathering in our living room to watch Christmas carols and drink hot chocolate. I would have baked a variety of Christmas cookies and would allow the children to each pick two, only after they had eaten their dinner. We would pretend things were great as we watched the kids get excited about marshmallows in their hot chocolate and sprinkles on the cookies. Mac would make remarks that hurt and I would ignore them, savoring the taste of the warm hot chocolate as I tried to push the depression down and smile my way through the evening. Tonight wasn't so.

Luke was playing with Tinkertoys in his room at the end of the hall. Carroll was digging through her clothes looking for a Christmas dress in her little room across from the bathroom. I sat anxiously at the stained wood table in the small dining room, staring at my Bible. I felt too guilty to read it. Surely, if Mac got home and saw me, he would make a comment about it. He would remind me that I was a fake Christian. A real Godly woman wouldn't ever leave her husband. He would tell me that I was a hypocrite. He would shake his head and tell me how disappointed my dad was. And he would be right. God was likely looking down right now, shaking H*is* head in disappointment at my behavior from the day before.

After I had sat for another five minutes, tapping my fingers nervously on the table, I heard the low rumble of Mac's truck outside the window. The familiar sound of the garage door rolling up came next. Kitten, who had been stretched out on her blanket underneath the rocking chair by the fireplace, let out a low howl as she perked her ears and turned towards the door. Mac peeked his head in, an angry scowl on his face. His grey eyes burned with intense anger as he looked me over. His black hair, which had begun greying early for a man who was only thirty, was damp. I wondered if it had started raining.

He came all the way in, folding his muscular arms across his chest. "You were with Corey, weren't you?" I looked at him then, seeing how tense his whole body was. A chill ran over me. "I always knew this was about him, this was about you having someone else!" he remarked. I told him no. I hadn't been with anyone else. I had known it would come to this. I knew he would bring up Corey. He slammed the door behind him with enough force that our wedding picture, which sat above the piano, shook, on the living room wall. "Where were you last night, then? If you didn't have anything to hide, you would tell me where you went. I am your husband; you know you shouldn't hide things from me." He glared into my soul, unwilling to break the stare.

Biting my lip, I replied in a tiny voice. "I only left to give you time to calm down because talking about this stuff when we are both mad, never works" I pleaded with him, looking for any glimmer of understanding in his dark eyes. "I'm not leaving you. Can we please talk about what happened?" No words for a moment. "I knew this was about Corey," he said after the pause. He then turned around, opened the door to the garage, went out, and slammed it behind him. The curtains in the kitchen window fluttered out and back in against the window.

I sat down at the kitchen table again, resting my hands in my arms. I began to cry, trying to stay silent so I didn't scare the kids. I was trying so hard to work through things. I was trying to do what was best and safest for myself and the children, while still working with him like a good wife would. I didn't understand why he couldn't just listen to me. I felt guilty for leaving him, but I only left for my own safety and to help him calm down. I would never desert our marriage. I wished that he could just see it from my perspective. I wished my dad would understand and that they both wouldn't assume the worst about me. It hurt.

Sitting there, my mind began to drift to the events of the day before. The anger came back to me as I thought about what had led to this latest fight. It had started when I asked him to come to the gym with me. I had explained that Corey and the others wanted to meet him. His response was to tell me he needed alone time. He said he was going for a drive in the woods and would be back in a couple hours, in time to leave for my parents. Well, if he's gone, I had thought, I can go to the gym without making him angry. I could get in my programmed workout and be back in time to drive the two hours to my parents' house. I had put on leggings, making sure to choose a tank top that was long enough to cover my legs and butt. I didn't want him to think I was going specifically to show it off. I didn't want guys staring at it, and I would show him by dressing carefully. I had gone to find my truck key then, looking on the shelf in the kitchen where I always placed my keys, next to the phone charger and the little stick of lip balm. It wasn't there. I looked on the table. Not there either. I checked our bedroom and then the bathroom counter. I checked my coat that was hanging in the shoe closet, knowing that I never left my keys in my pockets. I called for Luke, who hadn't seen the keys. I looked on the work bench in the garage, noticing the safe was locked. As I turned away, I saw something that made me angry. My key was inside the safe. He had locked my keys in the safe so I couldn't leave.

Instantly, I filled with rage. I didn't ask much of him. I cleaned and cooked and took care of the children full time. I had just begun homeschooling Luke, who would be entering kindergarten the next fall. I managed the money and set up automatic payments for all of the family bills. I mowed the grass and split the firewood in the summer. I weeded the flowerbeds and grew vegetables that I always preserved at the end of summer. I raised chickens in a little coop in the backyard, making sure they always had food, water, and fresh scraps from the table. I walked Kitten and picked up her poop. I washed the vehicles, often surprising him with vacuuming out his truck and hand washing it on the weekends while he slept in. I obliged his mother on her weekly visits to spend time with my children, though it was all about her. I stayed awake past midnight, even though my kids would wake up by 5 or 6, knowing that he wanted his alone time in the garage after work, but he would also feel hurt if I fell asleep without him. I gave him what he wanted in the bedroom, even though I never felt any love or connection from him during those times.

I had tried my best to explain how the gym would keep me looking hot for him. It would keep me fit and keep my butt nice and round, the way he liked it. I was doing this for him, at least in part. I was trying so hard to be a good wife. I began to cry again, thinking about how I had only ever wanted to be a supportive wife. I wanted to fulfill the role of the Proverbs 31 woman. To be available to my husband, to care for my children and keep my home in order, to keep myself physically fit and healthy. It was part of being a good wife. This was what God had called me to, after all. I would do everything to be the perfect wife, but I refused to give up the gym. Not now. Not when I had just been introduced to powerlifting. I wanted to compete.

I put the kids to bed that night, trying to stay calm. I read a book to Luke, tucking him in, before going to my own bed. Mac was still gone. I didn't really care. I showered, thinking about what personal record I might hit next in the gym. Powerlifting was saving me and if I focused on it, I didn't have to think of all the pain. I didn't have to think of how my life was falling apart, from the inside out. My mind began wandering to the first day I had been made aware of what powerlifting was. I had been training in the gym for about 3 months at the time. One Wednesday in early fall, I was getting ready to go do squats, when Mac had called. He had forgotten his wallet and needed me to bring it to where he was working. His crew was stationed about an hour from us, working on clearing some powerlines in a residential neighborhood near one of my favorite hiking trails. I loved coming to bring him things at work, sometimes bringing him coffee or hot lunch if I could. However, I knew that the childcare at the gym closed by 12 that day, and in order to make it back in time to take advantage of the childcare to complete my lifting session, I would need to hurry. In addition to taking an hour to drive to his location from our house, it was forty minutes in the opposite direction to my gym. I packed up the kids and went to find him. When I got close to the pin-drop he had sent me, I pulled over to text him that I was there. He didn't reply.

I drove farther down the road, looking for his lift truck. Still, I couldn't find him. I spent about 30 minutes looking for him, then called again. He didn't answer this time either. He was probably in a tree somewhere. Oh well, I thought, I'll leave the whole lunch box next to a road sign, hidden in the deep grass, but obvious enough that he can find it. No one was around and the road sign was right at the pin-drop he had sent me. I tucked the lunch box into its hiding spot, sent him a quick text and a picture of where I had put it, and got in the truck to leave. I had gotten ten minutes away, when he called me. I answered immediately, putting the phone on speaker. He asked me to come back and said he was waiting by the lunch box now.

I reluctantly turned around, knowing that this was cutting into my time to go to the gym now. As soon as I got back to him, he kissed the kids and then immediately told me how stupid it was that I had left the lunchbox unattended. He explained that someone might have stolen it and then where would we be? I could have risked our bank account being compromised, and all because I was so focused on getting in a workout. "I wish you would think more about our family, Sharon!" he chided. "You know that you could just go on a hike on the way home instead of wasting money on a gym membership just so that you could show off your body to all those thirsty guys at the gym."

He continued on for another 15 minutes, my frustration growing with every moment. I *needed* this time at the gym. By the time I was allowed to leave, I was in tears. I cried the entire drive to the gym. I felt so helpless. I felt ignored and misunderstood. When I pulled into the gym parking lot, I wiped away my tears, putting the truck in park. I dropped off the kids at the gym childcare and started warming up in the squat rack. I felt guilty for putting my own agenda above my family's needs. Maybe Mac was right and I shouldn't have wasted the gas to drive to the gym. Maybe I really was in the wrong; after all, I wasn't being submissive. I knew what my dad would say about this.

I refused to look around at anyone. Surely, they could all see what a bad wife I was. I wore the shame of my selfishness on my face as I stood there, deep in my negative thoughts. No one would want to be friends with a woman like this, I told myself.

I was trying to avoid the tears. I blinked hard, fumbling with the squat belt, getting ready for another set. "Hey, how's it going? Need a spot?" I looked up to see a man of average height, about 25, with thick blonde hair that was combed over to one side. He had white teeth and a bright smile. He looked friendly. I took out my earphones and smiled, slightly grudgingly. I wasn't in the mood for a conversation; I just wanted to slump down, bury my head in my arms, and cry. "You look like you're really strong! I've been watching you squat and you are definitely doing more than a lot of the girls in here! That's impressive!" he continued.

I was slightly interested, although I felt unworthy of the praise. I thanked him. If only he knew what I had done, to be here. He wasn't done talking though. He introduced himself as Corey Jacobs and asked my name. He told me he was a weightlifting coach. He continued on to explain that, if I wanted, I could come train with him and two other guys who were both signed up for their first powerlifting competition. He wasn't sure if I competed or not but he felt I would be competitive. I was intrigued. He told me a gym name. "Jonah and Lucas will be there with me Saturday morning for our deadlift session. See you there?" That infectious smile again. He seemed truly happy about life and wanted to include me as a fellow lifter.

That weekend, I decided to lift with them. The childcare was open for half a day Saturday morning, so I could get in at least a little bit of the session with all of them. Corey introduced me to Jonah and Lucas, telling me that if I wanted to compete on their team, we could possibly win a team award. He showed me some technique improvements and was patient with me while I adjusted my form.

It may have been a little thing, but the kindness meant so much. Someone telling me I was doing something right felt so good. Being encouraged and told that I was good at something felt good. They were all deadlifting that day so I decided to as well. I wanted to pull something

I hadn't pulled before, so I went for 245 pounds. It came off the ground easily. "Go for 275!!" they told me unanimously. They loaded the bar with two 45s and a 25 on each side; I got set up. I tightened my belt, getting into position and pulling on the bar. It was the ugliest lift ever, but it came off the ground and I successfully locked my knees at the top.

They told me this was more than any girl they had seen pull. They said that, because I was 24, I was a year past being able to compete in the junior category, but I would probably win the open women's category if I competed. They said I should come watch when they did their competition. I determined to go. I knew it would cause strife in my marriage, but I also knew I really wanted to compete at some point. Watching a competition would be the perfect way to get involved. I felt positive with the community I was starting to build at the gym. I wanted people around me who built each other up, people who encouraged one another and created positivity.

When I got home that night, Mac had been making coffee. "Babe, I deadlifted 275 today!" I told him, still on a high from getting a personal record. I pulled out my phone to show him the video. "Nice! I suppose that was extra fun for Corey to watch! It probably made him hard seeing you in leggings like that! Did you kiss him after that, to celebrate?"

My face fell instantly. "I seriously just wanted you to know that I lifted more than I have ever lifted! But you had to make it about him!" I responded. "It's not my fault you are choosing to hoe around with men like that who are just inviting you so they can eventually sleep with you!" he said. This conversation strengthened my resolve. I would go watch them compete whether he wanted me to or not. I may not have a happy marriage, but I could take out my frustration on weightlifting and I would sure as hell have friends, whether I was allowed to or not. This had been my introduction to powerlifting. As I recalled all of it, I realized that the competition they had talked about was coming up in the near future. I still planned on going.

Chapter Three

Christmas morning came and we were up early. Mac's mom had offered to watch the children so that Mac and I could have a couple's date. Because we had no other family that would be in town for Christmas the whole family had agreed that we would celebrate together on New Years Eve, allowing for Christmas to be a day for each of our families to do things individually. It felt fake, but we were trying to work things out. Mac wanted to go target shooting, but I really wanted to get to my favorite river and wet a line to find a steelhead.

As excited as I was to fish, I knew it would be a time of conflict. Mac wasn't too impressed with the fact that I had caught a steelhead on my first trip going out to try, while he hadn't had any luck even after multiple trips. I had asked our friend to show me how to properly setup a bobber-and bead setup, the most common way that local anglers chose to fish for steelhead in the winter. Our friend had showed me how to rig my line, starting with a bobber stop, a small bead, followed by a ½ oz float bobber and inline weight. He had showed me how to setup a leader, including tying the egg loop onto the hook, tying a bead stop about three fingers width above the hook for the bead to sit on and then adding one or two small pieces of lead, known as split shot, to make sure I was properly fishing. Our friend had explained how steelhead fishing took a lot of patience. "A lot of people try without success for sometimes a year or two before they catch a fish. Lots of them give up, but the ones who stick it out eventually find the fish and have success."

After his little lecture, I had made my way to the first spot. After two casts, I had one on my line! Although Mac had told me good job, and that he was proud of me, secretly, I don't think he was impressed with the fact that it had been me and not him having instant success. I think it also hurt that our male friend, and not him, tried to coach me through it. He had hated our friend since that day, refusing to fish with him after this and discouraging me from keeping in contact with him as well.

Despite my husband's disdain for my success, I had continued to fish with just the kids. On one memorable day, I had even caught one with baby Carroll in the backpack on my back. Luke, who had been age 4 at the time, had grabbed the net and helped me scoop the fish out of the river, dragging it onto the bank. Walking back to my truck later, with my baby in the backpack, a fish slung over my shoulder, and Luke dragging the net, had been the best victory walk ever.

The old guys at the parking lot had been standing there complaining about the lousy fishing conditions and how no one was catching anything. When they saw me, a young girl in a pink jacket and teal wading pants, with my entourage of small children, they looked at one another in shock, unsure how to respond. "Where is your husband?" one had asked, peering down the trail behind me. I had explained that I fished alone a lot, leaving out the part about how my husband couldn't stand to see me succeed. I felt proud of the fact that I could do this alone. Deep down, I also felt the sting of Mac's jealousy and the fact that he refused to come with me. Central to our arguments recently had been the fact that I had the ability to go and do fun things like fishing while he was at work. He found it highly unfair that I had the flexibility to do this. Besides my responsibilities at home, I also found the time to manage a part-time home business, altering wedding dresses and sewing custom creations for my community. Many times, I would rise by 4 in the morning, making sure I had time to read my Bible before making Mac's lunch and then working on alterations until my husband woke up, when I would stop work and make his breakfast and coffee.

I wanted to always be available to my family above anything. I had a fear of being a woman who was too focused on outwardly things like her career. I wanted my family to come first. Even so, the tension was mounting. Because of the pressure he had been putting on me relating to this situation, I had recently asked him if I could get a part time job. He had told me no. He didn't want me working outside the home. At all. Providing for a family was a man's job. I had talked with him about working weekends so that we would have extra cash and also because I felt he needed to experience parenting more than he was.

I had reasoned that, if I got the experience of working outside the home and he got experience taking care of children solo, which he had never done, we may be able to reconcile our differences by experiencing what the other dealt with daily. He had turned down this idea as well, without even a moment to think about it. It seemed there was no solution I could suggest that would solve any of our issues. "What are you staring off into space about this time?" Mac jarred me from my thoughts. I had been staring vacantly out the window, contemplating everything, feeling like a counterfeit for even going on a date with him in the first place. This all felt like a show. No one knew the truth. No one knew that we fought constantly, not even his parents. Still, we had just pulled into the parking lot and it was time to act like a happy couple who fished together. I would take a selfie for social media, captioning it, "couples who fish together, stay together!" I had needed to remind myself of this often lately.

The fishing that day was slow. I showed Mac how to tie an egg loop knot and he rigged up some translucent red hard beads I had provided. We tried four different holes, managing, miraculously, to not anger one another for several hours. The day was cold, the water was low and the fishing was slow. To wrap up the day, I suggested a spot where I had been told the fish liked to congregate on days similar to today, with less water in the system.

When we arrived at the spot I had suggested, the trail was still covered in blackberries. I felt it would be worth trying to get to anyway, but Mac didn't want to get scratched. I told him I wouldn't mind being the one to cut my way through the blackberries. This was a popular spot and others would benefit from this trail being made as the season progressed. My suggestion made him angry; he felt that I was threatening his manhood and ability to be the leader, by offering to be the one to whack my way through the blackberries. The fishing trip ended with him yelling at me, asking me why I always had to be in control. He reminded me that our marital problems stemmed from the fact that I always wanted to do his job and try to lead our marriage instead of letting him do that. If I was a submissive wife, he reminded me, I would have allowed him to choose the activity that day. As we drove home to collect our children, I wept softly in the passenger seat. I felt bad for controlling the day. I felt guilty for even asking to fish. Maybe he was right and I should simply have gone to the range to shoot with him. I had only wanted to help him get better at fishing and to bring the joy of angling to the one I loved the most, but my effort had ended up hurting us both.

Chapter Four

The holiday season dragged on, each day passing slowly and painfully. The days between Christmas and New Years always seemed to drag, feeling like a void of space before the reset known as the traditional new year arrived. The sky outside had been producing a heavy drizzle since Christmas night. Although we always hoped for snow on Christmas, the climate usually offered rain and cold, damp conditions. Because of the days of rain, I had kept the children in, only going out for short walks with Kitten, bundling up the little ones in rain boots and raincoats, letting them stomp in puddles for fifteen minutes, then bringing them in for hot chocolate and snuggles while reading them books.

As hard as I was trying to stay positive, the depression lingered. This time of the year was the hardest, there was no denying that. The dreary weather, combined with the never-ending tension I felt from Mac, was wearing me down. I asked Mac if we could have company one night that week. Somewhat grudgingly, he agreed. Albert and Daniella were two of the only people he liked. Mac wasn't a fan of most of the women I befriended, usually offering me a reason as to why he didn't feel they were good company for me. I understood, knowing that, as head of the household, it was his duty to help me pick good influences as friends. Still, it did get frustrating some times. I was glad he liked Albert and Daniella and their three girls. He had known Albert since childhood, having attended the Mennonite grade school with Albert, who had been a couple of grades ahead of him. He often asked Albert to help him with projects when his car was broken down; both of them were mechanics. Part of the reason for inviting them was that Albert needed to pick up his engine hoist after we had replaced the transmission on my pickup in September. It seemed Mac always chose people who he could benefit from to be our friends.

Albert and Daniella knocked on the door just as the gray clouds in the winter sky were turning to black outside the window. Mac was in the garage listening to rap music. I had been busy baking cornbread. A large pot of chili, made with pinto beans and ground turkey, sat simmering on the white stove top. I had placed a stack of red glass bowls on the dining room table, along with spoons, napkins and a glass jar of raw honey to top the cornbread I would serve. I opened the door and the smell of freshly baked cornbread wafted out into the cold street beyond.

Albert, who was tall and lanky and wore a baseball cap to cover his partially balding head, smiled between a gap in his front teeth. "Boy, does it smell good in there!" he remarked as I ushered them in, taking their coats and hanging them in the closet in the hallway. Daniella, who was preoccupied with helping her youngest, a six-year-old named Abigail, take off her pink coat, turned to him then. "I bet Mac is in the garage! Go find him so us ladies can catch up!" she said teasingly. After he had showed the older girl, Bridgette, where to put her rain boots, he meandered that way, peeking his head into the garage to find his friend. The couple's oldest child, who was already 17, had stayed home tonight.

After Luke had taken Abigail to see the table with his train tracks in his room, Daniella was able to take her own coat off, revealing beautiful black hair that reached almost to her waist. Her green eyes sparkled as she smiled at me, shaking her hair loose from the coat. Opposite from Albert, she was little, standing only maybe five feet. However, I never thought of her as little; her attitude was big and she knew exactly who she was. She would stand up to anyone who treated her in the wrong way. I admired her so much, although part of me felt uncomfortable with how outspoken she was; she had a mind of her own. Albert had left the Mennonite church before they had married. Although they were still closely connected to all of his family, who were devoutly religious, they stood out as a couple who had flown the coup of religion early on, not conforming to the gender roles of the cult.

Thirty minutes later, everyone's belly was full of warm chili, all having enjoyed the deliciousness of a hot, homecooked meal on a day like today. The drizzle carried on outside the window, but inside the house it was warm and comforting. The fire crackled in the woodstove and everyone felt warm and cozy. Having eaten, the men headed for the garage again, while Daniella and I washed dishes. Settling into the flowered fabric couch across from the fireplace, we were finally able to talk.

After a couple of minutes of calmly petting Kitten, who lay stretched out on the blue rug in front of the fireplace, Luke came up with the brilliant idea of jumping off the couch into a pile of blankets. Abigail helped him bring each comforter from the hall closet, piling them up to make a safe landing. They then took turns climbing up onto the arm of the couch, poising for their jump, and launching themselves feet first into the soft landing of down comforters and quilts made by the Mennonite women of Mac's family.

This game had been going on for about five minutes when Mac came in to check what all the ruckus was about. "Sharon, I can't believe you would let him jump off the couch like that! I can hear the thumping all the way in the garage! I really wish you would think before letting these kids run wild constantly!" he chided. I explained that Luke was having fun and I was supervising. It did no good. He continued,

"I go to work all day in the cold, climbing trees, while you sit around on your ass, scrolling on social media while the kids run wild. Often, I come home and the house is a disaster, just like it is tonight with all these blankets out! Your lack of attention to the mess makes me wonder who you are spending your time with…but then I remember, it's probably Corey at the gym…or outside of the gym!"

He turned around and slammed the door, shaking his head in disgust. I was embarrassed. Red crept up my neck and to my face. I put the backs of my hands against my warm cheeks, biting my bottom lip and looking away from Daniella, whose mouth had dropped open in shock. No one had a perfect marriage, but this outburst taking place in front of guests was humiliating. Daniella was dumbfounded, but not for the reason I had assumed. "You shouldn't let him talk to you like that, you know? He shouldn't put you down like that! It's not normal and he's treating you like a child!" she exclaimed. I sighed, still unable to meet her gaze. "Well, he's been upset a lot lately," I explained, after a pause. I stared out into the darkness, unwilling to look at her. "I have been spending a lot of time at the gym lately and the house does seem to be a mess because I always clean it and the kids mess it up again instantly. He thinks I don't get anything done." I blinked, trying to keep the tears at bay. I wouldn't break down in front of a friend. It was embarrassing enough that she had witnessed any of this in the first place. Daniella shook her head. "Come, I need to go to the grocery store and buy stuff for our New Year's Eve party. I was going to do it after we were done here, but let's you and me go do it right now!" she told me.

We loaded all four of the children into her black minivan and she put the van in reverse, slowly backing out into the quiet street. She began, keeping her eyes on the road as she moved the stick to drive, focusing on the street ahead. "You know I was married before Albert, right?" I hadn't known. Being in a community like this, it would be highly frowned upon for a Mennonite to marry someone who had been married previously. Albert had been brave to marry her and she had been brave to marry so close to a community full of judgment, such as his family's community. "It didn't end well and once I left my ex, he made my life hard every day after. He used to treat me this same way."

Her face, which was illuminated by a street light, looked sad. She told me how she had been married to Albert for almost ten years, and she agreed that marriage was challenging sometimes. "Albert pisses me off sometimes. Last week, he left dirty underwear in the clean laundry bin and I folded them and put them away for him, not knowing. No matter how annoying he gets though, he wouldn't *ever* treat me like I just saw

Mac treat you!" She looked straight at me. "When we get back, I need to talk to Mac about this separately."

The next morning, while I was frying his eggs for breakfast, I brought it up to Mac. He was sitting at the table watching YouTube on his phone. "So, what did Daniella say to you?" I turned from the oven, trying to make eye contact. He didn't look up, his eyes glued to the screen. "I really don't like her. The way she talked to me was disrespectful. Even Albert said he didn't like how she bosses him around all the time. If you keep spending time with her, you'll probably become like that."

Turning to the opposite counter, I ran cold water into the coffee pot, pouring it in to the 6-cup line and starting the coffee maker. Sighing, I turned away from him. I didn't want to be un-submissive. My dad always talked about Aunt Genevieve and Aunt Kathryn; they were the prime examples of un-submissive and worldly, immoral wives. He brought up his own mother often and how she had talked back to Grandfather. He often talked of how his biggest goal in life was to raise daughters who were submissive to their husband; this was the calling of God, to be wives who obeyed their husbands in everything. I wanted my father to be proud of me. I really did want Mac to be happy, too.

I rinsed out his coffee mug, pouring hot black coffee to the fill line. I added a splash of milk and a spoonful of sugar, the way he liked it. I finished making his lunch of sandwiches, freshly baked chocolate chip brownies, potato chips, and a piece of cornbread from the night before. I placed everything into his blue lunch box and put it by the door, along with his filled coffee mug. I grudgingly kissed him goodbye; no matter how bad things got, I always wanted the last thing before he left home, to be him receiving a kiss from his wife. I walked out to the garage to let Kitten out of her cage. I opened the sliding door and she went out to poop. Time to start another day.

Chapter Five

I didn't want to go, but I preferred spending the day with the in-laws to explaining that I didn't want to be there because we had been fighting again. I didn't even want to get in the same car with Mac. It was New Years eve, though, and there was an appearance to keep up. I packed up the kids and the strudel apple pie I had made to share, carefully wrapping it in a red bath towel to make sure it didn't spill in the car, or burn my feet, since I had just taken it out of the oven.

The ten-minute drive to Macs' parents' somewhat dumpy mobile home was silent. We had opted to drive the Pickup and I grudgingly let Mac drive. I didn't even look at him once. We had spent the morning fighting again; I had no energy to even interact at all. We had woken up slowly and I had patiently given into his desires, staying in bed with him for over an hour, making sure he felt appreciated, doing everything that made him happy. Secretly, I had hoped that this would be enough for him to allow me to go to the gym while he watched the children afterwards. I had gone only once this week and I was feeling the lack of energy that I always felt when I missed my regular workouts.

The morning had gone smoothly until I mentioned that I planned to get a quick workout before going to his parents at three pm. There was plenty of time. Could the kids stay home with Mac for an hour? I had asked timidly, afraid of his answer. It had begun then. He had told me he really needed some alone time this morning. He had asked why I always made everything about myself. He was the one who went to work all the time, giving up his time and energy all for the sake of his family, he had reminded me. I did nothing other than waste my time fishing and picking mushrooms and sleeping all the time. Why did I sleep so much? He asked then, noting how I always needed a nap during the day and had been so tired I hardly could get out of bed to get his lunches ready before work recently.

From there, things had only gotten worse. He was disappointed with the woman I had become lately. It wasn't who he had married, he remarked sadly. With this, he had left abruptly, shutting the garage door behind him with a bang. I had heard his pickup start, back up and backfire as he did a partial burnout on the way down our street. I had felt instantly angry. My only option now was to go on a run. Kitten needed to be walked too. How I would do that with a five-year-old, a two-year-old, a five-month-old puppy, and only one stroller, I didn't know. Mac had returned later in the day, kissing me and telling me he was excited for the delicious food his mom always made at New Years. Clearly his alone time had helped. There had been no mention of the fight or the fact that I had missed another day at the gym.

Now, two hours later, Mac used his patient voice to talk to Luke and Carroll, as he turned right onto the short driveway to his parents' house. It would have been a pretty driveway if they had maintained it. On both sides of the roadway, blackberry bushes had grown up, un-managed. Now, in the middle of winter, they were just ugly gray vines with leaves that were shiny wet in the drizzle that seemingly never stopped. On one side of the driveway, a little farther down, sat a car body that was probably from sometime in the late 1980s. It had likely been one of Mac's father's abandoned projects, long forgotten as he moved to the next thing. He had a pattern and it never involved completion, always bouncing from one thing to the next. One year, it had been starting a new home lawncare business. Another, it had been a dog grooming business. This had gone well for only a couple of months until he had discovered he didn't have patience for dogs, after allowing their own dog to get run over by a passing car. This year, it had been hiking across the US on foot. He had left, only announcing the journey to Mac's mom a week before he had quit his job as an online sales representative. Mac's mom, who had stayed home with Mac and his brothers for their entire childhood, had been forced to start a second job to pick up the slack and pay not only the home mortgage, but also the business expenses from the latest business venture. Bryan, Mac's Dad, might want to run it again, when he came back, he had reasoned.

Such was the way with this family. The men did as they pleased, while the women submissively held everything together, smiling and pretending their man meant well, keeping the family image to save themselves from embarrassment. Mac's family had been Mennonite from the time he was a baby, until three years ago. In the church, it had been easy for Bryan to hide his extracurricular activities like seeing multiple women. However, the abuse he had inflicted upon his boys had been harder to hide, especially when they showed up to the local

44

Mennonite school with black eyes or stripes on their backs. Although it was evident, most turned a blind eye to the obvious facts. What would they do, anyway? For most who followed the rigorous rules of the Mennonite church, abuse was simply part of keeping one's family in check. After all, a man was to be the leader of his family. This attitude had likely made it hard for church members, even the well-meaning ones, to intervene with the regular abuse that went on in the family. In spite of the freedom that Bryan had to behave in this unseemly way, he and Mac's mom, Amanda, had eventually left the church, saying that they felt their religious beliefs no longer aligned with the strict traditions and rules of the church.

Secretly, I wondered if all the impulse decisions that Bryan had been making recently were the result of being free from keeping up the image of a good church member. I also wondered what other mental health issues he might have, as his behavior seemed nothing short of strange, at best. As we pulled into the driveway, after passing an old train car that Bryan had used for storage, and then a broken-down garden tiller, two more car bodies, and a white work truck with the hood propped open, Mac pulled up in front of his mother's white sedan.

The yard was almost as messy as the driveway had been. The yellow mobile home, which had once been beautiful, looked old and tired with paint peeling on one side. Someone had begun replacing the siding on the east side; the home wrap rustled in the breeze where they had left it un-sided since last summer. A gutter with green moss growing on it hung down off the front porch. Smoke wafted from a chimney on the right side of the slanted roof which needed to be re-tiled. Last time we had been inside, I had seen a bucket where a leak had been allowing drips to slowly soak the outdated red carpet in the living room.

The yard, which was gracious in size and could have been well managed, was instead full of dandelions and dead grass that had never been mowed and was ankle length, despite the winter making it grow slower. The garden beds along the house looked as though they hadn't been weeded in years. An empty pig pen with a roof that had halfway caved in sat in the side yard next to a chicken pen that was no longer in use. Taking in the dilapidated sight, I silently got out and helped Carroll out of her seat. Mac came and offered to help me carry things. "Here babe, let me take that pie in!" He always seemed willing to help when his parents were within sight or hearing distance. Still, I had no words for Mac. I was still angry about the gym.

Mac's mom met us at the door, taking Carroll from my arms, hardly noticing me. Her white hair hung to her waist and her blue eyes sparkled at seeing her granddaughter again. She was short, with a big bust and proportions that only widened from there down. Mac's dad, on the other hand, who was about the same height, was skinny, almost too skinny. He looked like someone who had done too many drugs and could never keep on weight anymore. Maybe it was because he had; I could never be sure. He was missing most of his teeth, due to a continual lack of poor hygiene habits. He was missing all of his hair too, except for tufts of blackish gray that hung from the sides of his large head. His gray eyes looked deceptive and dishonest. I always felt he was doing things behind my back, no matter how friendly he acted to my face.

I helped Luke take his shoes off and he went to find his cousin Dane. Mac's middle brother, Alan, had recently moved back to live close to his parents after ten years as a pastor for a Mennonite church on the east coast where he had run a part time business on the side. I didn't mind Alan and his wife Rebekkah, although I felt they would probably judge me just as harshly as the rest of Mac's family if they knew the extent to which I was rebelling from my husband's command. I didn't really care anymore. We were here for appearances and that was it.

His entire family was devoutly religious, at least to the outside world. Mac's other brother Benjamin and his wife, with their eight children, had been missionaries for the past ten years in Zambia. I wondered if both brothers felt they needed to be extra religious, to make up for their father's lack of love for them. Or maybe religion was the only thing keeping them from turning to drugs and alcohol? The high that one got from attending church, from following a rule book, could help any person feel good about themselves.

The only one in the family who I had ever felt truly seen by, was Mac's grandma Dorothy. She had been my only friend when I first moved to marry Mac and start out in a new state and new town, alone, as an 18-year-old. She had never once judged me, and, although she didn't live here anymore, I knew she saw the marital struggles we were having. One day, after I had ignored her calls, finally answering out of guilt, she had told me she knew. I had never said anything, but she knew, because she had been through it once upon a time as well. She had told me once, after asking me not to tell her son, Mac's father, about all the abuse she had gone through at the hand of an alcoholic husband. Maybe this was why we were so close. She knew the dysfunction that ran in Mac's family and she didn't try to sugar coat it as something different. I wished she were here now, to help make the evening less awkward.

Mac's mom had prepared snacks for the evening, as was the family tradition on New Year's Eve. Processed cheese melted with ground beef and salsa made up a dip that she served with tortilla chips; everyone loved it. She had laid out trays of cheese and deli meats with crackers, a bowl of trail mix, a tray with veggies and ranch dip, and a mix of Chex cereal coated with melted chocolate chips, peanut butter, and powdered sugar. This snack was a favorite among the children. Rebekkah had brought a lemon meringue pie and leftover ham from their Christmas celebration.

After twenty minutes of small talk, Mac's mom announced that everything had been laid out to eat. Everyone got their plates and we sat around the dining room table. The darkness was settling in outside the dining room window as Bryan said a prayer and told everyone how thankful he was that we were all there. It would be a long night. I hoped Mac wouldn't insist on staying until midnight to welcome in the new year.

I wasn't excited about another year of struggles and fighting. "So, how's the gym been going, Sharon?" Mac's dad asked, breaking me out of my depressive thoughts. I didn't want to talk to him about it, knowing that whatever I said would likely get used against me later that night when Mac and I were alone. I briefly explained that I was doing more reps to build up my muscle mass and eventually I would reduce the reps and put more weight on the bar to go for a personal record lift.

Alan chimed in then, telling everyone how he had also been in the gym lately and he was benching more. Everyone acted amazed when I told them I had benched 135 for the first time. I was uncomfortable. It was all fake, a show that everyone put on because it was easier than asking why we weren't talking or commenting on the fact that I hadn't even looked at Mac that evening. This was how Mac's family lived. They all lived as if they were on camera, playing by a script, pretending there were no problems. It was better to be cheerful than honest.

Just then, Carroll announced from her high chair that she needed to poop. I sighed in relief and took her to the bathroom. I hoped she took a long time. At least in here I could be alone, away from constant stupid questions and the feeling that everyone was wondering what was up and judging me for my part in it.

Later, after pie, vanilla ice cream, and coffee for anyone who wanted some, Luke asked to stay up and watch fireworks. I reminded Mac that Luke had woken up early that morning and really needed his sleep. I thanked Amanda for dinner and took the kids to the car, sighing in relief as I made it into the cold and quiet darkness of their yard. Mac slowly came out, following me to the truck. Immediately upon shutting the door, he turned to me "I really wish you wouldn't act so sullen around my parents!" He glared at me. "All you do is stare at your phone and get

49

on Instagram constantly, it's like you don't even care about the family or your own kids. You never used to be like this, I don't know what changed you for the worse". I had no reply. I was tired of using words that would never be heard.

Chapter Six

One Week Later

I was getting ready to go to the gym. The house was clean; I had just finished putting away laundry and started the last load in the washer. The kids were fed and I had just pulled on my blue capri leggings and a black tank top that reached to mid-thigh. Today was squat day. My favorite day. Going to the gym was the highlight of my week.

Now that the holidays had passed, Mac was back at work and there were no family obligations to be managed, I had freedom to manage my days without him controlling every aspect. Training regularly again had been good. The thought of signing up for a competition had been weighing on my mind. Watching Jonah and Corey compete had inspired me. Their competition, which I had attended the previous weekend, had been a fun and invigorating experience. The environment at the competition had been a stark white compared with the blackness in my home. The competitors had all encouraged me. I had made multiple new friends, even being introduced to a couple of other girls who competed. This made me happy, as women powerlifters seemed to be few and far between.

I grabbed my white gym shoes and had just tied them when there was a knock on the door. I figured it was probably the neighbor wanting to tell me some important piece of neighborhood gossip or to bring me back one of my egg cartons from the eggs I had shared the week before.

Our neighborhood was close knit and everyone knew everyone's business. It was exactly how a small town should be.

Opening the door, I was unimpressed to see my dad standing there. My dad, who had looked like the perfect nerd during his prime in the 80s, was now a conglomeration of overweight hippie and just plain weirdo. On this January day, while rain pelted the ground outside, threatening snow with white flecks appearing every few seconds among the big droplets, he wore cotton cargo shorts and a dyed green t-shirt. Ever since I could remember, he had created his own fashion by buying white t-shirts and tie-dying them an ugly green that reminded me of a popular green colored cleaning spray. They always looked like they had come straight out of a pond full of algae.

He completed the same treatment with the knee-high socks that he wore in place of long pants. Why he never wore long pants, I couldn't guess. Today was no exception. The black shorts were accented by the green knee-high socks and a pair of sandals. On his balding head he wore a hat that reminded me of a cross-country hiker, with a string underneath his chin to keep it in place. His thick nerd glasses were flecked with water, but he didn't take them off or wipe them. He just stood there smiling at me. I instantly felt bad for not being excited about his presence. I opened the door for him to come in.

Both kids, excited to see their grandfather, came running over, wanting to give him hugs and tell him all about the toys they had received from their other grandparents on Christmas morning. After a moment, he turned to me, offering me a side hug. I could tell he hadn't showered in a few days. I felt bad for my mom, knowing that a lack of personal hygiene was normal for this man I called Father. He never had time to shower, he said. He had to stay focused on his work as a remote IT tech. Sometimes his clients needed him for so long that he couldn't step away from his computer or take a break, even for a shower or to sleep.

He used his most patient voice as he asked how I was doing. "I know it hasn't been easy lately, Sharon, but no one ever promised that it would be easy! Mac isn't perfect and he knows that. He is doing the best he can to be a good husband though!" He smiled ruefully.

"Father, he yells at me if I hang his shirts in the wrong direction in the closet. If I fold towels the way Mother taught me, instead of how his mother taught him, he tells me I'm a bad housekeeper! I can't even walk around the house without him getting mad that I'm walking on my heels and making a thumping noise. I have tried to learn to walk on tip toe but he still gets mad! I can't win with him no matter what!".

By this time, I was crying. My father opened his arm and gave me another hug. I cried on his shoulder for a moment. "Mac tells me you try to leave when all he wants to do is discuss your marriage problems. You need to listen to him and work through them or you won't ever get anywhere." I tried to explain how, when he got to the point of yelling at me and even throwing household objects at me, I didn't feel safe to continue the conversation.

"I know that Mac has a hard time with his temper, Sharon, but he told me you called the police on him and left for the night last week! You know that getting the law involved never did anyone any good, right? All it does is creates a paper trail that can never be undone. You wouldn't want him to lose his job because you created false abuse allegations against him, would you?"

I was ashamed. My reporting could yet cost him and I hadn't meant that. "I only wanted to make sure I was safe, Father, because he dragged me across the floor by my hair! It hurt." He took off his glasses, wiping them on the green shirt. He sighed and put them back on.

"I think you know Mac would never actually hurt you, Sharon. You have always been dramatic. I love you and I know that's just how you've always been. If something were to *actually* happen with someone hurting you, we would deal with it man to man. Your brothers and I would all come down and beat him up like proper men. We have no need of getting the law involved in this family. Your brothers and I will always protect you if there is a *real* need!"

He continued on for another hour, telling me how his mother had always forced his father into being submissive and how it taught all his sisters to talk back to their husbands. He reminded me of all the times that I had been dramatic as a child and teenager. He recounted a time I had put ketchup on my arm and told my mom it was a cut, asking for a Band-Aid. "It was really cute, Sharon. I always say you would make a wonderful actress!" I had been six when that had happened, but there was no use trying to correct my father. He was the leader of his house and his word was law, under every circumstance. I was defeated.

My time to go to the gym in the morning was gone by this point and the childcare was closed for the afternoon break. Later in the day, if I went, Mac would get home before I was done. I tried to always be home to greet him and ease the tenseness of the situation. I began crying again, this time because I would miss squats. But there was no sense in bringing it up. I already knew what my dad thought of the gym.

Chapter Seven

Mid-January 2020

"There! Done!" I said, submitting my payment to the online portal. I had signed up for my first powerlifting meet, facing my fears of not being ready. I had approximately 8 weeks to train for it, after all. Corey agreed to train me. My new program was easy. I would squat once, bench press twice, and deadlift one time in each week, to end it. When I had watched Corey compete, I had learned some details regarding the rules in a competition. My main concern with being ready for this competition was that I might not have enough practice waiting for the commands to do my respective lifts. If I missed a command, I risked getting disqualified from the event, which would make it so I didn't get to place in the overall event. I would practice these technicalities with Corey though. I was also doing my first diet weight cut.

With knowledge from Corey, I was adjusting my diet to begin dropping weight. I was beginning to look ripped and for the first time ever, I had six pack abs. Although Mac had recently let me know he didn't find muscular women attractive, I determined to continue with the weight cut. It made me happy to work hard toward a goal and nothing would get in the way of that. For as long as I could remember, he had compared me to my sister anyway, regularly stating how she was more attractive with such a large bust, than I was, with my small cup size and muscular upper and lower body. Even before the weightlifting, my arms and shoulders had been strong from splitting firewood, shooting a bow, and carrying my children around. Although I naturally had curvy hips, nearly perfect thighs and perfectly proportioned legs, Mac still looked at many other women regularly. I would never measure up to his standard of perfection in female bodies. It was time to choose what made me happy for once.

Chapter Eight

Over the next few weeks, the gym continued to be my reprieve from the struggles we were facing at home. Although we were at least talking again regularly, the tension was still there between Mac and me. Things weren't improving. One day, Mac surprised me with talking about how we should work on trusting each other more. He then asked to be added onto my bank account, our family's savings account. He wanted me to show him that I still trusted him. He had been losing trust in us after my leaving for a night and throughout my continuing to go to the gym against his wishes, he confided. Adding his name to the account could help me show him that I still loved him.

My goal had always been to buy a house, and although he hated saving money, he had agreed that the money I made through my home business could go into the savings account and I would be the sole keeper of this account, to make sure he didn't spend it. Whatever he made through his job, he could spend, after our monthly bills were paid. We also put in money from tax refunds, although this had caused an argument as well. He had reasoned that, because the money was a refund mainly from money he had earned, he should be able to spend it. I had pointed out that, if I hadn't born his children, we wouldn't have qualified for tax breaks. Additionally, if I had been working outside our home, we would have needed to pay for childcare. If he wanted to talk about whose money this was, he should pay me to babysit our children. It was a petty argument, I knew, but everything was a business deal between us these days. Love, that pipe dream ideal I had come to this marriage with, had long been gone. We could function as a business and think logically, since survival was all that remained of this union.

After the request from him to be added to the account, I immediately agreed. After all, he was the head of the household. I wanted to show him loyalty. It felt more like a plea for peace than a healthy compromise. Still, the paperwork was signed and he was given an access card.

One rainy afternoon, a client came by with some linens she needed me to hem. Living in a small town meant everyone was either a client, or a friend, or both. Leann was a friend who had listened to me more than once. Standing in my living room, her arms full of white linens, she looked into my eyes, daring me to be truthful. "How is everything going? Are things getting better?"

I looked out the window for a long moment, watching a robin that had landed on my daughter's baby swing. After a few seconds, it flew up to the top of the tree, landing next to another robin. I sighed and gave in to the need to talk about it, beginning with how Mac had taken the keys. I couldn't stop after that and I told her everything. I told her how I didn't know what to do, how I didn't feel safe at home anymore, and how he had left the house the day before, threatening to go and kill himself. I explained how he had taken his handgun and told me, in front of the kids, "I might not come home! This is just too tough, Sharon!" I told her about going to stay with Dex for the night and how he had gotten mad when I called the police. I explained how I felt I could do nothing well enough for him, how I was constantly failing but I didn't even know how to be good enough. How I was exhausted. How I was afraid of sleeping at night because he was home and I didn't know what he might do to me in my sleep. "I have a friend who went through a lot of this," she told me. "You guys should connect!". Later I messaged Greta, copying the number Leann had given me to her friend. Greta told me her story. She explained that she had been married to a veteran with mental health issues. She had tried therapy and sticking it out, but ultimately had left him because she found out he was cheating, after many years of physical and mental abuse. She told me she knew my situation was different; she hoped it wouldn't come to that. She said to reach out if I needed anything.

That afternoon, after the linens had been hemmed and folded neatly, ready for pick-up, I prepared to take Kitten, our hound pup, for a hike. We had gotten Kitten the previous October from a breeder several hours to the east of us. Kitten was purebred hound. She had the energy of a puppy combined with the smarts of a dog who wanted to track blood and tree predators. I had always felt nervous because I didn't know how to train a dog; I felt inadequate for the task. Still, I loved her. I was trying to follow Mac's advice and keep her entertained during the day. I got the kids ready and loaded Kitten into the truck, noticing that she had raided the trash in the garage while I was getting the children ready to go.

Driving towards our favorite spot, I thought about Mac's goal to train her to shed hunt for deer and elk antlers, and eventually track blood. After he had lost a bull elk he had shot the year before, he had thought getting a hunting dog would benefit him. I hoped maybe we would find an antler, or shed, today, although January was a little bit early for fresh ones. Deer and elk shed their antlers each year, but not often did it happen before March in this area. Once we had driven about five miles back onto the private timber property we often visited, I found a dead-end road. Parking where a log blocked the remainder of the road, I helped the kids into coats and snowpants, hoping to help them stay dry among the ferns and Oregon grape bushes. We hiked up the overgrown road about half a mile before dropping into the ditch and cutting across a small creek to start hiking through the woods.

Carroll, who had been walking slowly next to me, her tiny legs trying to keep up, needed help to cross the slowly moving creek. Lifting her, I set her firmly on the other side, before helping Luke choose the best route so as not to fill his black rubber boots with water. Kitten had found her own way, the training bell around her collar dinging loudly as she jumped across, landing on dry ground. I picked up her leash then, making sure she stayed close for now. We climbed the short grassy bank on the opposite side of the creek, entering into an area that was characterized by tall fir and maple trees, blocking out most of the light from the gray sky above. I sighed in relief, stopping to look around. I could wander all day in these forests and not ever want to come home. This *was* home for me. Among the trees, with only the sounds of water running and more water dripping off leaves and branches since it had just stopped raining, I felt at peace. Both kids wandered around within eye sight of me as we spread out, climbing over rotten downed trees and down the side of one small ravine, to cross a creek and go up the next.

We made it to a mostly flat area with a few rocks and a lot of logs that were likely the remnants of thinning projects from five or more years prior. The forest here was about thirty years old and the trees overhead completely shaded out the mossy ground from sky light. I was partially looking for late season chanterelle mushrooms, a local wild delicacy. After a minute, I found a handful of winter chanterelles and was carefully collecting them, when I noticed that Kitten was sniffing and digging at the base of a tree. By the time I got to her, she was eating something that looked like charred wood. "Weird," I thought, "she's eating wood".

I pried her mouth open and looked more closely. Taking the chunk out of her mouth, it easily broke apart. I smelled it and realized it smelled sweet, like a mixture of some kind of fruit, and an onion. The consistency was softer than charred wood, too. It broke apart like soft cheese. The inside was pearl like with bits of white running through the darker particles. I was ecstatic! Kitten had found black truffles! I had secretly hoped she might someday learn to find truffles; I had been picking and selling chanterelles for the last couple years, every season, to local restaurants. Truffles were much better money, often averaging around $75 per ounce if sold to the right buyer. I prided myself in finding ways to not only provide for my family through harvesting or killing our own food, but also making money off my passion for the outdoors. This was a huge accomplishment, and the fact that Kitten had discovered this on her own was even more impressive. She continued to dig and found more during the next hour, before the kids got cold and we hiked back towards the truck. At home, I researched how to further train a dog to find truffles. I found that hiding them and giving her a small piece then rewarding her with a dog treat when she found more, was a good start. I planned to improve her truffle finding skills and couldn't wait to tell Mac about this. However, when he got home two hours later, he went straight to the garage. He let Kitten out of her kennel and went to the backyard with her.

I planned to show him how she could find the truffles in the backyard, but I never got the chance. He came in a moment later, asking why Kitten had blood and trash in her poop. I explained that she had raided the trash; I then realized she had likely eaten one of my menstrual pads. I was embarrassed. When he began yelling about how disgusting it was that I had allowed Kitten to eat them, I felt even worse. He went on and on, stating how disgusting it was that women bled monthly. He told me how men were cleaner and simpler, making it into some sort of nasty joke as his rant continued. I couldn't blame him, since he was the one cleaning up the poop that day, though. I began to feel guilty for not doing a better job cleaning up after her. He had worked all day, after all. I should help more. Later that night when I did tell him about the fact that Kitten had found truffles, he responded by telling me that she was his dog and he really didn't want her to find truffles. "She's a hunting dog. You're gonna' confuse her by teaching her to find truffles!" He reprimanded. I had thought he would be excited that she was so smart and could help the family make money, but apparently, being my idea, it wasn't something he was interested in. Oh well. I would take her out again, but there was no need for him to know.

Chapter Nine

On Friday, I got a message from Corey. He let me know that he had invited some friends from the gym over for drinks and to hang out. Jonah and his girlfriend would be there, as well as Lucas and a couple of girls I had met at the competition a few weeks before. I was invited to join them. I said yes, automatically. Mac hated my spending time with them, and I knew that, but he would be upset with me regardless, so I might as well enjoy time with new friends. I had always wanted a friend group.

Ever since I was little and got excluded because of being homeschooled and part of a highly religious family, I had craved friendship and inclusion. Making friends had been hard. I would never forget being yelled at by some teenagers driving to the river while I was riding my bike along the road to a popular swimming spot with my sisters and brothers. There were six of us riding bikes. All of the girls wore dresses; modesty was the family dress code.

Even among religious groups, I had never felt like I belonged. As a young child, my parents attended church, but they switched churches often, complaining that the pastors were not living pure enough lives to be called pastors. I would often hear my parents critiquing the pastor on their way home from Sunday services. I remembered my father approaching the pastor to tell him that, because he had gotten divorced and re-married, he was unqualified to lead a church. My parents had not only left that church, but also told everyone they knew that the church had no morals. By the time I was 7, my parents had given up altogether on finding a religious group to be a part of.

We lived 15 miles from the nearest town, down a gravel road, with only three or four other kids that lived on that road. For a while, we played basketball with the neighbor boys weekly, but I don't think my dad liked us having a schedule. He always told me that I was too focused on having regular social events and that I should put less emphasis on having friends. He told me I needed to be more content with my life as it was. He would rather my sisters and brothers and I socialize with the 70-year-old neighbor couple than spend time with friends our age.

By the time I was 11, we had moved, and there were no kids anywhere in the area. I could remember going to visit my 80-year-old neighbor, a widow with white hair, and the only other person with my name whom I had ever met. It wasn't until high school age when we had begun bike racing, that I had finally felt I had a social group. Even then, my dad praised us for having conversations with the older people we raced against, often making fun of us for befriending other teenagers.

Getting married at 18 and moving to a new city in a new state, where I knew no one, this pattern had started over again. The other 18-year-olds in this small town were either still in high school, starting college, or partying every weekend. I was just Mac's wife, the one who stayed home and kept house. He had never allowed me to work even back then. I had felt out of place. Before long, I had become Lukes's mom. This had given me a title and purpose again. Although Mac's family had been Mennonite at the time, the local Mennonite group never included me in the same way that it included its members. While they welcomed me to social events, the younger women didn't really interact with me, aside from one who was soon reprimanded by her husband for doing so. The Mennonites, like my parents, believed that only those who looked like they did were good enough. Dressing in any way other than wearing dresses and head coverings was immoral.

Because Mac had chosen to allow me to wear modern day clothing after marriage, I clearly didn't fit. Even if I had worn a dress, I had never done the ceremony to become Mennonite. I didn't want to, but it meant I had no one and didn't fit in. When I had begun the sewing business, I began to connect with more of the community. Still, Mac had never approved of my having friends. Something was shifting within me, though. I was ready to come out from behind his shadow. At a soul level, I was beginning to rebel.

When Mac got home that evening, I informed him that I was going to spend time with my gym friends for a couple hours. I knew he wouldn't want me to go, but I deserved time away from the kids and out of the house. As I presumed, he told me no. He didn't want me to go. I grabbed my keys and went to leave anyway. His truck was parked behind mine. Both were older, and both had many dings and dents. Seeing that he had parked directly behind me, I asked him to move his truck. He refused. I looked for the keys to his truck, but he was wearing them. I was angry. He had done this on purpose, to block me in. I was an adult and he had no right to control where I went or when. Going to leave, I backed into his truck, ramming it until it was out of my way. Neither truck was damaged more than a dent on his passenger door. I was free.

I drove to Corey's apartment, where I was welcomed by the gym family. Everyone piled into Jonah's car and we headed to a Mexican restaurant, ordering takeout. When we had finished eating, someone set up beer pong on the kitchen table. After a couple of shots, everyone was having fun. I had never drunk heavily, so having one hard lemonade and a shot of whiskey was enough for me to get a buzz. We strategized about powerlifting and I told everyone I had signed up for my first competition.

When I arrived home that evening, after allowing the alcohol time to wear off, Mac was still up, working on something in the garage. I tried to be quiet, heading straight for the bathroom to take a shower and get ready for bed. Mac came in, still angry about the dent in the passenger door of his truck. I settled into the couch and fell asleep. An hour later he woke me, begging that I come to bed. "I feel so alienated from my wife, Sharon. Why do you do this to me? I want to make things right and you know what everyone says, never go to bed angry." I didn't have words for him that were kind, so I said nothing, turning away and pulling the blanket over my head. I slept fitfully; I hadn't felt safe in my home for a long time and tonight was no exception.

Chapter Ten

Six hours later I awoke, feeling like a ton of bricks had been laid on my chest. My asthma had been worse than normal the last couple days. I often felt as though my world was about to turn black. I had needed to sit down, but not lie down, as being on my back completely closed my airways. Several times recently, I had wondered if I was about to die. My heart would race as the anxiety set in at the world becoming dark around me. Breathing deeply did nothing for my lungs. I had thought I was having a heart attack.

This morning particularly, I had a sore throat and felt something was terribly wrong. The asthma was even worse. I couldn't catch my breath. Standing up shakily, I made my way to the bed, where Mac was still asleep. I lay there on my side of the bed, curled up, struggling to breathe. An hour later, I awakened. Sitting up, I attempted to walk to the kitchen. The world became dark around me and I couldn't see clearly. I was dizzy. I felt bad because I couldn't get up to make Mac his breakfast and lunch before he left for work. Lying back down, I eventually drifted into a fitful sleep. When I awoke next, I was fighting a fever. By this point, the kids were up. I gave them a movie and rested on the couch. Mac had left for work, but I hadn't even heard him.

The rest of the day my body alternated between running a fever and then being suddenly freezing cold. I would wrap myself in a blanket, shivering, and then throw the blanket off and fan myself weakly with my hand. The sore throat worsened until I could barely swallow. Sleeping that night proved almost impossible; I was afraid to drift off for fear that I couldn't breathe and would die in my sleep. By the next day, I was developing a cough and the chills continued. The kids seemed to be completely fine and had as much energy as they normally did.

By the end of the second day, I was even worse. I propped myself up with extra pillows so as not to get any more congested while I attempted to sleep. I woke up once, in the middle of that night, to find Mac next to me, holding my thumb over my phone. I recoiled in shock, being halfway in a state of delusion and half of fear, at finding him using my thumbprint to attempt to unlock my phone; he didn't know the passcode. I couldn't believe what I was seeing. I had never tried to hide anything from him. However, he had expressed his beliefs that I was cheating on him so often since I had begun the gym, that I shouldn't have been surprised. He left the room at this point and I attempted to sleep again.

The following morning, I was awakened by Carroll, holding up her favorite book for me to read. Mac was asleep next to me. It was Saturday. I was feeling slightly better, so I got up and attended to the kids. They were both fine still, showing no symptoms of being sick. Mac, on the other hand, had contracted the same bug, it seemed. I tended to him the best I could as I slowly started regaining my own strength. I was able to eat again and felt almost back to normal, other than the ever-present asthma attacks.

A month later, the entire world would shut down after becoming aware of the global pandemic. The news would be full of cases similar to mine, with people getting even more sick and many dying. Without even realizing it, I had experienced the COVID-19 pandemic. I wasn't sure what had been more unsettling about this week: the fact that I had faced the possibility of death, or the fact that, even while I was very sick, my husband was attempting to go through my phone.

Chapter Eleven

We both continued to recover from COVID and things seemed to get slightly better for a couple of days, as our focus was on physically healing. There was a ceasefire, an unspoken agreement that we would use our strength to heal before going to battle again. After several days had gone by, I woke up in the middle of the night. I felt it was my turn to go through my husband's phone. I felt guilty for doing it, but someone had told me that signs of a partner cheating included accusing the other partner of cheating, out of guilt. I didn't want to disrespect his privacy, but I did want to know the truth.

He had reprimanded me for downloading Chat-app, a messenger service that deleted messages instantly after they were read by the recipient. when I opened his phone, I was surprised to find that he also had Chat-app. I then discovered his locked down browser; I wasn't surprised that he looked at porn. Most men did. I was only disappointed. Somehow, I had always believed that I would fall in love with a man who only wanted me, who didn't need multiple women or to watch porn regularly to satisfy his lower needs. Having been married for over six years, I had realized long ago that this was untrue. Although my husband loved only me, he checked out other women regularly. He flirted with others and had asked in the past if I would ever be okay with having another woman in the bedroom with us. Now I knew that he used porn regularly and hid it from me. He knew I wouldn't approve. As normal as it was, it still went against the religious ideals he claimed to uphold. Opening his messenger app, I noticed that on several chats, the messages were deleted. This couldn't be good. I noticed that the girl he had been seeing when I met him, was among the names with deleted messages. I then looked farther back and saw several messages from other women he had been keeping up with. Although there was no proof that he was sleeping with others, I did find a message from the week before; he had asked if he could come over, and been denied. I also found a message from his high school sweetheart.

Although they had chatted recently, the text that caught my eye was a message from after she announced her engagement to the public, two years prior. *"I am happy that you are happy, but a part of me wishes it was you and me; I still miss you!"* He had told her. The date of this message was October 7th, 2018. I couldn't look at any more. He had sent her this immediately after our daughter was born. While I was in bed, recovering from the agony and pain of delivering his child, he had been messaging other women. Of course he had, I thought. I had been out of commission for sex and he still had needs.

This was something he reminded me of often. More than once, he had told me, "I have needs. If you can't fulfill them, I am still going to make sure they are fulfilled". Finding out he had been talking to women recently was no surprise; I knew things felt off. This only confirmed my suspicions. Finding out he had been talking to others for several years, hurt more. Somehow, I hadn't seen any of it back then. Although I had known about what happened with my sister, I thought it was strictly about her. I had thought that, although our marriage had other issues, dishonesty wasn't one of them. I had trusted him, even telling myself multiple times that I didn't want to be the mistrusting wife and that my gut feeling was wrong. I had brushed off weird coincidences more than once, reminding myself that he loved me and I could trust him.

I had always thought that living by my code of morality would promise reciprocity. Doing the right thing, being the right kind of wife, doing my best to be honest and loyal, would guarantee me the same treatment in return, I had believed. This was how my parents had raised me and this was how I had tried to live my life for as long as I could remember. Lately, these beliefs, the ones that had kept me safe in my little protected world of make believe, were beginning to crumble. I wasn't sure what to believe in anymore.

Chapter Twelve

When I was 13, my baby sister died. Or, more accurately, she was never born alive. I will never forget my mom coming home from the fated midwife appointment that day. She was worried because the baby hadn't moved in a couple of days. After carrying 7 babies to full term live births, she knew how it felt to have a pregnancy where something wasn't right. "They referred me to the hospital in the big city," she had told my dad. The doctors had scheduled for her to stay the night and to deliver the baby there. Our home had been dark; an atmosphere of death lingered in the air.

My parents had been grieving. I don't think they realized how myself and my siblings were also hurting. All except for me, that is. I was still holding out hope. I had been taught to read the Bible and pray regularly, for as long as I could remember. I had been baptized at age 5 and had a personal experience with Jesus where he came to me in a dream, telling me it was time to be saved. Ever since, I had trusted the Bible and its promises. I had asked God for things and he would answer. This time, I was begging him to bring back my sister. If I prayed hard enough and truly had the faith to move this mountain, she could be brought back to life. She would be delivered and they would miraculously report that she had begun breathing. I would restore the joy to my family through my great faith. I had spent that whole day in my room. I don't think I ate. I focused on fasting and praying. I envisioned my sister being healed. I knew that if I simply believed in this miracle, it would be so. That is, until my dad called from the hospital with news. The angel baby had been born that morning: still-born. She wasn't breathing or alive at all. I will never forget sitting in that hospital room later that day, holding her tiny, lifeless body. At six and a half months along, she was fully formed and weighed over a pound. All seven of us took turns holding her, gazing at the tiny body of our sister, whom we would never know on this side of heaven.

In the days that followed, I was lost not only in grief, but also in deep anger towards God. How could a God who claimed to be trustworthy break his promise like this? How could he let me down in this way? His word was clear: "Jesus said unto them, if ye have faith as a grain of mustard seed, ye shall say unto this mountain, remove hence to yonder place; and it shall remove; and nothing shall be impossible unto you."

Matthew 17:20-21 KJV. He had said, again and again to his disciples, that if they truly believed, nothing would be impossible for them. I had always believed this promise was extended to those of us who believed as well. But he had lied. He had broken his promise to me.

For months, I didn't read my Bible or pray. I couldn't place my faith in a God like that. If he was okay with lying about his promises to me, I could do life without him. A couple of months had gone by with me in this state. I was blocking every aspect of spirituality. I didn't want to hear what God would say to me if I listened. My heart had closed up in its pain. I wanted to be protected from the possibility of being hurt by God if I trusted him again, so I had completely shut down the lines of communication. One day, my father's friend and his wife had started coming over to help my dad with stone work on the exterior of the house my parents were building. Instead of listening to country music like the other builders, this man and his wife, who shared a name with my baby sister, would sing hymns and praises to God. I didn't want any part of it, but one day the man had looked me point blank in the eyes and asked if I read the Bible. He asked why I didn't like the hymns they sang. He had talked that day with me and I had realized that hymns brought me peace. Reading my Bible brought me hope. Feeling Jesus' presence brought me comfort, even if I didn't know why he had allowed my little sister to die.

Slowly, I had opened my heart again, realizing that I didn't want to live without the love of God to guide me through life. I had begun to see that, even when I didn't understand him, I could trust him. I could trust the peace that came with letting true love in. This, if nothing else, was reliable for me. I had finally laid down the burden of feeling responsible for my sister's death, accepting that things had happened for a divine reason, even if I couldn't understand them. My parents were lost in their own grief. I don't think they ever knew anything about the battle that I had silently fought. This had been between me and God alone.

In those beginning days of 2020, I was struggling in a similar way. I had always had faith that God cared for me and had a good plan for my life. I had prayed for several years that God would work in my husband. I had prayed for strength, multiple times. I had prayed for the attitude to be able to grow as a wife, to be submissive and to be patient with my husband. I had prayed for a fresh perspective. I had prayed that I would make the right choices in our disagreements. I didn't know what God was doing in my life, but just as I had come back to him after my sister's death, I had come back to him many times during this marriage, asking for more grace and stamina to fight this fight, to stay the course as a Godly wife. I had read books that explained how to pray for your spouse, expecting for the last couple of years that God would soon step in and work in Mac's life, especially because I was doing what I could to apply myself to this task of marriage.

Recently, though, rebellion had begun to take root in my heart. While I still wanted to obey God, I didn't want to obey my husband. I wanted to think for myself. I wanted to experience oneness with God, but I was no longer sure if I had to go through my husband for it, as my dad had always taught me. These thoughts conflicted me, as much as they raised questions. The last time I had left, for one night, Mac had reminded me how God wouldn't want a woman to rebel against her husband in this way. This only made me feel like maybe a God who forced women to work it out with men who hurt their wives was not the God for me. I didn't know what I believed anymore. I felt guilty even picking up my Bible, knowing what Mac would say if he saw me. I could hear him saying "You run away from our problems and don't submit to me, but then you expect to learn things from the Bible when you read it. You are a hypocrite!" The way in which I was seeing God was beginning to evolve and I didn't know where this uprising, this spring of desire for something new, was coming from.

Chapter Thirteen

The following week, Pastor Gordon and his wife invited us over for a Bible study group that they were starting. We had been attending Gordon's church for a while now, ever since Carroll had been a baby and I had requested that she be baptized there. Recently, though, we hadn't attended Sunday services. I had wanted to, but I felt embarrassed showing up with just the kids. Whenever I asked Mac to join me, I was met with an excuse. Sometimes, it was simply that he was tired from the week and wanted some alone time. Other times, he would tell me that church was fake and pointless, that connection with God could be achieved outside of a church more easily than inside a church. If I was honest with myself, attending church felt fake to me, for different reasons. I felt like a fake Christian, just as Mac always told me. I hadn't been very submissive lately. I hadn't been the perfect wife who stood by and supported her husband.

I had pursued my own goals, namely going to the gym against his will. The guilt ate at me and I felt that stepping in a church would be lying to God. He would look down and immediately point me out to the leaders of the church as a farce. "That one, right there!" he would say, into the ears of Pastor Gordon, "that one is the biggest sinner of all!" Surely, anyone who was a real Christian could see my sins laid upon my shoulders, plain as day light. No, church would only expose me to more judgment. Although attending church had been irregular, Gordon had offered us counseling after a particularly rough patch in our marriage.

As we got in the truck to drive to the Bible study, my mind drifted back to Mac and my sister's near affair, two years earlier. It had been October and the leaves were changing. Fall had always been my favorite time. It was always a joyously busy time. Between mushroom picking, harvesting my garden, canning tomatoes and green beans, and picking apples, there was always work to be done. The plentiful harvests that always yielded themselves at the end of the warm summers made me happy. It was also bear hunting season. I really wanted to fill my tag before late season archery started and my focus became killing a deer with my bow. My sister, who was the huntress in the family, had come to help me. I was still learning; although I did enjoy it, I was a lot better at harvesting mushrooms than killing animals. Naomi, who was beautiful, blue-eyed, with blonde-hair, and two years younger than me, had killed a deer every season with her bow. I had killed one last season but that was the only one I had ever managed.

My dad had been taking me hunting since I was less than 8; some of my best memories were from elk camp in my young childhood. I wanted to be successful at it. Sometimes, I wondered if my sister and I were like Cain and Abel. I was Cain, the one who could only offer things that had been grown, such as wild mushrooms or my garden vegetables. Naomi was Abel, the one who pleased her father greatly with her offerings of deer she killed, and sometimes, elk or bear. She was the successful hunter who pleased God, or in this case, my father. Every time I went to see my parents, my dad was bragging about her latest kill or how skilled she was. Sometimes, I wondered if even Mac felt that way about her. He had assured me that, while he did find her attractive, he didn't love her like he loved me.

The plan had been for Naomi to stay with us for two days. We had spent most of the first day glassing for a bear, sitting quietly above clear cuts where loggers had harvested timber. These hillsides the perfect paradise for a bear getting ready to hibernate. Between endless clumps of grass, blackberry bushes, and the occasional ant hill, wildlife, especially black bears, had everything they needed to fatten up for the upcoming winter. After spending most of the day in the wilderness, walking slowly with the kids, exploring and catching up on all the latest boys Naomi had crushes on, we had driven back to my house. The week before, I had started an oil painting for my neighbor; his dog had died and I really wanted use my art skills to gift him a portrait of his dog.

After we had gotten back from hunting, I spent most of the afternoon and evening working on the painting, stopping only to start cooking some dinner. I would have spent the time with my sister, but it always felt awkward when Mac was home. He seemed to want to show her things outside constantly, or in the garage. I respected their friendship, but it still felt odd to me how much alone time he wanted to spend with her, especially considering that she was my sister. After a dinner of taco salad and watermelon, I put kids to bed; looking at the clock, I realized it was past 9. "You going to bed soon?" I asked Mac. He was sitting on the couch talking with Naomi, his arm stretched over the back of the couch and around her shoulders. Neither of them seemed in any hurry to go to bed. She was venting to him about her latest failed courtship. He had been listening intently, staring into her beautiful eyes as she continued with the tale, expressing how unfair it was that this man didn't want to be with her as much as she wanted to be with him.

Mac, who hardly heard me, muttered a reply after a moment. He said he needed to get some things done in the garage so I should just go to bed on my own. I took a shower, brushing my teeth and getting into bed. He came in ten minutes later and came straight to the bed. He kissed me and pulled my hair. "Babe, I want you to wear this!" I wasn't sure what he was holding. Looking closely in the semi darkness, I realized it was my sister's bra. I didn't feel comfortable at all. Replaying this scenario in my head, I have never understood why I said yes to him. The thing about abuse, though, is that one rarely realizes they are in it, while it is taking place. One often thinks only of pleasing their abuser in hopes of keeping the peace. I put it on. He began kissing me again, this time fingering me as he pulled my pants down. He got on top and continued kissing me. When he was about to finish, he pulled out and finished on the bra. "Oops, we made a mess!" He chuckled. "I think you'll need to wash that before you return it to her." I pretended to think it was funny too, telling him that I would have to lie about an excuse of why it was missing the next morning. I felt disgustingly dirty. If I had known how to feel the pain, it would have flooded in. However, I had been swallowing it down for so long that I didn't even know how to feel anything anymore. I rolled over and went to sleep, balling myself up and making sure I wasn't touching my husband at all.

The next day, Naomi and I took the kids hiking at a new trail covering more area. It was fun hanging out with my sister, when my husband wasn't around anyway. She updated me on all of the family drama and all the stupid things my brothers had done this week. She told me about my mother's sickness and how it hadn't improved. My mom got anxiety so extremely that she often got nausea and spent a day throwing up and had to rest extra for the next few days after one of these attacks. It seemed to be getting worse. When we got home that afternoon, I went in to make dinner. Mac was home by this point and wanted to show Naomi the progress on the grape vines. I was extremely proud of those grape vines, as I had started them from cuttings two spring times earlier; now they were successfully yielding juicing grapes.

I had just finished stirring the bear sausage and added the onions to the pot, when Naomi walked in, an unhappy look on her face. "We need to talk" she said "and then I'm going home". "I thought you were staying till tomorrow after our morning hunt?" I asked.

We sat at the kitchen table so I could keep an eye on the dinner cooking. "Mac took pictures up under my skirt just now. He tried to do this another time but I wasn't sure if that was what he was doing, so I couldn't say anything. This time, I *am* sure. He tried touching my boobs when he hugged me last night too". She looked me straight in the eyes. "I always felt weird," I told her, "But I wanted to trust that you guys had a solid friendship". I felt sick to my stomach. I remembered the pictures

I had found on his phone, of someone's legs and the panties that didn't look like mine. He had assured me they were, in fact, my legs, and my panties. I gripped the side of the chair, turning white. I didn't even know what to say to my sister. This had been going on for months. He always wanted to visit my parents and I had been completely right with my suspicion that he had something going on with my sister. Surely, she had recognized it too. Or did she like it? I asked myself suddenly. "Why did you always agree to hang out with him, Naomi? You allowed this!" I screamed, suddenly angry at both of them. She looked defensive. "He always listened to me and let me vent to him. He gave me the best hugs," She replied, unwilling to meet my gaze. "I never meant for things to go like this!" Venting to him was more than I was ever allowed. But I was just his wife, not his hot sister-in-law.

Naomi left that afternoon. My dad called Mac that night. The next day, he talked to me and explained how sorry Mac was. He told me Mac knew he had hurt me a lot. Mac had even cried, he said. He had never seen him this emotional; my dad was sure that Mac had learned a lesson he would never repeat. That weekend, Mac had work training several hours south of us. He wanted me to go with him, to spend the day together, for us to have some quality time together. He knew he had messed up; he wanted everything to be normal again, and quickly. I didn't want to even talk to him. I told him no. He explained to me how he was afraid for my safety, that I would do something to harm myself if he left me home alone. The last thing I wanted was to spend a day in the car with him. What was there to talk out? I had done everything I knew to do, to be a good wife. And here we were. I didn't have a choice though. As my husband, when he told me I needed to do something, I must do it. Back then, I had never argued.

The drive was long and tense, and I was silent. The only noise was the sound of the old car's engine. The car didn't have proper insulation on the doors, so everything was loud, but I welcomed the noise. I tried to sleep, or even pretend I was sleeping. I didn't want to talk about anything. When we got to the warehouse, he kissed me. I turned my head in the opposite direction, unwilling to acknowledge him even. He told me he loved me; he would be done in a few hours. I drove the kids to a hiking trail, welcoming the oak leaves that fell on the car in the parking lot. Ewe trees and oak trees lined the open hillside above us. I loved the difference in scenery that driving a few hours from home had offered. I smiled, taking in the sight.

Still, thoughts plagued me. I wondered if I had been wrong to marry him. Maybe it had all been a mistake. It was a moot point, regardless. I couldn't even allow thoughts like that to enter my mind. What I had committed to, I would stay committed to. My parents didn't even believe the word divorce should be in the dictionary. I was hurting but there was no way out. I would shove my pain down until I didn't feel it anymore, just as I had always done.

On the drive home, Mac had asked me to talk to him. He wanted to know my feelings for once. Secretly, I wondered if he was afraid that I was, in fact, considering leaving him. I brought up couples counseling, for the second time. Instantly, he shot it down. "You really think we need some random stranger trying to tell us how to be married, Sharon?" That was the end of that. Over the next few weeks, things had seemed to be a little better. He had stopped texting my sister, as far as I knew. For a while anyway.

Back in the present, we arrived at pastor Gordon's house. I helped the kids get out and carried in the brownies I had baked to go with the potluck dinner. Another younger couple from church was there, as well as a single woman, and an elderly couple. We exchanged pleasantries; I hoped no one could see how hard Mac and I were trying not to fight. All the kids began playing. After everyone had finished eating dinner, the adults gathered in the living room, seated in a circle around the floor. I was nervous. As much as I wanted to be a regular Christian and to have fellowship with other believers, I felt unworthy. The feelings of fakeness returned.

Each person was asked to speak about how God was using them as a disciple and to bring others to Christ through community. When it was my turn, I hesitated. I didn't even have to look at Mac to feel him glaring at me. I took a deep breath and spoke. "For me, I have begun to make friendships in the gym," I started, not looking towards him "Going to the gym and having people watch me workout took a lot of strength, but I am beginning to build community through working hard with others". I told them about my new friend Bonnie, an older woman who had talked with me multiple times. I told them how Jonah, Corey, and Lucas had included me, telling me that my hard work and stick-to-itiveness had inspired them to work harder in the gym. When I finished, everyone thanked me; they told me they felt it was inspiring to hear about how God was using the gym to transform me and my relationships with others. Everyone was impressed by how strong I was physically. All except Mac, that is, who continued to glare at me. I was glad to be done talking. My only thought was how I still planned to go train with Corey and Lucas the next morning, even against my husband's wishes. I felt so guilty. I wondered if I really was a fake Christian. I didn't even need God or my husband to judge me, because I was judging myself.

The tension was strong and others felt it as well. I was glad when the kids started to get tired and I whispered to Mac that it was time to go. As soon as we got back in the car, he began about the gym again, telling me what I already knew. He told me I was a fraud. He found it amazing how I could so easily disobey him. I had no problem talking about how great I was and how I was doing so many wonderful things for the Lord, while defying the commandments about wives obeying their husbands, in secret. Maybe a relationship with God isn't what I want after all, I thought once again.

Chapter Fourteen

Two days later

The evening had started off wrong and only gotten worse. Mac had asked me to take a shower with him, likely with the hope it would turn into more. I had told him I was tired. I had gone into the room, mindlessly scrolling social media, watching friends lift weight. I was tired of feeling like I was just there for sex. Mac had reminded me again that if I didn't meet his needs, someone else would. I felt like I was living in a trap that was slowly killing me. The life was being siphoned from my body, day by day, and I was powerless to change it. The depression was strong tonight. I didn't know how to get away from the pain or where to turn anymore.

When Mac made his way into the bedroom, I was still lying on the bed, staring at my phone. The kids were asleep, thankfully. "So you would rather look at half naked guys online than spend time with your husband," he remarked, dropping the towel onto the floor at the foot of the bed. "You're the one who talks to multiple women, hides your phone and told your ex you wished she was marrying you, while I was in bed healing from Carrolls' birth!" I snapped. A match had been struck and the gasoline had been poured. Flames of anger, an explosion ready to happen. He had begun yelling. I had reminded him of the children, walking out of the room in rage. I had run to the garage, unsure what I was doing. Something needed to break. I picked up his chainsaw, slamming it onto the concrete floor. He opened the door then, exploding in a fit of anger as he saw me throw it. I knew breaking his things wouldn't help, but he wouldn't listen and I didn't have a clue how to reach harmony or a place of middle ground anymore. He was accusing me of things I hadn't even thought of doing, all while lying to my face about doing the things he accused *me* of. We had gone in circles for months now, always ending with the same helplessness of me surrendering to him and his will. I was done.

He lunged at me, grabbing my wrists in anger. I struggled to free myself, pulling away. The result was a bruise on my wrist and a scratch on the other one. "Don't touch me!" I growled. "I'll call your dad," Mac said, "he can calm you down". By calming me down, he meant telling me how he would never allow a daughter of his to be un-submissive, as long as he was alive. Mac was already dialing. "Sharon just broke my chainsaw because I asked her to take a shower with me, Father. I was wondering if you could help us work through this." I heard Mac say, in his calmest, most condescending voice. He was glaring at me. I didn't wait to hear my dad's response, heading instead for the kitchen. Taking my phone and keys, I ran out the door. I didn't know where I was going, but I knew I needed space. We could talk it through the next day. Being at the point where we were physically hurting one another could never be healthy. Even pastor Gordon had said separation could be necessary, when there was physical abuse. I drove aimlessly, wiping away tears. I sent a quick message to Daniella, who assured me that leaving had indeed been the right choice. She reminded me that I wasn't wrong for taking space. I needed reassurance because I didn't know which way was up anymore. I didn't even know what was right, blinded by the brainwashing I had been through from Mac and my father. My friends all seemed to think that the situation was getting bad, but I had lived through it for so long that it was just life.

Eventually, I ended up back at Dex's. "I am sorry to be a hassle, but can I spend the night again?" I had asked. He had assured me that I was welcome whenever. "You know, ever since Mathew died, the yurt has been empty. If you and the kids need a place to stay, I can clean it up a bit and you guys are welcome to stay in it until you find something more suitable or figure out what you are doing." Dex had kindly offered. I told him we weren't leaving; I just needed a break tonight. I settled on the couch and slept fitfully, worrying about the kid's safety. Mac had never hurt the kids physically, at least not on purpose. Yes, he had slammed the door on Carroll when she was two, resulting in her shoulder becoming dislocated, but he hadn't *meant* to do that. He had cried and assured me multiple times that he would never purposely hurt his daughter, when he had returned home from cooling down after that episode, to find that I had been forced to take her to the emergency room. He had told me that it never would have happened if I hadn't made him angry. He had said it wasn't his fault she happened to be in the way of the door when he was angry. I didn't think my husband meant to hurt our child, but lately I had wondered if he was more dangerous than I had originally assumed. There was also the issue of Luke and how he disciplined. Mac never missed a chance to give him a physical consequence for his actions. Surely, he would leave them be tonight. I would make things up with him in the morning and they would both be okay.

The next morning, though, I was in for an unpleasant surprise. I arrived at the little white house, feeling that something was out of place. The kids weren't outside playing and Mac's truck wasn't even home. I called Mac, demanding an answer. "Your parents came and took the kids, but your dad said you can have them back after we work it out." I was furious. I called my parents. "Mac asked me to take the kids so you guys can talk, that's all," my dad explained. "After you come back and make things up to him, I'll bring the kids back to you," he assured me. How could Mac do this? How could my parents do this? They had taken my own kids in the name of resolving conflict, but were now using them as a pawn, a bargaining tool, a way to get me to obey. I didn't know what to do. I changed into clean clothing, having slept in my yoga pants and a hoodie. I went to the gym. At the very least, my kids would be safe with my parents so I could get in a workout. I didn't doubt their safety while staying there.

At the gym, I saw my new friend Josephine. Josephine was a young vet-tech with long black hair and olive skin. She was shorter than I was, and thinner too, with curvy hips and perfect legs. Her makeup was done perfectly today as she flashed white teeth at me. Reading my face, she asked what was wrong. Her dark eyebrows knit together as I told her about my parents and how Mac had asked them to take my kids. She didn't have kids, but she had compassion for me, feeling the anger as intensely as I did in that moment.

Although I had initially taken her to be in the gym to gain attention more than actually work out, I was beginning to see she meant well. She invited me to come and eat lunch with her after the gym. I agreed; I didn't know what else to do and needed to kill time because I couldn't go back home at this point. Over low carb lasagna made with cabbage and ground beef, she explained that she worked nights and she didn't have much time to meet new friends. She wanted more girls to train with. I was welcome anytime I wanted to come over. She told me how her fiancée, who was a general contractor, focused too much on work. She wanted to get him to loosen up. "You should come over for drinks soon," she said as I was leaving.

I took a shower at the gym, sitting idly in my truck after this, unsure what to do. I didn't really know what to do. I didn't feel safe at home but I couldn't just go back to Dex's and forget about my children. After I had spent half an hour in tears, then tried to clear my mind, I messaged Daniella. She responded immediately: *Come over. We need to talk.* Short and to the point. When I got to Daniella's house, she sat me down at the kitchen table. "It's time we have a serious conversation," she said. She told me about her daughter's dad, who had fought them in a nasty court battle to win custody, ultimately making Daniella and her daughter's life difficult for the remainder of her daughter's childhood. She told me how she had escaped that abusive relationship and that, although I may not want to hear it, she said, leaving Mac for good may be the only option ultimately. "I want you to know that it's not okay how he treats you and its definitely not okay that your parents have taken your kids," she said, looking me straight in the eye. "You can stay here tonight, but in the morning, you're going to march your butt up there and you're going to get those kids, whether your parents want to give them back or not. You can get the police involved if you have to. Your parents have no legal right to keep the kids against your will." I was scared. I didn't know what else to do, so I agreed. "Elizabeth can stay with my grandma tonight. You can have her room," Daniella suggested.

I was exhausted, but when night came, I was unable to sleep. Finally, after changing positions and stacking a pillow on top of my head to drown out my surroundings, I fell into a light sleep. I dreamt Mac had come to retrieve me, bringing a gun and shooting at Albert before finding me.

The next morning, I wasted no time. I had a mission to fulfill. It was time to face my greatest fear: my father's disapproval. My parents lived in a secluded, gated neighborhood, away from the busyness of the nearby big city. The road to their home, which was lined with cedar, fir, and maple trees, had recently been paved with my dad's second-hand paver that he had gotten at an auction the year before. Always the community-oriented man, he liked to go above and beyond to help make the neighborhood a better place. He had the money, if not the time, to make a positive difference for his neighbors. Turning off this main road, I thought about how this place had brought me so much peace over the years. My parent's home had always been a refuge. They owned several acres of wooded hillside and operated an un-certified tree farm. Over the years, my father had logged portions of the property to help pay for the high cost of building their own completely hand-built log cabin. On the outside, it looked like a primitive log cabin, but on the inside, everything was finished with stained cedar wood planks and roughhewn interior siding.

Today, as I drove up the tree lined driveway towards their home, it felt like a foreboding castle prison looming in front of me. I hoped they would release my children. The ground was muddy with small piles of dirty snow melting where my dad had plowed the driveway.

I parked my truck next to my sister's pickup, taking a deep breath. I called the number to my parent's landline, a number I still knew by heart. When my father answered, I told him simply that I had arrived to pick up my children. I didn't want to go in. I got out of my truck slowly, seeing that my mom was helping Luke to walk out the door already. Naomi was carrying Carroll towards me. Both my mom and sister looked somber and didn't say a word to me as they handed me Lukes's booster seat and then Carroll's car seat. I thanked them, buckling in my children to leave.

Driving slowly down the road once more, I sighed in relief. A weight was lifted off my shoulders. Standing up to my dad hadn't been easy. I could feel the disapproval in both my father and my mother, though they hadn't reprimanded me verbally. The energy they exuded naturally trickled down to each of my siblings, who all still lived at home. We had all learned how to believe, based on my father's religious beliefs. I was no exception. Only now was I was beginning to realize that I would have to start thinking for myself. This was uncharted territory.

Chapter Fifteen

Two hours later we arrived at home. It was 11:15. I didn't know what to do. I was afraid of Mac showing up, even though he was likely at work. I had defied him multiple times in the last twenty-four hours. I had left instead of working things out, gotten my children against his will, *and* disappointed my father in the process. I could feel Mac's rage without even being physically close to him. There was a heavy feeling in the empty house, a foreboding dread that pulled me down. I didn't know what the ultimate consequences of my defiant actions would bring to our family. I only knew that I didn't want to face Mac right then, if at all. I called Daniella again, unsure of what to do. She told me to come over; "Bring clothes for the night for yourself and the kids" she instructed. I brought food for the night as well, not wanting to invade on their space or resources any more than was absolutely necessary.

The kids were scared. They didn't understand why we were leaving home, but I explained that it would be an adventure. When we arrived at Albert and Daniellas', she told me we could stay as long as we needed to. I didn't know what to do with myself. The children all played together and I tried to pretend this was a normal playdate with friends. I paced, checking my phone often. I had missed calls from Mac by this point. When it got late, I tucked in Carroll in the room I had stayed in the night before, settling Luke onto the leather couch next to the fireplace in the living room. Snuggling next to Carroll, who had fallen asleep with her tiny arms wrapped around my neck, her head nestled against my chest, I tried to tell myself we were safe. Everything would work out. When I was almost asleep, I thought suddenly of Mac, envisioning him breaking in and harming Albert again in pursuit of his wayward wife. I slept fitfully, dreaming of dark energy and Mac yelling at me, waking several times and ensuring that the door was still locked. I hoped Luke was okay in the other room and that I hadn't put Albert and his family at risk by staying with them.

The morning came slowly, another February day blanketed in clouds and fog. This was now the start of the second full day in which I hadn't talked with Mac. I continued to ignore his calls. I could feel the rage building within him, like a furnace burning hotter and hotter. Even physically safe, I felt vulnerable, afraid, and unprotected from him, and even my parents. I knew they were all collaborating on how to get me to come back to him; when my dad called that morning, I let it go to voicemail. I didn't even listen to the message. I didn't have the energy to fight a battle today.

I sat at Daniella's kitchen table. She looked at me seriously. "The company that works with my cousin's daughter is hiring. You will make better money than most of the other positions available as an entry level employee. I think you could start at $18. They always have need of caregivers. You also need to apply for food stamps and medical benefits through the state. You can do it through the self-sufficiency office down the road. You can stay here as long as you need to, but you need to get started on making these changes right away. Becoming financially independent will be crucial to your and the children's future." I was silent.

I knew I had left for a couple days, but I wasn't sure I was completely walking away from the life I had with my husband. I didn't know what I wanted. I simply knew I didn't want to be controlled. I knew I couldn't keep living in the fear of what he would do to me if I didn't obey. "Well," I said slowly, "Dex did say I could stay in the yurt if I needed a place for a while. Maybe I'll go out there and ask him if I can stay for a couple of weeks until I figure out what to do.".

Daniella told me that she knew I was hesitant to apply for state benefits, but that I could get off of those supports as soon as I was making good money. She said that this was why these benefits existed, for those who were in crisis. My heart rebelled at these thoughts. I wasn't in *crisis*. Yes, I was scared of my ex-husband and had taken space, but he wasn't *that* bad. He had never actually tried to *kill* me and had only hurt me physically twice. He wasn't one of those abusive partners that we all heard about on the news. If I stayed with him, I had steady provision for the kids. I really didn't want state benefits. I could still hear my parents' voice, talking about how God would always provide our needs; government help was a trap. *The rich will provide for the poor*, my dad always said. But where was he now? He wouldn't help his own daughter if she needed it. "Go work it out with Mac," he had said. "Stop being dramatic and go back home to your husband!" I could hear him now, influencing my thoughts as I tried to see clearly. A memory flooded to me then. I thought about my neighbor in the tiny apartment Mac had gotten for us when we first married. I remembered how she had befriended me, only to eventually ask for help babysitting her children weekly so she could go to the bar.

I remembered how she had convinced us to let her use our Wi-Fi connection for free and had even asked for my help with all her clothing alteration needs, for free. She was a prime example of someone who used state benefits so that she could avoid work and not take responsibility for her life, Mac had said. "Single moms always need help and they will take whatever they can get," he had repeated, again and again. If I chose to apply for food stamps, I was only one step away from going down that same path she had gone.

I remembered her standing in the middle of the common parking area, a cigarette held between her fingers, blowing out smoke and venting to me about her ex-husband. "He never takes any responsibility for these kids and he has all this money, but he's so selfish," she had said. "Because he won't pay child support, I can only afford to live in this cheap apartment and my kids have to share a room and struggle constantly!" The mere idea of applying for any benefits, combined with leaving Mac, brought up the same emotions in me. Internally, a war had been waged.

Amid the feelings of shame at the thought of applying for state help, something inside me was stirring. I felt excited for a change, ready to shake up the life I had known. Though the fear shouted "NO" loudly and clearly, a different voice whispered "yes". Softly and quietly, like the first rose budding on a bush in the early spring, a tiny bud of hope was beginning to form in my mind. Maybe there was a future. Maybe, just maybe, things would turn out. I thanked Daniella and asked her if I could come back to use the internet the next day, to apply for that job she had told me about. We drove to Dex's, expecting to stay for a few days.

Chapter Sixteen

I called Dex on our way there, to let him know. When we arrived, he let me know he had made a fire in the yurt. I parked near the road in the usual spot, walking quietly up the little path to the front door. As I pushed it open, I felt thankful for someone who was willing to support me. The house smelled of marijuana smoke, incense, and fried potatoes. It was warm and I could hear the fire in the woodstove. Dunagen came to meet me, wagging his black tail and pushing his nose into my hands.

I rubbed his head, thankful for his comfort. Sitting on the dusty red couch, it hit me how life had come full circle in a strange way. Mac had once lived in a teepee on Dex's land; he had been living there when I met him. Dex had been the one to introduce me to Mac. I had been so young and beautiful and full of light. I was only 17 when we had met. A dreamer, waiting for prince charming to sweep me up so we could live happily ever after at the castle together.

I would never forget the feeling I had when Dex talked about the young man who lived in a teepee in his meadow. I had a feeling, before I ever met the man, that he had a story. When I shook his hand for the first time, standing on the track after a bike race, I had known we would share a large part of our lives. Before he spoke a word to me, I had *that* feeling. Not like love at first sight, but the deep knowing that my soul was meant to collide with his. Most of the time that I had been courting

Mac, who was six years my senior, he had continued to live here with Dex. When we had gotten engaged, Mac had worked hard to afford an apartment, ultimately giving Dunagen, who had originally been his puppy, to Dex so that he could move into the apartment.

Now, here we all were, minus my husband. This house held a lot of memories for me, from the last six years of our lives together. I remembered carrying in my brand-new baby, who was fast asleep, and swaddled in a stretchy green blanket. I remembered handing him to Dex, uncovering the blanket from his face so that Dex could meet my son for the first time. I remembered having Luke stand against the wall as a toddler, marking his height on the height wall. I remembered sitting on the couch, covering up with a blanket as I nursed baby Carroll a while later. I remembered bringing Dex Christmas cookies.

A couple of years later, I remembered stopping by on my way to hike in the woods, explaining that Mac was out hunting. I hadn't wanted to explain that Mac was hunting alone because things were getting worse in our marriage, or that he wasn't with us because he never spent much time with us anymore. I hadn't wanted any of it to come out. I hadn't wanted anyone to know that I had failed at a healthy marriage. I had tried to keep it secret for so long. I had worked hard to preserve the façade, to hide the abuse and the dysfunction that I had married into. Yet here we were, sitting in Dex's living room, waiting for him to put boots on so he could show us the way to his yurt.

The trail behind the house was slightly muddy but Dex had put gravel on parts of it to make it less treacherous. We hiked down, carrying a backpack for each of us, the kids favorite blankets slung over my shoulders. At the bottom of the hill, the path joined the main trail that headed towards the creek. This one was wider, and covered in large rocks that were lodged in the ground, making it uneven. As we reached the final stretch towards the yurt, I was reminded of walking this same trail with Mac, Dunagen following, as he had showed me Dex's property for the first time, right before we had gotten engaged. Mac had led me down to the creek.

I remembered a moment of connection between just the two of us, my father not trailing along for once. I had felt so in love with him, simply standing there watching him as he stood on a rock in the middle of the river. It had felt so beautiful at the time, so magical. This place was still magical. The maple trees that surrounded the path to the yurt were bare this time of year, but leaves still covered parts of the path where they had fallen three months before. As we got close to the yurt, I saw a hand-built stone sauna, currently used as a storage room and filled with stacked firewood.

I saw the ax lying next to the large round of wood that was clearly used for splitting smaller pieces. I took in the beautiful wood doorway to the yurt as I stepped inside for the first time. Dex left us then, inviting me to get acquainted with the space alone, while the children milled about, exploring it, just as I was. The yurt was toasty warm, thanks to the fire he had built. The wood floors were covered in several large oriental rugs; there was a wooden bed frame with a thin mattress directly inside the door. At the foot of the bed stood a wooden chest which spanned the width of the bed. To the right, there was a clothing hanging rack, currently empty.

Next to this was a small white cupboard for food storage, with the doors closed. On the other side was a makeshift sink, placed in a wooden structure which included a countertop and shelves directly underneath. The shelves were neatly covered by cloth curtains. On the other side of the sink sat a dish drying rack. The countertop held a small propane powered burner; on top of it sat a red tea kettle and a cast iron skillet. There was a porcelain tub in the corner, but it hadn't been hooked up. Futuristically, it would become a storage bin for me. Next to this was another small mattress, set on top of cement blocks. Through the yurt and to the back deck I went, taking in the beauty.

I silently surveyed the maple trees that provided a covering above the yurt, and the steep slope down to the creek below. The sound of the water was soothing as I took it all in. Being that it was the beginning of February, the air was cold, but the fog had lifted. The sky was sunny for the first time in many weeks. The birds were starting to wake from their sleep. My mind filled with the noise of birds chirping, combined with the creek gurgling below, and the fire crackling behind me, through the open door of the yurt. All was chaotic on the inside, but in that moment, I felt peace. I felt nature enveloping me, caressing my mind. Everything would be okay.

Chapter Seventeen

After that day, changes began to happen at a rapid-fire pace and life began to look vastly different. I determined to stay in the yurt for a while. In the meantime, I got to work. I applied for a job with the caregiving company Daniella had pointed me to. A day later, I talked on the phone with a recruiter; I was hired instantly. There was a family who needed an immediate caregiver for their seven-year-old, who was in a wheelchair with cerebral palsy. Pending a background check, I could start within the week. I spent the next two days filling out applications. I completed one for food benefits and another for healthcare.

Before I even had a chance to worry about childcare, Dex stepped up. He told me that he could take care of my children during my evening shifts, for the time being. Between Dex, his girlfriend Alana, and Jonathan, the 40-year-old, unemployed know-it-all who lived rent free in Dex's spare room, there was a true village to raise my children. All I needed to do was focus on stabilizing my life, doing what I could to give myself another option while I tried to gain perspective on my marriage.

I went back home a couple of times during the day that week, cooking and meal prepping, both for myself, and for Mac. I cleaned the house for him, feeling guilty even as I stayed away. I was leaving to clear my head, not to abandon him and the marriage. He called me three times that week. First, they were angry voicemails. Then sad. He pleaded that I come home. He wanted to talk and make things right.

Throughout the next few weeks, I began to slowly develop a routine. I would rise early, stoking the small fireplace in the woodstove. I would splash ice cold water, the only temperature that came out of the tap, onto my face. I would then fill the red tea kettle, placing it on the propane burner to heat. I would place coffee grounds into the French press, pouring the hot water over top of the coffee grounds as soon as the kettle had hummed, letting me know it was ready. After pouring myself a cup of hot coffee, adding a thin line of half n' half, I would sit in the rocking chair to drink it and wake up slowly.

I would either watch the children sleep or look out towards the creek, trying to create an environment of calm to start my day. After coffee, I would go up to Dex's house, check my messages, brush my teeth and get ready for the day. The kids, who normally woke by the time it was light, would be starving by then. Often, I cooked in Dex's kitchen. While it was physically possible to do it in the yurt, I found it more challenging. Many times, I made the children pancakes or fried potatoes, Dex's go to. After breakfast, we would pack up the truck and go to the gym. The gym was the only thing that really motivated me to wake up each day and go after my goals.

Josephine had introduced me to Sophia, her main lifting partner. Together, they had begun including me more and more. Sophia, who looked as though she could have been my sister, with bright green eyes and nut-brown hair, had perfect legs and a beautiful face. She was my age and we had a lot in common. While she had also married young, and had long since become unhappy in her marriage, she was handling things differently than I was. I knew she was seeing someone, but that wasn't my secret to break to her husband. I was thankful to be included and we made a very attractive and strong trio in the gym.

After my bi-weekly lifting session with the girls, I would come home, not knowing what to do with myself. In truth, I didn't know where home was anymore. When I lived in our little home on the edge of town, I had at least some sense of normalcy. I would clean, watch the kids play in the yard, do gardening or mow the lawn, bake muffins or cookies for Mac, or do any number of other "normal" activities that people do in their own home.

Being in the yurt suddenly, with nothing that belonged to me other than the clothing I was wearing, I felt off balance. I felt that I had too much time on my hands. Although I had committed to working three nights a week, this schedule left a lot of time that was unaccounted for. Besides not having access to the normal pastimes of my life with Mac, I didn't really know what to do mentally. I was supposed to be figuring things out, but it seemed that the opposite was happening.

After three weeks, I was even less sure than I had been when I had left. I knew life couldn't go back to the way it had been, but I didn't know what I wanted or where to go from here. Mac seemed to be making changes. He had texted me multiple times a day; he wanted to be able to show me that he could love me the right way. He told me he would never give up on our family. He missed me. He told me he missed the kids;

they needed him in their life. I knew he was right about that at least. He had even found a therapist and scheduled our first meeting together.

One evening, mid-February, I came back to the house. I knew he was home. He seemed happy to see me. There was no trace of the anger from weeks before. He made dinner for the family, breakfast food; fried potatoes, eggs, and bacon. He hadn't cooked for the family since the week Carroll was born. This was a big deal. I felt like an awkward guest in our home, like I wasn't meant to be there. I wasn't sure how to act. Being treated well made me nervous. He was trying. Maybe I had been too hasty to leave. I didn't want to give up on a marriage where kids were involved. I could see he was suffering without me. He didn't even pack himself lunches anymore. The house was dirty. He needed me here. I couldn't leave again, in good conscience.

I stayed that night. And the next and the next. He agreed to watch the kids in the evenings so that I could still go to work. It was easier than having Dex do it and it gave him time with the kids. Although I still didn't know what I wanted, I felt I couldn't stay in his house and not give him sex. We both had needs and it just made sense to fulfill them. I didn't even consider love. It had never been about love with him, even when our marriage was good. It made no difference if we slept together. Maybe I had made too much of a big deal about him wanting other women as well, I told myself. Maybe humans *were* animalistic with basic needs. *I* had been the one with unrealistic expectations. On a subconscious level, I began to feel that the only way this would work, was if I compartmentalized everything, turning off all feelings. *Love was a fairy tale, an ideal from another lifetime.*

Chapter Eighteen

Though I had been staying with Mac again, and he had tried to make changes for the first couple of days, the same problems lingered. The fighting had come to a physical standstill, but the currents still ran strong beneath the surface. I tiptoed around Mac, trying to not say or do anything that would upset him. This seemed to be the only way to maintain any level of peace. I hoped therapy would help. The first session went probably much like marriage therapy often does. It started with the therapist asking for us to take turns talking about our situation. Neither of us wanted to let the other talk, so finally I allowed Mac to start.

He explained how I had left and he missed me dearly. He was unsure if I was committed to the marriage at this point. He felt that, while he was all in, I had given up on our union. He then went on to explain that the problems had started when I had become lazy. I never kept the house clean anymore and he didn't understand what I did with my days when he was busy working to keep the family afloat financially. He continued, explaining how I had energy for lifting heavy weights, but never enough energy to spend time with him.

He was concerned this obsession with lifting weights was affecting my parenting as well; he wanted to see me helped before it was too late. I stayed silent until the therapist asked about his family history, at which time I interrupted his description of a happy upbringing and a positive relationship with his father, to remind him that his father was never reliable and could be counted on only to disappoint him. I said that, regardless of how I felt about our marriage, seeing Mac suffer because of his dad made me hurt. I didn't like it. Mac interrupted and we began arguing.

The therapist held up a hand reminding me that it was, in fact, Mac's turn to talk first. I should wait for my turn next session. I sat silently for the remainder of the session, wishing I was at the gym. I didn't say a word to Mac on the drive home.

While life at home continued to be tense, my powerlifting strength progressed. My competition was now only a week away. I had asked Mac if he wanted to come, hoping that he would bring the children so they could see their mom compete for the first time. Maybe we could even make a family vacation out of it. Angry that I hadn't given up my lifting goals, he refused. I didn't know what to do, so I settled for doing what I had been lately. Following my heart, regardless of the anger that it invoked within my husband.

Three days before I was to leave, I went to the bank, planning to take out cash for the cost of the hotel. When the teller handed me the money and a receipt, it showed a total balance for the savings account, of $900. My heart dropped into my stomach. An awful feeling began to creep over me and then dread set in. When I had brought Mac in to add his name to the account a month before, I had proudly noted that we had saved over $15,000. "I think money has been stolen," I said in disbelief, immediately beginning to panic. The teller looked over the recent transactions, putting her finger on a spot on the touch screen in front of her after a moment. She read, "It says right here that Mac, that must be your husband? Took out $14,500 on the 15th of this month." I went pale. "That wasn't his to take out, I had added him but it was *our* money, mostly *mine*!" I told the teller, panic now evident in my voice. She looked at me over her glasses, compassionately, but firmly. "Well, because he was legally added, there is nothing we can do; I can take him off now if you want though" she offered, trying to be helpful. I was numb with shock.

I called my dad, in tears. We were back to speaking again since I had come home. "Mac told me about that, but Sharon, you need to trust him. He was really concerned that you would go and spend it all," my father explained patiently. He reminded me again how the leader of the house always did what was in the best interest of the family. I was fuming. It was *I* who had saved all of this money. All of the effort had been mine and yet my father actually believed Mac. My father actually thought that I might spend it. Or had he advised Mac? I didn't know anymore.

Two days before the competition, I began my final process to sweat and drop a few more pounds, by sitting in the sauna for an hour, then swimming a lap around the pool at the local recreation center near my gym. I repeated this process again, weighing myself a second time. I was half way to my desired weight. I would go home, sleep, and then come back early in the morning to do the process one more time before driving the four hours to where the weigh-ins would be held. I wouldn't drink or eat again until I had weighed in the next morning.

That night I went to sleep hungry, thirsty, and cranky. I was stressed about leaving the children for this long with their father. I planned to be gone two nights. I knew this was a big sacrifice for him. He wasn't eager for me to abandon my duties, but he agreed. I think he was afraid I would leave again if he didn't. I awoke at 3 the next morning. Grabbing my gallon of water, I quietly tiptoed out to my truck, headed for the gym and the sauna. When I arrived, ready to get into the sauna again, the door was locked. There was a paper on the door that read: *Closed until further notice, due to the outbreaks of the COVID-19 virus.* I was annoyed. I hoped this COVID thing would be done in a week or two so that everyone could go back to their routines. I knew I wouldn't make it to my goal weight. I could still compete, but not in the weight class I had hoped to compete in.

The next twenty-four hours passed quickly. On competition morning, I woke up nervous and excited. I ate a blueberry muffin, drank some electrolytes, and went over to the facility to begin warming up. I didn't know what to expect. When they called my name, I went, and after this, my nervousness turned to sheer excitement. Stepping onto the platform for the first time, I successfully squatted 252 pounds. I had followed the commands effortlessly; I was on the board. I finished out squats with a 300-pound squat. On to the next part of the event, I bench pressed 135. I was a big girl who could successfully lift full 45-pound wheels off my chest! While I was waiting for others to finish so we could move to the final event, deadlift, my phone rang. It was Mac. He was upset. He told me Carroll had a runny nose; he was worried about her. He wanted my advice about what to do. I told him to let her rest and give her warm tea, if she would drink it.

I began worrying. The mom guilt, which had never left me, crept in quickly. I thought how Mac was having to deal with a sick child alone, while I was enjoying myself. I had abandoned my family to compete. I began beating myself up mentally, reminding myself of everything my parents, brothers, and Mac had said about me over the last few months. My responsibility was with my children and I was probably a failing parent because I had chosen myself this weekend. I quickly became engulfed by stress, fidgeting and squirming as I sat in a chair watching others lift. I bit my lip, hoping the event would be done quickly.

When it was time to deadlift, I completed a 341-pound lift for my final attempt. After I had finished, I began to relax, swelling with pride at how well I had done. That is, until my phone rang again. This time, Mac was even more stressed. "Luke got mad and hit Carroll, and now she has a bruise. I don't know what to do. I wish you were here!" He told me, on the verge of tears. He went on to say that he wasn't sure if he would make it until I got home. He wished I had considered the consequences of my actions before abandoning him for two days. I fought back, reminding him that I had asked if he wanted to come.

The conversation went on for a few more minutes; at this point, his voice was elevated and even with the phone to my ear, others were looking. People could hear him yelling at me. My friends looked on helplessly. Finally, I hung up. They advised me to turn off my phone. I did. The rest of the afternoon I spent meeting new people and being social. At the end, judges called my name; I had won my weight category, by a lot. I happily received a medal and then we left. My original plan had been to stay that night and go home leisurely in the morning. The guilt was strong and I couldn't allow myself to neglect my family any longer. I hoped I could stay awake while I drove through the night.

Alone in the darkness of my truck, I re-lived my glory moments from the day. I would never forget this day, as long as I lived. This little bit of freedom had showed me how much power I truly had. I felt strong. Even as I was to go back to the struggles that were taking place at home, this memory could never be taken away. I would tuck it safely into my heart, remembering it as the day I had showed the world my true strength.

When I got home, well after ten, my kids were calm and ready for bed. Mac said nothing to me, retreating to the garage immediately. I showed Luke my medal. At least someone was proud of me. I wanted to tell Mac all about it, but he wasn't in the mood to listen. He never was. After both kids were tucked in, thankful that their mama was back, I curled up on the couch, exhausted. Mac asked if I was going to come to bed. He had missed me, he said. I didn't feel like it. I felt hurt. This had been a big deal to me. I had really, really wanted him to be proud of me. I had won and done something new. The excitement of the day was dampened, once again, by my husband's contempt.

Chapter Nineteen

In the days that followed, I became even more confused about what to do. I felt as though I was stuck between two worlds, surrounded by fog and unsure which way I should go. The chasm that had opened when I had left for two weeks was widening. I was afraid to make a decision, knowing that either way, I would cause upset. I knew I couldn't trust Mac after finding out about the stolen money. I knew he hadn't changed when he freaked out during my competition. I knew I wasn't happy, but I didn't know what would bring me happiness. I felt like I was using Mac for a secure and stable place to live, in exchange for sex and cooking for him. But what did secure even mean?

While the house was clean and dry and I wasn't being murdered by gangs in the street, I felt mentally unsafe in every way. To make the decision even harder, I had lost my client due to the COVID outbreak. While caregivers were considered essential workers, the amount of work that each one was given depended on the preferences of the family. It seemed that no one wanted a new caregiver when the whole world had shut down, in fear of contracting a potentially life-threatening virus that could spread from person to person through many forms of contact. I felt stuck. I felt dumb for leaving in the first place and also weak for coming back. I didn't know who I was or where I was meant to be. I knew that God wanted me to be a submissive wife, but I wasn't sure if I even aligned with God anymore. How could I be in agreement with a God who supported my husband's behavior toward me? Did I even *want* to serve a God like that? Not really. Maybe God was actually against me. Mac had reminded me again how women in the Bible would have never been this wayward. These women knew their roles as wives; to step out of that role was disrespectful to God. I had begun attending a weekly Bible study a few weeks before, hoping to find answers. Even this, I knew he didn't support. These women worked and had dynamic lives. I think he feared they might influence me negatively if I spoke up about my situation. They weren't in any danger of knowing the situation though. Although I enjoyed the fellowship with these women, I felt guilty because they didn't know the real me.

They saw me raising my kids and they saw Lukes's behavior issues, which had started manifesting more during the time he was playing with other kids while I attended the meetings. They knew that I was a young married woman who was also a stay-at-home mom. They didn't know that I had directly disobeyed my husband by powerlifting, or that I was thinking about leaving him for good, even while still living with him and getting a free place to stay in exchange for sex.

The Bible study had been focused on a teaching about discerning God's voice from other voices. This was why I had signed up. I wanted truth, though I was unwilling to share the truth of my situation with others. Even there, I felt trapped. I felt trapped by the picture that I had painted of the life I lived with Mac, which most thought was still a beautiful Christian marriage. My leaving would tear down all the illusions. There would be no more fantasy among my community about how Christianity had kept our marriage intact because I had followed rules and made it work.

It was now mid-March. Spring was approaching, ever so slowly. The nights were cold, but occasional days of sun graced the world, thawing everything out and bringing the first flowers of the season, dandelions and the occasional daffodil. The clusters I had so carefully transplanted to bloom in the flower garden in front of my house began blooming, blasting yellow and white into a world that had been dark during the long winter. Birds began to sing more, illuminating the positive aspects of a changing season.

The grass would soon begin to grow again too; soon it would be time to work in the yard. Even with the season bringing positivity, I felt dead inside. I felt as though my winter would never come to an end. Little by little, the hope that I had felt when I had left, was dwindling. I couldn't see the light anymore. I was aimlessly floating through life, doing the motions, smiling the smile and playing a role.

One day, I got a call from Corey's mother, who told me she was throwing a surprise birthday party for him. She hoped I would come. She knew it would mean a lot for all of the gym family to be there. She let me know Mac was welcome too. I was afraid to even bring it up, already knowing how he would respond. When I eventually did, Mac declined and told me he didn't feel comfortable with my being at Corey's house, especially at night. He could only imagine the things we would do while together. I went anyway. It was at his parent's home, not his, after all. Corey had a younger brother, who brought his two boys and his girlfriend. Jonah came, with his girlfriend. Coreys' parents, who had been together for several years, looked happy, thankful that all his friends had come to celebrate him. A pang of sadness hit me as I realized I was the only single person there, other than Corey. I wished my man had come with me.

When I got home, Mac was in the garage. "You fucked him tonight, didn't you?" he asked, as soon as I had shut the door. "Mac, please, don't talk like that in front of the kids!" I begged, ushering them in to the bathroom to brush their teeth and get ready for bed. He didn't say another word to me until I was in bed. He walked in, turning the overhead light on. "I'm going to kill him," he announced. "What are you talking about?" I asked, sitting up in the bed. He continued, "I know what you guys did tonight, and he's not going to get away with fucking my wife". He had his handgun in his waist holster. "I'm not joking," he said. He turned and left the house. I sat in bed, frozen in fear. What was I to do? If I called the police, he would be angrier at me later on. Not only that, but my dad would hear about it. If I warned Corey and Mac wasn't serious, it would raise an unnecessary alarm to Coreys' family, who would probably do all they could to press charges.

I didn't know what to do, so I did nothing. I lay there in the dark once more, shivering in fear. Not only was I scared for my friend, but I was afraid for my own life. Recently, I had faced the real fear that Mac could, at any point, decide to take my life. I felt helpless. Mac never returned that night and I eventually drifted into a fitful sleep, surrounded by darkness and the dark energy that resides where hate has made a home. I checked on Corey the next morning; he was fine.

Chapter Twenty

Time continued to creep on. I continued to go through the motions of my life, repeating the basic actions that constituted survival each day, living in fear and paralyzed by my lack of direction. I knew I needed to make a decision, and whatever I decided needed to be final. I needed to commit to it. One morning, I woke up with a knowing. It was April first. Spring had fully sprung and this was truly a day for a new start. For the first time in weeks, I had clear direction. The time had come. My soul had spoken and I was ready to listen.

As distanced as I was from God, I felt a peace like I hadn't felt in a long, long time. I had doubted my choice to leave for a long time. I didn't want to do this, but I knew it was the right choice. The chasm had widened and it was time to jump. It was time to take a side and stand upon my action, no matter what the consequences of the decision would bring to me.

I cleaned the house. I packed my kid's clothing, my sewing machine, the sewing machine desk, and some of my clothing. I filled the back of my pickup, which still had the canopy on. When I arrived at Dex's, the warmth of spring welcomed me. I opened the door of the truck and breathed in fresh, outdoor air, smelling the newness of the season. It took me a couple of hours to take everything to the yurt and clean the space up. Because I hadn't been sure what I was going to do for the last few weeks, I had left it unorganized; it needed some work. I put my sewing machine table in the corner, hung my dresses on the clothes hanging rod and put some food in the mini fridge.

I cooked my kids' lunch on the propane stove. I boiled water over the propane flame, pouring it into the sink one potful at a time. I put soap in, relishing the calmness of washing dishes while looking out the window towards the creek. All of this felt like a new adventure. I was ready to start it. After lunch, I took a moment to hug both kids. I told them this was home now, that we were lucky to get to live next to a creek and be surrounded by wilderness. I told them we were going to go on a little hike. Up the creek from Dex's house was a little waterfall. We walked to it, following the dirt trail that meandered through salmonberry bushes, maple trees and ferns, toward the sound of water.

Robins chirped in the trees above, calling to one another, discussing the warmth of the day. As we climbed down the last of the steep trail towards the creek, I was surrounded by the sounds of rushing water and once again, the scent of newness. I stopped and pulled a mini fern out of a moss-covered log. I bit the end of it, tasting the faint hint of licorice in the root. This environment was home. This was where I could be at peace. I helped the kids onto the bank of the creek, which was covered in tiny gray pebbles. I took my shoes off and waded in. The water was ice cold. I stood there, completely in the present. In that moment, I felt the peace again. There was nothing but nature; it was enveloping me and calming me, holding me, and caressing my skin. This day was truly a new beginning, more so than I would even hope to understand for several months.

Chapter Twenty-One

If you've ever had a big change in life that happened suddenly or unexpectedly, you may know the feeling of waking up after a sleep where you had forgotten about the change. You may have woken up, thinking about your routine for the day, only to have reality hit you in the face like a bucket of cold water, jarring you out of the unconscious escape of slumber. This was how I felt on April second, when I opened my eyes in the yurt on day one after making the biggest decision of my adult life. I lay there, taking everything in. The rushing water in the creek below me, steady with its pattern but ever changing slightly as the water flow constantly changed tones.

The pattering of rain on the clear dome of the yurt roof, the sound of maple branches scraping against the side of the yurt as the wind rustled them. I was in my *new* home, without my partner by my side. There was no lunch to be packed, no coffee to be made and there were no eggs to be fried for Mac's breakfast. There was also no need to perform for him, to pretend that I was excited about pleasuring him while inwardly cringing. There was nothing on my agenda today. No one to answer to. There was no pressing matter that I had to deal with, no calls that I needed to make.

Only nature sounds and sleeping children, who had both ended up next to me in the bed. I leaned over and kissed Carroll's blonde curls. I watched Luke make a face in his sleep; his little hand was stretched

125

protectively over his sister. I didn't know what I was doing. I had no clue how I had ended up here, how I had defied my husband, the leader of our family, and disappointed my father. I didn't know what would come next. As much as I often spent hours day-dreaming about the future, I didn't even know what this day would look like. Somehow, that was okay.

Later that day, I talked with Dex. He told me he had been unsure if we were coming back. I asked about a fair rental price since this was more permanent now. We agreed on $300 per month.

I needed to work, but I didn't know if anyone needed a caregiver since COVID was now in full swing and most people were concerned. Even Dex was talking about how many people had died. He mentioned how this was just the beginning. He was concerned for anyone in his house to go in public and possibly contact the sickness, bringing it into his household. He was sure that if he contacted it, death would be the result, just as it had been for so many others.

My calmness from yesterday was quicky evaporating. Even out here, surrounded by nature, living with Dex the Zen filled hippie, the reality of the nationwide event was catching up. The weight of the world and my situation was slowly settling around me, like a heavy blanket.

Chapter Twenty-Two

I didn't have phone service at Dex's. In his house, I had Wi-Fi, but this didn't include phone calls. When I drove into town to get gas and buy groceries the next day, there were two voicemails from my dad. The guilt tripping was stronger than ever.

At the gas station, I quickly discovered that my debit card had been declined. After only two days away from Mac, he had taken me off our joint account. Panic began to set in as I realized the only source of income I had was the money in the savings account; what was left of it anyway, after he had taken so much out. Mentally, I began doing the math. I thought about all the expenses I had. I needed a job, and fast. Thankful now that I had applied for state help with food costs, I filled the cart with my children's favorite snacks. I would do my best to make this adventure a positive experience for my children. They didn't need to know about my worries. When I got home from the grocery store, I went into Dex's house to take a shower. One downside of the new living arrangement was that there was no way to shower or even use the bathroom without sharing with Dex, Alana, and Jonathan, the prospectless roommate.

Regardless, I was thankful for a place to live, and definitely not in a place to be picky. I would try to not get in anyone's way, making sure no one needed to use the bathroom before taking a shower and trying to make myself scarce. While I savored the hot water, washing out my long brown hair, my kids created a whirlwind of disaster. Ultimately, a cup of milk was spilled on Dex's oriental rug. A trinket that had some very important spiritual symbolism, was dropped on the wood floor, shattering. Dex wasn't impressed. Alana was even less impressed.

Although Alana was beautiful, with long brown dreadlocks, green eyes, and glowing skin, I felt the current of jealousy that ran deep within her. She had moved here to be with Dex only a month before I had, hoping to live a peaceful life with her man as they approached retirement. Yet, here I was. Me, with my natural beauty, youth, and enthusiasm, but also chaos, and energetic children. We were less than a week in to this new life and I had a feeling Dex was already re-thinking his choice to allow us to stay.

Later that day, my fears were confirmed. "Have you had any luck looking for a place?" Dex asked. He wanted to know how soon we could leave. Job searching meant I was exposed to multiple people, all who could carry the COVID virus and expose his household to COVID. Even if the kids were calm, the COVID issue would continue to present itself. This situation was temporary and he wanted to make sure that I knew that.

That afternoon, while my kids played outside of the yurt, I had my first melt down, lying curled in a ball on the thin mattress in the yurt. The weight of the world had literally landed on my shoulders and it had all happened over night. I had gone from a familiar, though unsafe and unhappy, environment, to one where I had no answers and I needed *all* the answers. Although the weight had been there mentally, I hadn't been able to feel anything while I was still with Mac. I had been able to keep everything in compartments, thinking only of the fact that I had provision physically.

I had been in survival mode, accepting the crumbs that had been thrown at me, in place of forging my own path. Now that I was trying to do it on my own, I felt it all. Dex didn't want us, I couldn't afford to live, I didn't have work, and even if I found work, I didn't have full time childcare so I couldn't go. Dex would only do it for three hours, a few times a week, and he was already annoyed with my children. I needed something full time and someone who was more equipped for this task. Even if I did find childcare, there was no way I could afford to pay for it.

I was basically screwed, and even God hated me. Even God was looking down, judging my pitiful self who had thought I was independent enough for this. *Look at her now*, he was probably thinking. I had gotten myself into this because I listened to the quiet voice inside, instead of being practical and real with my situation. At least Mac had been security. Maybe he had been right that I wouldn't make it on my own. He had often reminded me that I needed him to make it financially, stating how I would fail at finding a job and providing for the children by myself. I was too proud to go back to him; even pride set aside, I would rather be dead than face the pain of another day living in limbo, waiting for him to blow up or threaten me or guilt trip me again for not being enough. I had never considered taking my life, but in this moment, it crossed my mind. Face down on the pillow, I sobbed. Long, gut wrenching sobs that came from my soul, as I began to feel reality hitting me. I allowed the tears to soak into the pillow as I lay there, feeling like even in my grief, I had no privacy. Dex would likely come down if the kids touched anything in his yard; I had to be on guard. Maybe this was it, I told myself. Suddenly feeling the anger towards my father, my husband, Dex, even God, I looked up at the sky and made a dare to God.

"God," I said, shaking my balled fists in anger, "if you actually care about me, if you aren't up there judging me for my life choices, if you truly want me to succeed without Mac, and if you want me to stay alive and not take my life, then make a way! Open the sky and pour answers into my life. Direct me to people and places that can help me! This is the only way. If you don't, I will know that you, like my family, truly hate me. I will take my life."

Chapter Twenty-Three

The next morning, I started making realistic plans. I called a homeless shelter, asking if they had any room for a family of three. The receptionist told me that they currently did not, but if I really needed a place, they could make room within the week. I hadn't ever thought that homelessness would be my reality, but a shelter was a step up from being on the street. We would be welcome and safe. I would do anything I had to, to prove to Mac that I could, in fact, do this alone. The stubbornness was kicking in. This wasn't just about being freed from Mac, but about remembering who I was. I wasn't the woman who would grovel for basic necessities to be provided, in exchange for sex and abusive treatment. I was the woman who would make her own way.

Later that day, I received a call from the caregiver company. "I see your name is affiliated with our company still. You are on a list to be called if new clients become available. We have an urgent request for a family who wants support for their child. Are you interested?" The lady asked. She explained that the pandemic had made it harder for the family to find a provider who was still willing to work. They weren't concerned with the risk of bringing COVID into their home. She gave me a number. I called this mom, who wondered if I could meet her child that Saturday and do my first four-hour session then. This would occur in two days. I agreed immediately. I texted Mac, offering him some time with the kids on Saturday, not telling him it was so that I could work.

This would have to do for now. I checked my phone, seeing I had a message from a lady named Martha. She had been an assistant midwife at my child's birth.

"I heard you were looking for childcare; I recently opened a full-time childcare in my home. I take state pay. All you have to do is apply through the state program; you will get approved. I can take your kids starting Monday. Because Luke is preschool aged, I can do pre-K work with him. It's free to you assuming you get approved and even if it takes a few days, we can back date pay so that you can start bringing them right away".

When I returned to Dex's, he apologized for getting upset about the broken trinket. He let me know that we could stay until we found something better, and he understood how hard it was right now with the pandemic.

In less than 24 hours, God had answered on *all* accounts. Not only had he provided work, but childcare in an unconventional, unexpected manner. He had sent the people to me, before I had even the chance to go looking. Heaven had truly heard my prayer and faster than I could even have orchestrated things on my own. I was in shock. The way was being paved. Had this been a coincidence? Was this truly God's answer? How else could this have fallen into place so perfectly?

The first day at the new job went well. The mother was kind and patient as she observed me working with her five-year-old daughter. She explained to me that she worked from home, but struggled to meet the demands of her child, who had been diagnosed with autism the year before. Because her husband had a high-level position with the military, he was often gone for weeks at a time, leaving her to manage things with this child, and a younger one, who was only two, independently. She asked if I could come three days a week, starting next week. I felt instantly that this family would be a good fit for me. I was in awe that this opportunity had lined up so effortlessly.

I finished the application for childcare services. My children would start Monday. Because the kids did well with their father that Saturday, we agreed that they could come over twice a week. They still needed their father and I wouldn't deny that. Mac had texted me nearly every day, asking if I could just give him time to talk. He told me that he had done a lot of thinking and realized he had been wrong. He wanted to be a Godly husband. He let me know that he was still attending therapy. I had given up after I had been told to listen and not interrupt. I wasn't sure I would go back. I had asked Mac for marriage counseling since the time I had found pictures of my sister on his phone, over two years before. He had told me no, even when I had left for a night after the first episode of physical abuse. Why I should attend now, made no sense to me. Therapy was for people who wanted to fix their marriages and I wasn't sure if I fell under that category any more at all.

Even if I was to eventually try to work it out with Mac again, it would take a lot of effort and time to know he had truly changed. Right now, my priority was getting stable on my own. I couldn't work on the relationship if it was focused only on survival. Besides that, Mac needed to see that I could, in fact, do this on my own.

Chapter Twenty-Four

A week had gone by. A week that showed me what my routine would begin to look like. I had gone to work Monday, Wednesday, and Friday, spending the other days with my children. I was afraid that if I worked too much, I would become a typical *working mom,* as my father had always referred to them. I would abandon my children and put my career first. I didn't want to do that; I told myself I would never work full time.

Because my regular gym was closed due to the pandemic, I packed up children after work, taking them to Corey's garage where he had offered Jonah, Lucas, me, and a couple of others to train weekly. I was getting stronger and I needed the outlet, now more than ever. When Friday night came, I spent it with my children, relaxing on Dex's front lawn, then retreating to the yurt to prepare for another night in this tranquil setting. Relaxing was hard for me, especially now. My mind never truly shut down, but I forced myself to read my children their favorite book before collapsing into the yurt bed next to them, exhausted. In the morning, Josephine called, inviting me to go to the beach with her and Sophia.

At the beach, we sat in the sun and tanned while the kids played. It felt like summer and I wore a bikini top with short black jean shorts, making sure to get some pictures that accented my growing shoulder muscles, my mostly intact six pack I had worked so hard for, and of course, my leg gains. Sophia updated me on the latest with the boy she was seeing. I felt a tinge of guilt at the fact that she continued on in her marriage while sleeping with someone else. Josephine, on the other hand, justified her behavior, telling her that she had a right to be happy. When I sent a picture of all three of us, in our bikini tops, to the powerlifting group chat, Lucas replied that Josephine was "hot af" and he would "like to hit". I told her, laughing. She asked for his Chat-app, adding him.

When we got back to the yurt, there was a paper plate with apple bars on the counter, covered in plastic wrap. A note was left on top.

"These were from mom, for you and the children. I don't know if I can, or I'm strong enough, to keep living like this, Sharon. You tell the children that I'm a bad dad and that you can do it all on your own. Well, you're stronger than me then, because I can't and I won't do it alone (life, family, raising our children with anyone else). I can't do this. I want life with you and the children, or I want God to take me. I love you. Till death do us part". –Mac

The guilt started to come back, flooding in again as I wrestled with thoughts I had tried to ignore for the last few days. I *had* agreed to never leave him. I *had* said those vows. I *had* committed my life to him. I was concerned for his life and I knew he was struggling. Maybe I had been too hasty to decide to leave him.

After work two days later, I went to get some items from the little white house. Daniella had told me that I should probably collect important documents from the house in case things changed and I wasn't able to get them in the future. Although I didn't feel that this was a grounded worry, I did need birth certificates for the kids to complete their enrollment to the childcare assistance program. I had made a list of items I would need so that I could spend minimal time in the house, feeling awkward even going back anymore. Although I was very inwardly conflicted on what I was to do with the situation, I needed to continue taking daily actions to make myself more independent of the marriage. I needed to be able to function on my own. Doing this, was one of those actions.

When I arrived I went straight to the bedroom. I opened the cubby built into the back of the king size bedframe, shuffling through papers. I had pulled out the kid's social security cards, birth certificates, my own birth certificate and social security card, and was deciding on what else to get, when I noticed something that decided the trajectory of my future. An opened box of condoms sat on the back of the bed. A wrapper lay on the sheet where one side of the comforter was pulled back. Looking around, I saw a bra and a bathrobe lying on the bed, partially hidden by the comforter. My heart dropped into the pit of my stomach. My knees went wobbly. I took in a sharp breath, then another one, trying to stay grounded. It had been less than three weeks since I had moved out. Although I knew he had been talking to other women throughout our marriage, I found it gut wrenching that he was seeing someone else, especially since he had told me in his letter just yesterday how he didn't want to ever do life with anyone but me.

I could hardly move. I stood frozen in my place. The truth hit me then, like an arctic wind, a blast in my face that blew right through to my soul. There was no stipulating or guessing anymore. My fears were realized. My deepest fear had come true. Being cheated on by the man I thought I would spend forever with. I knew I had been unsure of our future, but to be hit with cold facts was more than I could take. I reached for the bedframe, steadying myself. I didn't even want to get close to the bed, thinking how dirty the room suddenly felt. Our room. The room we had made love in, the place we had conceived my daughter in, the bed we had rested in the night after she was born, where we had both watched her sleep and dressed her for the very first time. The bed we had woken up in, that fateful night I had received the call about my brother in law's unexpected death. The bed we had cried in together after a fight, before having make up sex. And now, the bed where he had broken the sacred bond of our commitment to one another. I needed to leave.

I gathered papers and left. Once I was in my truck, I took another breath. There were no tears, only shock. Only the disbelief that comes with the truth settling in, truth that was long questioned, but truth that was easy to shove back to the corner of my subconscious, to tell myself I was overthinking, until now. In a shaky voice, I called Daniella. I didn't know what to do. Daniella knew exactly what was needed.

"Oh, honey, I am sorry it has come to this, but I can't say I didn't see it coming. You need to file for divorce and you need to do it now." Thirty minutes later we sat at her table again. "You need to file first," she told me. I didn't want to think about what my dad would say. I was becoming the woman he despised, the one who not only defied her husband, but also was going to get the law involved. The fear instantly began to rise and I went silent. "Listen honey, I know your dad won't approve, but he is probably advising Mac to file; based on how he has supported Mac so far, you can't trust his advice. You need to do this for the children, if nothing else." Still reeling, I took the name of the lawyer she gave me, written neatly on a piece of note paper. Standing in her kitchen, I called the office.

I scheduled a consult, grimacing inwardly about spending $200 for a consult that would only bring more pain and chaos, not to mention negative responses from my parents. This wasn't what I wanted. However, Daniella was right. It was time for drastic measures. I must not get caught up in my emotions right now.

Chapter Twenty-Five

The next week went by in a blur of chaos. I didn't have time to be in my feels. Though I had told myself I would work only part time, this illusion quickly faded as I realized how expensive any legal action would cost. The day for my consult with the lawyer came and I pulled in, noticing how my truck barely fit into the tiny parking lot between all the more compact cars. I already felt out of place here. I walked in, tucking a printed cloth mask behind my ears.

The office was small; the immediate entryway had two chairs, a potted plant that looked like something tropical, and a water cooler in the corner. I stepped up to the counter and told the receptionist my name, in a tiny voice. The lady was kind and asked me some basic questions, before taking me to a conference room with a long black table. The leather office chair she directed me to was comfortable, but I felt less and less relaxed as I waited for the lawyer to come in. She handed me a worksheet to fill out in the meantime. It asked more questions, mostly related to my financial status and my cost of living. She left me then and I quietly wrote answers on the white sheet of paper.

After five minutes, the assistant came in, followed by a tall man with a balding, shiny head, and broad shoulders. He was probably in his mid-fifties and looked every bit as lawyer-like as I had imagined he would. He waved a hand in greeting, remembering that shaking hands was unsafe right now due to COVID precautions. He introduced himself as

Jordan Carol; we all sat down. I explained to him how I was needing to legally separate from my husband of six years and how I had recently found out that he was cheating. My main concern was for getting full custody of my children. I let him know there had been some recent domestic violence. "Can you prove all of this?" He asked, point blank. "Well, I called the police once, but I haven't really wanted to involve the law until recently". I explained, feeling less hopeful the longer I sat in this chair. "Doesn't the fact that he cheated make him look worse to the court? Is that something that will help me with custody?" I asked, hopefully.

"We're in a no-fault state. That means that it doesn't matter if he cheated or not, it won't make you look any better in court because the judge doesn't care." He was so matter-o-fact. It wasn't like we were discussing the future of my kids or anything. The law was the law.

"I also want to let you know that, while judges used to favor moms over dads and grant more full custody for one parent, times are changing. In many cases, the judge likes to rule 50-50 custody for both parents these days. With that being said, the fact that you have stayed home with them for the last 5 years may help you if you state that you don't want their routine to change too much, since they have spent most of their lives with only you up to this point. Also, you should know that if you file for divorce instead of a separation, you have a better chance with the custody. That is what I would advise. If you hire me, your $200 from this consult can go towards the retainer fee of $2000. Once I have that, I can file your divorce petition and we can serve him papers. From there, he will get to decide if he wants to accept your offer, or get a lawyer of his own and fight this".

That was that. Ten minutes of his time and he had it all figured out. I sat in stunned silence. "Well, what do you think?" He asked, folding his hands on the table top. He was polite, but stern. I suddenly felt small. In front of this man, I felt like an uneducated back country hick. I wondered if I had dressed professionally enough, as I noted his suit and tie. Besides feeling out of sorts, I wasn't used to making decisions on my own.

Normally, I would say something like, "let me talk this over with my husband and get back to you." I would then tip toe around the subject until the right moment, before bringing it up with Mac, telling him why I thought it was a good idea, then telling him how much it would cost. I would then call my parents to get my dad's input. I would come back with an answer, knowing I was doing what would make both of them happy, and therefore make me feel confident I was on the right track. But now, here I was trying to make the most difficult decision of my adult life, without either of their support, and forced to make this choice because of their own actions.

I took a deep breath, looking him in the eye. "I'll see how fast I can get the money and we can start. Thank you for your time," I smiled and tried to look confident as I stood up. I took the folder the assistant handed me on the way out, along with Jordan's business card and a free pen. The most expensive free pen I had ever been given, I thought, tucking it into the folder. I stopped at the bank on my way home. I needed only $700 more in addition to what I had, to start the process.

When I got home, I had an idea. The children's bank accounts, which were still in my name only, had $350 each in them. I had wanted to start early on a savings account for each of them, to be able to someday support them as they left home and began their lives. Right now, their safety and our future had to come first. Between these two accounts, I would have enough. I would get paid again in two days, but until then, this had taken every last penny in my name.

The next day around noon, I got an email from my lawyer. The sheriff had served papers to Mac that morning. The day got more tense as I missed a call from my father. I didn't need to listen to the voicemail to know what he would say. The energy spoke for itself, loud and clear. Even if I had wanted to listen, I was at work. I didn't need to cry at work. I couldn't avoid my parents forever, but talking to them now wouldn't serve a purpose. When my mother-in-law sent me a text, however, I knew I couldn't ignore her. "Let's sit down, woman-to-woman, and you tell me what's going on!" I agreed to come the next day.

For now, I needed a break. After getting the kids, I headed to the park by the water. I had gotten the kid's bikes when I had gone to Mac's the week before and I would take them to ride today. I opened the back of my truck to pull the bikes out. They were gone. Instantly, a wave of rage washed over me. No one knew they were there. No one had had a chance to steal them, except when we were parked in the yard at Dex's. The obvious explanation made me so angry. Mac knew how much the kids loved their bikes. Why was everything about him? Even if we couldn't make things work, he could at least be considerate of our children. But no. Again, he had chosen to win for the sake of showing who had the most power. He had taken their bikes. I wiped away tears, stubbornly refusing to show my children the grief and anger that bubbled up inside me. It was already hard enough for them without seeing mom cry constantly.

Chapter Twenty-Six

I drove the short distance to see my mother-in-law the next afternoon. Dread had been building all day as I thought about how this conversation would go. I didn't want to talk with her about any of it. I didn't want to be subjected to her fierce protection of her son who could do no wrong. I hoped that she would listen to reason. I wasn't crazy. The abuse had been going on for a long time. Even the Bible justified ending a marriage because of cheating. I had done no wrong. Surely, she would see.

The day was cold for May. It was always colder at her house too. The sun never hit their yard until late afternoon due to the trees that were planted in and around the yard. In the winter, frost never melted off the ground. Even though it was mid-spring, I shivered as I walked up the steps and across the porch toward the sliding door. I had left the kids with Daniella for this visit. I didn't want them to feel anything negative toward their grandma. They were going through enough as it was.

Amanda met me at the door. It was always weird seeing her in jeans and a sweater after all of the years of her being a devout Mennonite. I wasn't sure I would ever get used to her hair being down, or worn in a ponytail. In my mind, she would always wear a black head covering and a flowered dress that barely fit over her rounded body. "C'mon in," she smiled, trying to look cordial. Her southern accent was strong. She had moved here from southern Texas before Mac was born. I walked in, seating myself rigidly on the edge of the overly firm couch. It was ancient, probably from the eighties, and one of the most uncomfortable couches I had ever sat on. It felt perfectly matched to the conversation I was about to have. Amanda sat in her lazy chair that overlooked the yard and the trees beyond. She crossed her arms and stared me down. "So," she began, "tell me what's been going on". I looked her in the eyes and began with the incident with Naomi two years before. I told her about the abuse and how it had been getting worse. "Mac doesn't always do well at managing his emotions," she admitted. "He really can't help it though. At least he has never hurt you." I wasn't done. I continued, explaining how the final straw had been finding the condoms a few weeks ago. She sighed and looked out the window. After a few seconds, she turned around and chuckled. "I'm not saying I don't believe you," she started. I sighed inwardly. I had known it would go like this. "I'm not saying I believe you, or I don't. Either way, divorce is really extreme, don't you think? Why not separation? Why not just take a break until you guys figure it out? He doesn't need any more pain in his life. It's been hard enough on him lately without this."

I was in shock. How could she not believe me? When had I ever lied to her? Why did no one take me seriously? I fought tears. "Has Mac's dad ever talked to another woman?" I looked at her point blank. I knew the answer already. "Well, yes," she looked away. "How did that feel? Why did you put up with that?" I pleaded with her. "I didn't like it. He has cheated before and it hurt," She confided. "But sticking it out is the right thing to do. Think of the children!" She sounded so final. "Well, this is where you and I differ on opinions." I said firmly. "You chose to

145

stay and your children were abused and you put up with the cheating. Your son paid the price for the abuse and became abusive himself. I don't plan to offer my children the same life."

I had heard about Bryan beating Mac with a belt, throwing things at him, and how they had gotten in fist fights when Mac was a teenager. I had heard how his dad had punched holes in the wall because Mac made him so angry. Bryan was abusive, in every right, just like his father before him had been. I had seen it myself, in all the times Mac tried to get his dad to be proud of him. Each time his dad brushed him off, made him feel insignificant and less than, added an emotional welt to the physical ones that had long since healed.

Mac had learned from him. His mom had enabled both of them, by choosing to stay. I wouldn't leave my children to the same fate. The cycle had to end somewhere. *I* was the chain breaker. Looking at Amanda now, I knew this had been a waste of time. I had known this woman for 7 years and she had never once taken my side. No wonder I hadn't come to her with anything over the years. It had always been superficial. I hadn't wanted to believe I would be brushed off in this way. And yet, I knew I must stand behind my choice. My resolve became even stronger after this conversation.

When I finally had the courage to face my father, the conversation went in a similar direction. I wasn't surprised; this was how he had reacted the entire time. It was just more final now since they all knew I had filed to end the marriage for good. My dad reminded me that I always had a flare for drama. He said he had known me to stretch the truth and he was disappointed I had made the choice to leave over making the assumption that Mac had cheated. "You don't have any real proof, Sharon! I was worried it would come to this with you." He reminded me that, even if it were true, I was still disappointing God. I was still going against the Bible. By leaving, I was being un-submissive. This wasn't who he had raised me to be. My mom got on then, letting me know that Mac had called, in tears, when he found out. He was heartbroken and he was struggling. He was already drinking more and I was to blame. The conversation ended when my dad began crying. He had been using this one for a while.

I could remember being 8 years old and seeing the sad look on his face when I disappointed him. I could remember not doing the chores my mom had asked me to do, and how he would respond with crying and telling me how sad I had made him. Sometimes, if I was bad enough, he would make me spank him instead of the other way around. He would get out the belt and roll it up, handing it over to me. "Do it ten times," he would say. I never wanted to hit him hard. I didn't want to hurt him. "Harder!" he would yell, until he was grimacing in pain. I would be crying, begging to be done, before he would finally tell me "That's enough".

He would then go and show my mom all the stripes I had left on his back. "I wish she would obey," he would sigh. Nothing had changed. He still used the same tactics to get me to conform. He still reminded me how much of a disappointment I was. He knew exactly how to make me feel bad and the conversation with him this day had been no exception.

I already knew I was a disappointment to God. I had accepted that, in leaving Mac, I was leaving God. I couldn't do life the way I had before. If the choice was between God and being free from Mac, I would choose freedom.

Chapter Twenty-Seven

The next day, my client's mom asked more questions. I had expected being a caregiver to be all about showing up professionally. I hadn't expected that it would include answering personal questions. I had mentioned my kids early on, but that was all I had planned to share. However, it seemed that God had different plans. On my second shift, she had asked about my husband. I had explained that I had just consulted with a lawyer and was about to get a divorce. "I don't think you are wrong!" She had said immediately.

They were Catholic. She had also been raised in a conservative environment where marriage was upheld as a sacred commitment. However, she had stated, "I would do the same thing if my husband cheated! He doesn't even look at other women. Men of God don't. A *real* man wouldn't treat you that way. The Bible allows for divorce in the case of unfaithfulness." She had let me know that whatever days I needed off for legal issues, I was welcome to take.

The next weekend was Mac's weekend with the kids. I planned to drop them off Friday night and head to the garage gym for an evening lift. I found solace in lifting alone, staying late, listening to music, and pumping iron. I took my time with each set, allowing myself to unwind slowly from the busy week. As per our normal, I showed up at Mac's around 6. The garage was open and he was at his work bench. He came out and came over to say hi to the kids. He helped get Carroll out of her car seat and I took it out of the truck; we had only one. I helped both kids get inside the house, gave them hugs, and turned to leave. "I have something for you, Sharon," Mac blocked me from walking out. "Here," he handed me a black jewelry box. "I don't want it," I pushed it back at him. "Please, just let me leave." I attempted to walk around him. He moved out of the way and I walked out. He followed me to the truck and shoved the box onto my seat. "The kids can't be here this weekend," he said suddenly. "What do you mean?" I was angry. "The kids need some sense of normal. You can't cancel on them when they are already here!" He was already heading in, pushing both kids out the door. "Please, don't do this!" I begged. It didn't seem to matter to him. He was now shoving the car seat into the backseat. He turned and roughly picked up Carroll, shoving her into her seat. He was cussing and yelling at her to "just let me buckle you!". I came up behind him, pulling at his arm to remove him. He shook me off and finished, slamming the door in her face. "Get out of here before I hurt someone!" he yelled. By this time the neighbor was watching us.

I didn't need to be told twice. I took a deep breath and got into the truck. I clicked my buckle in. Both kids were crying in the backseat. I felt so helpless. I wanted to scoop them up and hold them both, but I knew we needed to leave. I didn't want things to get worse. I didn't feel safe.

When I got home, I took both children in my arms. "I'm sorry you guys," was all I could manage. I held them tightly, burying my wet eyes in their hair and kissing their little heads. I had cried the entire drive to Dex's. Not only could I not provide stability for them, but I felt helpless in keeping them safe. I had never known it would be this hard. I had only known we needed to leave. None of this was fair.

When I unloaded the truck the next morning, I noticed the jewelry box. Opening it, I found a wedding ring. It wasn't ugly but it wasn't pretty either. It was a simple diamond, complete with paperwork from *Diamond Company*. I covered my mouth as the tears came again. The tears weren't happy tears. An experience I had never been given when I became engaged to this man, the part of our wedding that had never been, was now a ring box thrown at me as an afterthought to a failed union. A tactic to reel me back in? Memories came to me then, flooding from my long forgotten childish dreams.

Ever since I was 13, I had listened to ads for Diamond Co. on the radio, in between breaks from early 2000's country hits. I remembered imagining that someday my prince charming would take me there; we would pick out a ring together. It would be perfect. I had known since I was born that there was a perfect counterpart for me somewhere in the world. I had always had the deep feeling that he was out there. When I was 14, I had written a letter to my future husband. Throughout our marriage, I had never showed that letter to Mac. At first, I felt I didn't know him well enough. Later on, I didn't feel safe enough. Something deep inside me didn't want to expose my soul to him. The letter had been lost since then. I wondered suddenly if I had walked away from my soulmate. I remembered the words of my dad, the reminder that I had given up on my God ordained life partner. Marriage was for life! Now, I didn't know what was right. Looking again at the ring, I wiped away more tears. Mac's family didn't believe in rings; neither did mine.

My parents had stopped wearing theirs before I was born. It wasn't something that bothered me when I became engaged to Mac. He had never even asked me, getting on one knee in the traditional sense. Instead, he had asked my father. My father had delivered the news to me and the next thing I had known, we were planning our wedding. Even at this point, my dad hadn't wanted me to spend time alone with Mac. He had grudgingly let me ride alone with Mac to run errands one day, shaking his head in disappointment, even as 18-year-old me looked to my father for approval.

I don't think he trusted Mac with me alone. And probably with good reason. I was a virgin. Mac wasn't. Mac and I had never even kissed before our wedding day. However, that didn't mean that he didn't push boundaries in other ways. I would never forget the guilt I had felt when more had happened than I agreed to. I had gone to my dad, confessing that Mac had touched me inappropriately. To my parents, sex before marriage was a sin punishable by excommunication out of the family. I had been honest with my dad. If I had actually had *sex*, I don't know what he would have done.

Regardless, he was highly unimpressed with *me*. Looking back, I suddenly wondered why I had taken all the blame for this? Why had my father not gone to Mac at the time? I should have seen the red flags right then with Mac. However, no one told me anything about boundaries in sexual relationships, as a child. All I knew, I had learned from the encyclopedia. That, and the library computer. I had gone to the back room, in the teen section, carefully making sure no one was around. I had then googled my questions. This was my sex-ed. It didn't include talking about the importance of choosing a partner who respected my boundaries. My parents didn't really respect boundaries, so they weren't the ideal candidates for teaching them. I sighed, looking down at the ring again. Why now? I had been wearing the rubber one to the gym for the last year. We had agreed that it would be wise to show others we were taken. Why had he not bought it at that point? At least I knew where $3000 of my money had gone. After another moment, I tucked it into the center console of my truck. It was a problem for another day. Right now, I needed to get ready for work.

Chapter Twenty-Eight

A week had gone by since the ring incident. It was Saturday morning, Mother's Day. I was lying in bed looking up at the maple leaves directly visible through the glass dome in the middle of the yurt roof. The leaves were finally full, showing the newness of late spring, flapping softly in the breeze that had come up. Down here, in this safe haven, I could almost forget about the stress that loomed in the air. I could pretend there were no problems and this was just another day in paradise. Afterall, whenever I told anyone that I lived in a yurt, they were a little jealous.

When I showed my friends pictures of the back deck overlooking the creek, they all said something like "I wish I could stay in paradise like that; you're so lucky!" They were right, of course. I should be thankful. Only, I had omitted the part about the mice, which had become an increasing problem. Dex had asked that we didn't kill any. He believed in peacefully co-existing with nature, even when nature came into our living quarters, climbed on our counters and pooped on our dishes in the dish rack.

Last night, I had heard the mice scurrying across the countertop, gnawing at something that I had forgotten to put away. I hoped they weren't chewing through any of my clothes. I looked around, seeing one peek its tiny head out from behind the curtain that served as a cupboard door. Its tiny pink nose was cute, its large ears almost adorable. It reminded me of living in the travel trailer as a kid. My mind began to wander, thinking back to those days as a child and teenager. I remembered the old travel trailer my parents had housed us in, parked next to the shop they had built before I was born. I remembered doing schoolwork, sprawled out on the bottom level of the iron bunkbed I shared with my younger sister. It wasn't so bad in the summer.

Aside from the mold and the headaches I always got, that is. It was warm and we didn't need to spend much time inside. I spent most of my summers lying in the hammock, reading novel after novel, keeping track for the summer reading program. Winter was what really got me. I remembered standing next to the coil heater, taking turns with my sisters to put our dresses over the heater and absorb all the warmth. Because portable heaters were the only source of heat for the entire trailer, we would alternate between doing school work and taking heater breaks. I remembered taking showers and seeing my wet hair freeze in icicle shapes on my back, while someone else was taking a turn at the heater. I didn't miss those days.

I shivered inwardly, thankful that it was currently summer. I had experienced a month of winter in this yurt and it wasn't fun. Hopefully, I would find something better before summer was done. Back to the present, I looked around, blinking. My eyes settled on the stack of plastic storage bins moved to the side of the entryway. Heaviness settled around me as I remembered the happenings of the day before. On Monday, my parents had emailed me that Mac had a bunch of stuff of mine that he was cleaning out. They wanted to get it to me. I asked them if they could store it for me. They had agreed. I hadn't thought about it again.

When I had gotten home from work last night, I had walked into the yurt to find all of the items my parents agreed to store, neatly stacked just inside the yurt, topped with a note. The note was written neatly in my mom's cursive, on a homemade card backed with construction paper. My parents trademark card style.

Sharon,

We love you and I am sorry to do this, but we cannot support you in your sin. We can't store your stuff so we have delivered it to you. I hope that you will turn from your ways and do what you know is right. We really do care about you. -- Love, Mother

Below her letter she had carefully written out the most applicable Bible verses she could find for the occasion.

But your iniquities have separated between you and your God, and your sins have hid his face from you, that he will not hear. —Isaiah 59:2 KJV

Therefore, to him that knoweth to do good, and doeth it not, to him it is sin— James 4:17 KJV

Marriage is honourable in all, and the bed undefiled: but whoremongers and adulterers God will judge. --Hebrews 13:4 KJV

This recent one had stung. My parents knew exactly how to hurt me. I already knew I was judged. I didn't need my parents to remind me. I wasn't even dating anyone, but they still assumed that I was? It didn't make sense. They would always see me as still married; if I did eventually find someone new, they would tell me I was wrong. There was no hope with them. I sighed, flipping back the blankets. Today would be a good day. I may not have family support, but I was free. And it was sunny. The plan was to hike an old railroad grade with the kids. Being outdoors always eased the tension.

Six hours later, we returned home. The kids had hiked well, exhausting themselves. Arriving back at Dex's parking area, I gently woke Luke from his driving induced nap, and then lifted Carroll from her sleep. She was instantly awake, rubbing her eyes with her tiny fists. I smiled, kissing her soft blonde head. I stroked her curls, pushing hair from her eyes. She squirmed to get down and I set her on the ground. Dunagen had come to meet us and Luke was rubbing his back while he wagged his tail. Carroll started toddling towards the garden space, where Dex was diligently digging and hoeing. Alana was sprawled out in a lawn chair, her head back and her eyes closed. Bees buzzed and I saw a butterfly. The air smelled of spring and I was thankful I was wearing a tank top and shorts. I headed to the yurt, grabbing my white laundry basket. Time to do laundry. I went into Dex's house, taking in the familiar scent of marijuana and fried potatoes. The new normal. I headed into the mudroom, which was still cold. It was uninsulated and open to the back yard on one side. I shivered just a little bit as I dumped the clothing into the washer.

Checking the dryer, I found that Dex had changed the laundry while I was gone. The first load was dry. Good. The kids would have clean clothing for next week at daycare. I sighed with contentment, pulling out a big armful of clothing. A sock dropped. I bent to pick it up and a pair of underwear fell out. Picking it up, I filled the laundry basket and headed out the door towards the yurt. The kids were still in the yard with Dex, so I figured I was fine to take the clothing down and fold it. Upon making my way down the first trail, I turned onto the bigger pathway to the yurt and the creek. As I rounded the corner to the yurt, my heart dropped into the pit of my stomach.

I stopped suddenly, frozen in place. I couldn't move. There was Mac, arms crossed across his shoulders, blocking my path, his eyes locked on me the way a hungry mountain lion looks at his prey before he pounces. "Happy Mother's Day, Sharon!" He glared at me. "Why are you here?" I asked, in a tiny voice. He was wearing his handgun in a hip holster. I felt even less comfortable than I had previously. "I came to see the children. Where are they?" I ignored him, unsure how to answer. "I don't feel comfortable with you coming out here. Can you please leave?" I managed, trying to think of a way to escape before I angered him even more. "If you only knew how much cocaine I snorted this weekend!" He reached down, unholstering his gun.

He didn't point it at me, but waved it around as he went on. "I've been having a great time; I did so many drugs this weekend! I've been partying like you wouldn't believe! I'm here for a good time, not a long time! Might as well go out with a bang," He shrugged, waving the gun around some more. I turned around, heading for the trail back up to the house and safety. "Please just go," was all I could manage as I cautiously walked back up the trail. He didn't follow me. Good. I sighed as I made my way back towards the yard, where everyone was still working in the garden. "Did you see Mac just now?" I asked Dex. He had seen him parking but wasn't sure what he was doing. "You should get a restraining order against him," Dex said.

I was still afraid of how my dad would react. I bit my lip. "I don't know if we have enough proof," I looked toward the trail where I had just come from, wondering if he was gone. I waited another 30 minutes before heading back down the trail, this time with Dex, just in case. Mac was gone. I sighed in relief, heading in and plopping the laundry basket on the bed. How could I send the kids back there again, knowing he was doing cocaine? I had wondered in the past if he was doing drugs, but even now, I had no proof.

Chapter Twenty-Nine

On Monday, I updated my lawyer. He informed me that, because Mac had verbally stated that he was using drugs, we needed to try to get proof. Maybe if any friend of his knew about the drug use, he could vouch for it so that we could get it documented. Without a paper trail, it meant nothing. I was irritated. How long would I be told that none of his threats were valid, simply because there wasn't a paper trail? How long would it be before someone took me seriously? I didn't even feel safe in the yurt anymore. What if he came back again? What if, this time, he wasn't as careless with the gun and decided to end my life?

I had been here before. I thought of all the nights lying in the king size bed in the little white house, tense and curled in a ball, jumping at every creak in the floor or car driving by outside. I remembered how I had waited for his mood to change, waiting to see if he would murder me while I lay there. I had been at the mercy of his mood; here I was again, even living separately from him.

I decided not to send the kids back to Mac's after that. I knew it would be harder having them full time, but with the news of the drug use, their safety must come first. There was no court order requiring him to have any visitation and my lawyer thought that I was justified in keeping them, at least until things settled down. Amanda had asked to take the kids the next weekend. I agreed. At least they would be safe with her, even if she didn't understand my side of the story. Surely, she could understand the need to keep them safe; if they did visit Mac, it would be supervised. Mac wouldn't do drugs around his mom.

When I dropped them off that Friday night, the whole family was there. Alan and Rebekkah watched me from the house, while Amanda came walking out, focusing all her attention on the kids. She gave me her typical smile, the one that felt forced as she tried to pretend to be cordial. She then helped Carroll out of her car seat. Luke was out already, showing Mac's Dad the paper airplane that Dex had helped him build. Bryan stood watching; he looked even worse today, in a white wife-beater tank top, with a brown stain on the front and a pair of checkered shorts. I wondered when he had last showered.

Grimacing inwardly, I tried to be polite. I waved hi, hoping he wouldn't talk to me. He smiled then, revealing two missing teeth. "If you need anything, I can always help you." I did need to change the oil in the pickup. "Come over on Monday and I'll help you!" he sounded serious. Maybe I should take him up on it. It would be cheaper than taking it to a shop. Maybe, just maybe, they would be a support to me after all. This was how it should be. Families should support one another, regardless of individual differences. The kids needed to see us working together. "Thanks Dad," I smiled. "I'll plan on coming up after work."

As uncomfortable as I always felt around him, I wondered then if I had judged him too harshly. I got in my truck and drove back to the yurt, changing into the blue dress that showed off my tanned thighs. I put on mascara and lip gloss, the most makeup I ever wore. It was party time with Josephine. I was excited to go out and drink. I had never done any of this as a teenager or a young adult. I never had gotten the chance. I had been a mom, by choice, at 19. I didn't have any need for partying. But now, things were different. Now, I was single.

Maybe I would meet someone at a bar and maybe he would take me home. I had never experienced any of hook up culture, and this was what most people did nowadays. This was the way. Sex didn't have to be about love and deep connection. It never had been for me, even when I wanted it to be. I might as well explore and learn.

Josephine had invited Sophia and Corey, and her fiancée, Daniel, would tag along too. Jonah couldn't come because he had a girlfriend and they were hanging out. Being tied down sounded so miserable. Oh well, his loss. When we got to the bar, everyone started off with shots. I don't remember a lot about that night, but I remember getting drunk enough that when I got up to go to the bathroom, I swayed a little bit and had to grab the table for balance. There were no cute guys to flirt with, other than Daniel, who was flirting with both Josephine and myself by this time. By now, it was past my bedtime.

I planned to get up early to go to the gym in the morning. Josephine and Daniel had agreed to let me stay the night. We were home by 11 and I had climbed into the bed in their guest room, with the yellow comforter and too many throw pillows, quickly becoming sleepy. Somehow, I felt safer here. Mac didn't know where I was. The door had locks. I fell asleep instantly.

I must have been asleep for about an hour when I was awakened suddenly by Daniel. The overhead light was on and he was standing in the doorway. "Get up!" he said, almost yelling. His arms were crossed as he glared at me. "What's going on?" I blinked sleepily. "We need to talk, and you're not welcome here anymore." I sat up, finding my t-shirt and pulling it over my sports bra. I grabbed my backpack and came out of the room. "Come on, you're leaving," He led me to the door. Still confused, I followed him blindly.

As I made it to the truck, he began talking. "You told Josephine to cheat on me, didn't you!" I was shocked, trying to remember what he could possibly be talking about. "She told me that you told her to message Lucas. How dare you come and ruin my relationship just because you fucked up your own marriage? Divorced women are all the same, always ruining everyone else's relationship!" I was still only half awake. "You mean because I was the one that introduced her to him? I told her Lucas said she was hot. Then she added him. How is that my fault?"

He was angry, convinced that I had forced her to talk to him. I couldn't argue. I *had* been the one to tell her what he had said. But then again, she had made the choice to talk to him. The alcohol hadn't worn off, but I wanted to leave. I hated being treated like this. All of a sudden, I didn't feel safe at all. "You can't drive like that," he put a hand on my arm. "As much as I despise what you've done to my relationship, I won't allow you to drive like that".

I don't remember all of the next few hours, but we talked, and then talked some more. Daniel told me about how he got cheated on with his last partner. He was afraid that Josephine would cheat on him. I didn't say that I felt like he might be right; it wouldn't have done any good. He needed someone to blame, and I understood. I knew the pain all too well. I knew what it was like to think that your partner wasn't actually capable of hurting you in that way. No one wanted to face the reality of their own partner being at fault, or lying to them.

It wasn't my place to convince him that Josephine had chosen to flirt with other guys, or that she chose friends like Sophia who were actively cheating on their partner. None of that was my place to reveal. It stung, though, and I realized then how easy it was to blame a woman who had chosen to leave her marriage. It was easy to see me as the homewrecker because I had done something that most never would. Although the alcohol had numbed my reflexes, it had sharpened my mind.

During that strange night, while I sat in my truck, with the door open, breathing in cold night air and listening to Daniel tell me his life story, I could see clearly the battle that this man was fighting internally. I could see that he was in denial and was choosing to stay that way. As much as he had hurt me, I could empathize.

As soon as he felt I could drive safely, he told me good luck with my life, shut my door for me, and went into his house. I cried the whole way home. Arriving at the yurt, the dashboard clock on my truck said 4 am. So much for lifting at 7. This was going to be a long day. I was sad, but I didn't need friends who would treat me like that. I knew then that the friendship was over. Somehow, I saw the truth. I had triggered a wound in him that he wasn't yet ready to heal. This experience had triggered something deep inside me, also. Something that I wouldn't process for a long time. All I knew, in that moment, was that getting betrayed hurt and that it had been happening a lot lately. What I didn't know, was that this was only the beginning.

Sunday evening, I texted Bryan, asking if he could still get the oil change done for me on Monday. He never replied. When I picked up the kids, he wasn't there. I suddenly felt dumb for asking him for help, remembering all the times he had cancelled on Mac when Mac had also needed him. I had known that it was all for show, all to make himself look like a loving father, when in reality he probably didn't even remember making that offer to me. He had deceived me with his fake words, while emanating an energy of hate and deceit. Intuitively, I had known all along. I felt suddenly like a sheep among wolves. I knew I was in unsafe territory. The entire family hated me. It was evident in the way Mac's mom glared at me, then covered it quickly with a fake, almost menacing smile, as she had helped me transition Carroll to her car seat at pickup.

Chapter Thirty

When I got home, I had a missed call. Patty had been a customer of mine when I was doing alterations full-time. I had originally been contacted by her at the recommendation of Mac's mother. Apparently, she lived next door to Mac's parents, on a large grass seed farm. She had expensive tastes and an eye for perfection. The first time I had completed an item for her, which was a cushion for an antique rocking chair, I had been nervous. She had let me know that she didn't trust many other people and that the fabric had been expensive.

She hoped I could get it right the first time. Although her attitude had put me on edge, I knew my work was high quality. Everyone had always raved about my eye for detail. It helped that I was a perfectionist. I never wore clothing that had wrinkles or stains. I had to present myself perfectly to the world, and this ideal transferred to my work. When I had finished the project, she had loved it. She had let me know that she would be back when she had other projects. After that, I never felt nervous. I respected her high standards, understanding that this was one thing that we had in common.

Her message that day was about a cover for an antique lazy chair. I read it, thinking about how I could accommodate. When I had run the alterations business, I had always instructed people come to me. I worked out of my home. Often, the work involved fittings. The easiest way was to have people try on garments; I would measure, make notes of what needed to be altered and they would then leave them with me until I could get them done. Because I now lived in the yurt, I didn't feel comfortable asking people to come to me. Or, more accurately, I didn't think people would feel comfortable coming to me. Not only did I live 15 miles out of town, but the trail to the yurt made it seem even more remote.

On top of that, the yurt itself was in a remote corner of the property. Finally, I was embarrassed about the mice. I didn't want people worrying that their clothing could get ruined by mice. In reality, I wouldn't ever allow that. Either I would keep the items in my truck until I could work on them, or I would store items in a clean trash bag, hung on the small clothing rod in the corner. Because of the changes in my living situation, my current solution was to offer to drive to clients. I told them it was due to COVID-19, not mentioning that I had almost become homeless and was now living in the wilderness. I let her know that I could come over the next afternoon and we could discuss it.

I hadn't ever been to her house. When I drove in the driveway, I wondered if my soon-to-be ex parents-in-law would see me and get angry that Patty was still giving me work. I knew they were friends and I was nervous to get in the middle of it. Still, I needed the extra income.

The driveway was long, lined with newly planted fir trees. The driveway had recently been graveled, with bright, sharp pieces of gravel that crunched as I drove over them. On either side of the driveway, I saw the fields, tall green grass blowing in the breeze, stretching out on both sides until they reached Mac's parents' home to the west. Getting closer to the house, I saw flowers planted everywhere. The sign above the gate to the yard read *Greener Grass Farms*. From the sign hung honeysuckle plants which were in full bloom, lighting up the sign with their yellow and white vibrance. Flower beds surrounded the gate, yielding red, pink, and yellow roses. Patty met me at the gate, pulling it open so I could drive through. I parked in front of a large, two-story farmhouse that was bleached white. A tired looking brown and white sheep dog, who had been resting on the front porch of the big house, stood up as I got out, wagging her tail in a friendly manner and coming over to sniff me.

As I stood waiting for Patty to walk back up from the gate, I heard the distant sound of roosters crowing their afternoon announcement. Looking towards the barn, I saw a gated enclosure that apparently housed alpacas. They watched me warily from the fenced barnyard, curious to see who had come to visit. A black and white cat walked up to me then, arching her back and rubbing herself against my leg. Patty had made her way to me by now, waving a greeting. Patty was tall and slender and wore designer clothes. Just as she had an expensive taste with her furniture and high standards for the work that I did, she had high standards for how she presented herself. Her bright red hair was perfectly styled, reaching just below her shoulders.

She wore a V-neck black top which was exquisitely embroidered with beading and contrasted her off-white dress pants perfectly. Her nails were perfectly manicured with a deep red that matched her hair. Her makeup was impeccable, making her look in her early forties, although I knew she had to be at least in her sixties. Even her sandals looked expensive.

"I heard you left Mac!" she exclaimed, no pretense or small talk. "It was about time! The first time I met you, I wondered what you were doing with a loser like that". She put her hands on her hips. Well. I wouldn't have to worry about justifying myself to her. Jim, her husband, lumbered up to stand next to her now, nodding his head in agreement with Patty. I had met Jim once, but would have hardly remembered she was married if it hadn't been for the large diamond she wore on her left hand. Jim, in contrast to the beautiful delicate figure that Patty was, looked like the ultimate farmer.

He leaned on his pitchfork, which he had brought from the barn, as we talked. He was tall, but his height wasn't evident due to the fact that he was also very large framed. Not only this, but his rounded belly stuck out from his blue striped overalls, giving him the look of a traditional farmer. His balding head was covered by a straw hat with a string that run under his clean-shaven chin. He smiled at me then, and I saw how kind his blue eyes looked. I felt at ease instantly.

After a moment, we all walked inside. Patty began telling me about the sewing project as she led me through a traditional dining room, with a wooden farm table, into a large living room. After she had showed me the project, she turned to Jim. "Jim, she could come and help you maybe," She explained that, after Jim had handed his construction company over to a younger man to run so he could retire, he had taken up farming full time. Although the grass seed, which was farmed commercially, still made them money, he raised alpacas and chickens and one cow as a way to relax and enjoy his retirement.

He carefully sheared the alpacas every spring, selling their coats every year at the local markets. "If you wanted to come help, we could pay you and it could supplement your part time work. I can't move as fast as I used to, and it takes me twice as long to get work done as it did when I was younger," Jim was explaining. Weird, I thought. Mac had mentioned multiple times that he didn't like them. I couldn't see why. They were both genuine, kind people, and were now offering to help me, when everyone else who had known me before leaving Mac had turned their back on me and cursed me. It didn't make sense.

I felt shocked that anyone would like me or accept me. I had become so used to being rejected. It felt almost suspicious that someone would actually choose to support me. Mac had even threatened Dex last week, telling him that he should watch his back if he continued to let us stay there. I knew this was part of why Dex was hoping that I found somewhere else to live. Coming back to the present, I realized Jim was talking again. He was telling me how he needed to till the garden patch and get some corn into the ground before it got too late. He wanted to make his own chicken feed and he always grew corn, snap-peas and carrots, as well as leafy vegetables, to supplement the grain-based chicken feed that he gave them from the local farm store. If I wanted to help plant, we could start as soon as Wednesday.

They would pay me every week and make me an official employee of their farm so that I could count the income on official documents.

Having more income on paper would help me find a rental. I didn't even need time to think about it. I knew I would need to start saving money. If Mac got a lawyer, the divorce costs could start adding up. "Yes!" I said, explaining my days off from my part-time job. I left, feeling thankful. God was providing, whether or not my parents supported his choice to help me.

I was beginning to wonder who was truly against me. Was it God, or was it just my parents? I had always thought that God could only reach me through my husband and my parents, but I was starting to feel as if God actually *wanted* me to be successful in this new life. Wouldn't he have ignored my pleas for help if he didn't want to plant me here, on my own two feet? Gradually, I was beginning to trust again.

Chapter Thirty-One

A week later, I looked at the calendar, counting the days and realizing the thirty-day mark for the divorce was coming. Mac had only two more days to reply to my divorce petition; if he didn't, I would get all I had asked for and it would be put into official documentation and filed. The kids hadn't gone to see their dad since the day he had gotten angry, telling me about the drug use. I knew that eventually they would start going again, but there was no official order right now.

Meanwhile, lifts in the gym were progressing. I was getting stronger. I had squatted 315 for a set of two reps the week before. I was feeling positive. I had found a competition that I wanted to sign up for in October. I was registered and getting ready to start training for it. Gyms were beginning to open again.

Between the upcoming competition and my experience with Josephine and Daniel, I had decided that I wouldn't drink and party for a while. I had come to the conclusion that drinking never left me feeling proud of myself the next morning. Not only that, but it always took away from being able to get up and lift early. I would wake up early regardless, feeling sick but unable to go back to sleep. I realized there was nothing that I was missing out on. While I still wanted to be a member of a group, I wasn't sure that I would find *my* group through partying.

Although I had decided to be done with partying, I wasn't done with the idea of casual sex. I was free now. There was no reason not to at least try it. I had tried doing things the right way, waiting for marriage, being pure. I had always believed that doing things according to Bible teaching would produce the result I wanted. Christianity was supposed to be safe, with the promise of reciprocity from others who also claimed the title of Christ follower. But being moral hadn't worked. Being moral had gotten me a broken heart. Being moral and obeying the Bible had gotten my ex-husband to cheat on me. It had gotten him to try to touch my sister. It had ended with divorce. There were no answers anymore. Many of my friends talked of their regular hook ups. Corey brought a different woman home every week. Hook-up culture was the new normal. One of my gym friends had even met her now husband through a Tinder hookup.

Trying things out sexually seemed like the only way, so I might as well jump on the trend. I knew that I could literally choose whoever I wanted for the job. I was one of the hottest girls at the gym and in my community, for that matter. Many guys had said that to me. I wasn't concerned with that part. I could afford to be picky. Of the several who had been hitting me up, one in particular came to mind. He was a local fuckboy, a college football player from a privileged family. His daddy had paid for him to get a free education, so all he had to do was keep his dick wet and post flex pictures to his female fans on Chat-app when he wasn't hanging out with the other boys from the fraternity at his college.

He was a little taller than me, but not too tall. Just how I liked them. He had a big chest, a perfect six pack, and was tan. His black hair was cut short in a fade and he had a moustache that made him look just a little older than his 21 years. When he flashed his white teeth smile at me, I got butterflies, every time. One afternoon I saw him in the gym. He came over, leaning his lean figure on the squat rack, a little too close to me. He nodded towards my shorts, biting his lip as he whispered, "it would be better if you took those off for me," He walked back to the deadlift platform where he was doing his back workout.

When I did my set of squats, he videoed it secretly, sending it to me with the devil emoji as he zoomed in on my butt. I replied with a picture of him and the drooling face. It was easier to flirt online when in a public gym. It didn't make a scene that way. The air was thick with sexual energy. We both wanted each other, that was plain to see. When I finished my workout and left, I told him to come over that night. Although I played it cool, I was nervous. This would be a first for me. It had been almost three months since I had moved out, and a month since I had filed for divorce. That seemed like a respectable amount of time to wait before seeing someone else, especially since Mac had been seeing others the entire time we had been together.

That night, I texted the address to the college boy, who responded with more devil emojis. He said it would be late before he got there. Good, because the kids needed to be sleeping. Maybe they could sleep in Dex's house for the night. At 11, the boy messaged me that he was almost there. Soon, there was a soft knock on the yurt door. I opened it, letting him in. There was no need to turn a light on. He kissed me, grabbing my hair as he tipped my head back in the pitch blackness; everything flowed naturally after that. When we were done, we lay there talking. I offered for him to stay the night. I didn't know the typical hook up etiquette or that staying overnight was boyfriend behavior. Hook-ups didn't normally include pillow talk after either. He was kind and we talked. He asked me what I was planning to do with my life. He asked if I had ever thought about college. No one had asked me that before. Food for thought.

At 12:30, he got dressed. We kissed and he slipped out the door silently. As I lay there, processing the events of my first hookup, I thought I heard a voice outside the thin walls of the yurt. It must have been him, talking to himself as he walked away, I reasoned. A minute later, the yurt door opened again. "What did you forget?" I said, turning to him. I was wrapped in my blanket, still not dressed. When I caught a glimpse of his face, illuminated by the full moon that lighted the pathway outside, it wasn't the boy who had just left that I saw. It was Mac.

He stood over me, glowering. "I videoed the whole thing! I heard all of it!" He waved his phone in the air, almost hitting me with it. I gasped. Shaking with fear, I couldn't move. Was this real, or a nightmare? Had he truly just walked in on me? Had he been stalking me all night? How did he even know I had someone coming over? "Please leave," I managed, in a small voice, trying not to show the fear that was bubbling up and overtaking me. I didn't know what to do. Calling for help would be pointless.

Dex couldn't hear from there and no one else was around. I tried to think if there was anything close to me that I could use to hit Mac with. I could fight, if it came to it. "I offered you to see other people while we were married, but you didn't want it! Why are you doing it now?" He growled.

"It's been almost three months, we're not married anymore, and you have no business being here". I shot back, as angry as I was scared now. "Just because you filed for divorce doesn't mean this is over!" He raised his voice even higher. "This will never be over! In God's eyes, we're still married! Just wait! Everyone will know about this! Imagine how your family will feel, knowing you just cheated!" He walked out then, slamming the door behind him, making the entire yurt shutter as the sound reverberated across the other side of the yurt.

I sat there, shivering in fear. After about 15 minutes, I got up and got dressed. I walked to the house, using Dex's landline to call the police. I told them about the whole thing. They couldn't do anything, but they said that my asking him not to come back was a good start. If he violated it again, they could press charges. Back in the yurt, I pushed the rocking chair up against the front door, sliding the bins of clothing up against the other door. At least I could hear if he tried to come in this way. I lay there, too stiff to sleep. For the rest of my time in the yurt, pushing furniture against my door would become my bedtime routine. I wouldn't sleep peacefully again for a long, long time.

Chapter Thirty-Two

The next day started with an email to my lawyer. I let him know about the incidents of the night before. He documented it all. He advised against a restraining order. He said a restraining order would be extra, and make me look like I was out to get Mac. He did have news, though. Mac had obtained a lawyer and had not accepted my divorce proposal. The lawyer he had chosen made me sad. He was an older man, my neighbor's father. I had bow-hunted on his property last spring. He knew both of us. Oh well, he had to make his money somehow.

As for the divorce proceedings, a draft order would go into place until the divorce could be finalized. Mac would be required to pay child support, back dating to May first. The kids would be required to go to his house every other weekend.

When I had finished responding to emails, I had other work to do. Once again, I called the local domestic violence line. "Hello, do you have any information on shelters that could take a mother and two children? I have heard that you have rooms available that lock at night and are guarded." I explained the situation with Mac to her. The woman replied that they didn't have any this week, but starting next week she could get us in. I sighed. How was I to make it another week like this? Last night had been nerve wracking.

I was terrified of ever sleeping again, without being protected. Finishing on Dex's phone, I went outside to find a woman walking across the grass towards me. "Are you Sharon Trammell?" she asked. She was in her mid-fifties with short brown hair and green eyes. She wore dress pants and a flowery button up shirt. She had a badge that hung from her neck, identifying her as Shirley Greene from child welfare services. "That's me," I tried to act at ease. I waved, engaging in the typical COVID replacement for a handshake. "I got a call about Luke and Carroll. Someone was concerned that their living condition wasn't safe for them." I wasn't sure who, but immediately my ex-parents-in-law came to mind. "Was it Bryan and Amanda?" "Well, yes," she replied. I guess, this time, it wasn't crucial to hide the identity of the caller. "They said you guys live in a yurt and they didn't think it was safe for the kids because there might be a deck and a drop off to the river. Can I take a look?" We walked down the trail, Luke leading the way. He had no problem chatting her up. She seemed friendly.

He led her in, showing her where he slept. He showed her the back deck. "Do you guys spend time here alone or is your mom here when you are?" She asked, bending down to their level. "Only when Mom is here," Luke answered. She turned to me. "How do you feel about this setup? Can you find anything else?" I explained how I had been looking, but due to COVID, there was a shortage.

She already knew. I then explained how Mac had come the night before, how I was scared for my kid's safety, and how the shelters were full. I was at my wits end. By this point, I was holding back tears. I hadn't meant to tear up, but she genuinely sounded like she wanted to protect me and my kids. This was new to me. I expected her to want to arrest me or tell me how I was failing. Instead, she began brain storming. "I'm going to get back to you on this," she said. "I want to see if I can find a safer option until you can get into a house."

As we walked up the trail, Luke picked up where I had left off. "Mom has to block the doors because dad might break in and kill us in our sleep! Dad also stole our bikes a while ago. I was sad. I loved my blue bike. Carroll had a pink one. He took our helmets too!" Shirley shook her head, just as disgusted as I was. "I will see what I can do for you guys," she said. As she was getting into her car, she turned to me. "I can see you are doing the best you can. No one can blame you for this situation. I just want you to know that. You aren't going to get in any trouble." She gently put a hand on my arm.

Growing up, my dad had always raved about how bad it was to get the law involved. He had told me that child protective services wanted to take children from their parents and ruin families. He had said that whenever they got involved, it was always bad. He had been wrong with advising me not to report Mac, though. Maybe some of these workers truly cared for people, after all. I was still slightly stressed, but I had been honest. There was nothing more I could do. The next day after work, I was at the gym lifting when I got a phone call. Wearily, I answered.

"Hey sweetie, I wanted you to know that I have some information for you and some resources that may help. First, I found a grant that you qualify for. It's a domestic violence grant and it will pay for your first month's rent or a deposit when you find a place. In the meantime, my supervisor approved putting you guys in a hotel to keep those kids safe.

It's close to your work, I think. Its located across from the university. Will that one do?"

I was speechless. They were doing what? Paying for a hotel for us? To keep us safe? I thanked her and she gave me directions to the hotel and information on how to check in. She said they had a room that would be ready by that night. I blinked, trying to avoid the tears that threatened to surface.

When I got in my truck, I searched the web for the hotel she had given me. It was the nicest hotel in the area! By this point, I couldn't hold back the tears. Alone in my truck, I began bawling, shocked at the love I felt from this woman and the support that the system wanted to give us. I hardly felt worthy of being taken seriously. Half of me felt as though I was still being dramatic, blowing the situation out of proportion. This woman apparently didn't see it that way. She actually cared about our wellbeing!

I drove home, listening to praise music. Maybe God really did want me to get through this. Maybe, just maybe, He truly was supporting this journey I was taking, in spite of my imperfections. Still emotional, I packed a backpack for each child. I grabbed my own bag and the ring, only because it held value and I didn't want to leave it in case someone went through my stuff while I was gone. I grabbed my sewing machine and my bag of utilities that went with it. I had a dress that needed to be altered by Friday. I went up to the house. Dex and Alana had been watching a show, but when I came in, Alana went to the backroom. She often did this, saying she wanted to give me time to spend with Dex. Oh, well. I didn't have time for drama today. I quickly explained the situation to Dex, who looked relieved.

I drove the thirty-five minutes back to daycare, picked up the kids, and told them I had a surprise for them. Check in time was at 4, and it was 3:55 when we arrived. The kids had never stayed in a hotel before. This was going to be a new experience. As I parked the truck and began to walk in, it hit me just *how* nice this place really was. The entryway was grand, with tall white pillars holding up the covered loading area. The sliding doors were impeccably clean. The lobby had dark colored carpet that looked brand new. I recalled seeing the construction for this building only a year before. As I stood waiting my turn to check in, I saw other families milling around. I didn't feel out of place.

No one needed to know that I was here because I was a domestic violence victim, fleeing an abusive and mentally unstable ex-husband who had been stalking me off for the last two months. All they needed to know was that we were another family on summer vacation. I handed the papers that Shirley had given me to the lady at the front desk. She sounded kind. She handed me a key card and told me which room. "It's just down this way to the right, then it's on your right towards the end of the hallway by the pool. They gave you a downstairs room since you have kids. Your checkout time is the end of next week." Ten days. I sighed, thankful. Walking into the room, I was again amazed at the cleanliness and high-class aura of the place. Directly inside was a bathroom. It had a large mirror with makeup lighting and a large white marble countertop. The white porcelain bathtub was large enough to almost stretch out in and starched white towels hung on the towel rack beside the tub. Two more towels were stacked neatly on the marble counter. Walking out of the bathroom, I noticed the large closet. Inside was a bathrobe and three hangers. On the outside of the closet door was a full-length mirror. I stood in front of it, flexing my quads and admiring my tanned legs.

The kids had already made their way to the bed, which was covered in a white down comforter. Fluffed pillows, which had been arranged neatly against the headboard, had already fallen on the floor. The kids were jumping on the bed, excited for this adventure. I looked around, finding the black polished desk that faced the large window. I set my sewing machine down, still slightly embarrassed that I had carried it in. What if people knew the truth? What if people knew I was practically homeless and I was living out of a hotel room? What if my clients knew that I was altering their clothing from a hotel room because I wasn't even safe in my little forest yurt?

The negative thoughts started to come then. What if my kids destroyed this hotel room? What if I couldn't find a place to rent and I disappointed the child welfare lady? Dex would be disappointed too if I had to move back in. What if my kids were too loud and people got mad? There were so many what if's. Opening the blinds halfway, I watched a family of four getting out of their car. They were carrying pool noodles towards the pool end of the hotel. My kids had seen them too. "Can we go swimming? Pleeeeeeeasssee?" They begged, looking more excited than I had seen them look in a long time. "You guys need to find your swimsuits in your bag and then we can go."

They were already digging through their bags, racing to get ready. I buckled their life jackets and they raced down the hallway. Calling for them to slow down did nothing, they were already through the gate and racing towards the pool. I caught up, opening the gate for them to go into the pool area. People here didn't seem to be as concerned with COVID precautions. While they were keeping their distance, no one was wearing masks. Then again, it was outside.

Chapter Thirty-Three

I found a table with an umbrella and sat down, watching my children splash in the shallow end of the pool. I felt comfortable with this environment, hoping that people wouldn't be upset at my kids for not respecting COVID personal bubbles. Luke especially struggled with this.

Since working with multiple kids who had neurological diagnoses during the last few months, and noticing some similarities, I sometimes wondered if Luke had a diagnosis I didn't know about. Not only was it manifesting through hyper behavior, but it seemed his focus was worse than it had ever been. I couldn't get him to do even simple tasks without prompts. Then there was the aggression. It had been bad lately. Even Martha had mentioned little things that seemed strange while he had been at her daycare during the last couple months.

When I had visited his doctor for his five-year checkup, she hadn't recognized anything as being off with him. She had told me that it was likely due to all the changes he was experiencing. While I agreed that he had gone through a lot, I felt that he was struggling more than other kids. Or maybe it was simply that I wasn't parenting him firmly enough. This was what Mac had always told me. Maybe if I disciplined him more, he would listen better. It just felt so overwhelming. I felt I was incapable of disciplining to the point of making an actual change. I wished my parents would have wanted to be involved more. However, my parents hated me now, even more than they had previously. After Mac's recent uninvited visit, I had received a text from my older sister. Esther was normally the kindest one of my siblings. Not this time though. "Is your new boyfriend still there? Mac told us all about it!" she had taunted. Naomi had texted me that she was disappointed in me; she knew I had left Mac so I could sleep with other guys. My brothers had taken me off their social media friend lists. Five different family friends had blocked me on the internet after that day.

If I hadn't already been branded as the black sheep, it was written all over my forehead now. Everyone in my parent's circle seemed to know about my hookup. I was now the whore of the family. It didn't matter that I had been faithful to an abusive cheater for six years. One instance of engaging in immoral behavior, and the whole world knew what I had done. This was the way for Christian women though, I thought.

Although it was the twenty-first century, it seemed our culture was one that still held onto the idea that women were to be labeled as sluts for having sex outside of a relationship, while men, who were naturally horny all the time, were just being men when they engaged in casual sex. Especially college aged boys. They had needs, after all. My lover had gone about his life, back to his parent's house where no one knew what had happened. The next day he had probably hit up a different girl, hardly remembering this night, aside from the drama with my ex. He had been able to keep the whole thing private, just like all of his other hookup experiences. But me, on the other hand, I was now famous. Mac now had the tangible proof he needed to share my immoral behavior with everyone. In all honesty, this hookup hadn't even felt fulfilling at all anyway. I hadn't become immune to developing feelings for people I had sex with. I had been disappointed when this boy had stopped texting me after we had hooked up. Some part of me had hoped that it would turn into something. I still felt that sex was something that only people who were in love should do together. Maybe that was my problem. I was so weak that I couldn't engage in casual sex and wanted to do it only in a committed relationship. The day after the hookup, I had felt a deep longing, even deeper than before the hookup, to find true love. I had listened to sad songs about relationships that had gone wrong, silently suffering as I realized how I was the last of my kind. What was wrong with me? Why couldn't I stop these big feelings?

I brushed the thought aside, determined to not stay stuck in the sadness. Sitting on a lounge chair in my strapless bikini, I swiped Tinder. Maybe I would meet someone. A guy named George had been hitting me up. He liked to fish. He had offered to bring his rods and go to the lake with me, even offering to bring rods for the kids. We could catch some bass and croppie from the dock, he had said. I had agreed, telling him we should meet up in town first to make sure we were both legit.

Two days later, after work and the gym, I met up with George. When he pulled in to the hospital parking lot where we had agreed to meetup, I saw that he drove a lifted red pickup. He jumped out, his belly jiggling. He was tall but it wasn't obvious since he was so round as well. He had a big beard and gave off a biker vibe, I thought as I observed him. He wore a sleeveless t-shirt with jean shorts. He shook my hand and we talked for a minute. He seemed safe enough and I was concealed carrying. I followed him to the lake, about 40 minutes' drive away. Others were out and about, so it didn't seem unsafe to me. He showed me how he set up the rods with Powerbait and we began fishing. Luke caught a crappie right away. George showed him how to unhook it and release it. I smiled, observing how he was making an effort to be helpful to my kids. I didn't exactly feel at ease with him, but I also didn't know him yet. We talked and he told me he had always wanted kids, how he had been married, and then how she had left him.

Poor guy. I didn't find him attractive at all, but I reasoned that I should give him another chance before ruling him out. We agreed to go to the beach the following weekend and then I headed back to the hotel. I didn't tell him I was living in a hotel or that I was constantly checking over my shoulder to see if my ex was following me. I didn't tell him that I had asked the security at the hotel to check their cameras and see if my ex had walked in. I didn't say that I was still having nightmares about him attacking me, even there, even with the doors locked. That was irrelevant to my future and I was moving on with my life.

Chapter Thirty-Four

The next day after work, I began house searching again. So far, none of the rentals I had inquired about had replied to me. COVID had been hard on everyone and many people were searching; this had driven the cost up and created a housing shortage. Searching for a rental had quickly become discouraging. Even if I qualified financially, I had no credit history. My dad had always said that credit was for people who wanted to live their lives in debt.

I had never even had a credit card in my name. On the one hand, I was thankful. If Mac and I had a credit card, he would have spent money we didn't have. At least this way, I didn't have debt to pay off. Still, I wasn't set up to qualify for anything on my own. The other issue that scared me, was thinking about how Luke would do in an apartment. I was terrified of getting kicked out because of my son. He was loud when he had his tantrums and no one in an apartment would put up with that.

All the worst-case scenarios towered over me. I needed to take a break. Opening up Tinder, I began scrolling again. I was still planning to see George again, but talking to multiple people seemed to be the only way. Being "exclusive" was that scary word that no one talked about until after at least 6 to 12 dates. Until then, it was best to play the field. Right then was when I swiped right on Austin. Match! This notification made me happy. His profile picture was him next to a lifted truck, wearing designer jeans and cowboy boots. He wore Pit Vipers and a ball cap. My type completely. His profile said he worked in some sort of skilled trade. I hoped he messaged me.

The next day I got a text from a friend I had met through the kid's daycare. She was a single parent who was in nursing school and had quickly taken me under her wing as the new single momma that I was. She wanted to know if I wanted to get together at the river and let the kids swim after work. The weather had been in the low 90's all week, so the river was finally warming up. I readily agreed.

Setting up a blanket on the sandy bank, I set out snacks for my kids. I snapped their life jackets on and let them play. Luke found a log and started dragging it behind him through the water, pretending it was his boat. Carroll sat and splashed in the shallow water, turning to look at me every couple of minutes, making sure I was still there. I opened a hard lemonade, thankful for the chance to relax. My friend sat next to me, holding her six-month-old in one arm and a drink in the other. "So, have you thought about what you want to do with your life?" She asked point blank. "I know it feels like you just started over, but you will eventually need to figure out what you want to do. You could probably get grants if you wanted to go back to school." What was with everyone asking me what I wanted to do with my life? Wasn't I doing it already? Working, raising the kids, staying alive, going to the gym? What was the rush? I didn't get it. She continued, "One income only goes so far. If you went to school, you could make more when you finish. When I finish nursing school in another 4 years, I'm going to be making really good money. It will actually be enough to get off of state benefits and thrive, even without a second income" she said. "My ex is supposed to pay me child support. If he does, it won't be so hard." I replied, beginning to think about her question. My parents had always thought college was stupid. They raved about how kids these days had no life experience but they got a degree and ended up working at a gas station anyway. It was pointless, they had always told my brothers. Higher education had never even been a question for me.

I was a woman. My place was in the home. I wasn't to even have a career. My dad had critiqued my side hustle as an alteration's specialist, saying that if I applied myself thoroughly to my parenting and house cleaning, I would have no desire to make money. That was Mac's job. I was taking away from his manhood by trying to add financial support to the family. It wasn't my place.

Even my parents' attitudes aside, I wasn't sure if I was smart enough for college. I had heard the horror stories of having to spend hours studying, writing papers and taking tests, abandoning one's physical health routine, only to graduate with student loans that drowned any potential of a successful future. No, college had never been a thought of mine. Only now, I wondered what life would be like if I *did* go to college. Either way, it wouldn't be right now. I needed to find a house first. And finish this divorce. Then maybe I could consider it.

Chapter Thirty-Five

I got another call from Shirley the next day. We were scheduled to check out the day after. A week and a half had gone by fast. The kids had spent most afternoons by the pool. We had been living off of microwave burritos since there wasn't an oven or stove in the unit. The kids were eating healthy snacks at daycare; I consoled myself with this knowledge. I was slightly worried how peanut butter sandwiches and microwave burritos were affecting my six pack, but I was thankful to be in a safer environment than we had been while at the yurt.

On the phone with Shirley, I filled her in. I hadn't found a place but I was still looking. She had found three apartments within 30 minutes of me. I had gotten on the waiting list for a local apartment complex, but management had told me it could be up to a year before a unit would become available. Shirley told me that she had gotten her supervisor to approve another two weeks for us at the hotel. She also wanted to meet up with me, because she had some stuff for the kids that had been donated. I agreed to meet her an hour later.

When we arrived, she wasn't there yet. The kids got bored with sitting in the car, so they got out and began playing in the grass. After a minute, she pulled up. She opened her trunk and I walked over, curious to see what she had gotten. When I saw what she had, I swallowed the lump in my throat, blinking back the tears that threatened to surface. She pulled out a blue bike, then a blue helmet. She leaned it against her car. She then pulled out a pink balance bike, also complete with a pink helmet. I called the kids over. Excitement wouldn't have adequately described their emotions. They couldn't contain their joy at the sight of new bikes. Carroll clapped her tiny hands together in pure happiness. "You got us bikes!" she yelled. Luke was already putting his helmet on.

He didn't care for shoes, and was riding across the parking lot before I could stop him. I barely had words to thank Shirley. I wanted to hug her, but this was a professional relationship. Besides that, COVID was still killing people. I would give back someday. This would become an experience I would never forget. Her kindness was already making me believe that good still existed in a world that, up to this point, had showed me a lot of heartlessness.

That night, while the kids played in the pool, I searched the internet for rentals again. An idea had come to me. If I could find a spot to park a travel trailer, I could make things work. Not only would it be cheaper, but it would also be more yard space for the kids, than finding an apartment. I would need to find a used travel trailer as well, but this might be a viable solution. I had emailed about three trailer spots so far.

As I searched listings again, I found one I had missed previously. There were no pictures, but it sounded promising. The posting said that there was a concrete pad to park the trailer on and there was a big shop right next to the parking spot. The property owner stated that the parking spot was housed on several acres, on the edge of his grass seed farm. He wanted to help someone who needed it. I texted the number listed. Within five minutes, I had a reply. The listing was available and the property owner wanted me to call to discuss it. I called immediately. The guy who answered introduced himself as Dennis. He said he had grandkids. He said that he was a bachelor and missed having his own kids around; having kids living there would brighten his world. He invited us to come look at the spot. He said that he would hold the spot for us until we made a decision. The price was well within my budget. I was excited!

The day I had planned to spend with George arrived quickly. I had let him know that I wanted to go slow with him, so this was more like hanging out with a friend. I was dressed for a summer day, in jean shorts that showed my tanned and muscular thighs. I wore a Stlhd Gear t-shirt, a memento from those first days of learning to fish. I braided my hair and put on mascara, the only makeup I ever wore.

George met me with an awkward side hug. I uncomfortably leaned into his large belly, feeling somewhat repulsed even though I wanted to be interested. This would be a good day. I would *make* it a good day. He had mentioned having a trailer that his dad might want to sell me. Part of my reason for spending the day with him was to see this trailer. If the worked out, I could be done with the yurt and Dex. There would be no more feeling like I wasn't welcome or that I was coming between Dex and Alana. No more having to feel uncomfortable whenever I asked Dex for any help, because of Alana's hate for me. And there would be no more feeling guilty for using state money to stay in a hotel, just to make sure Mac didn't try to murder me in my sleep. The date was mediocre at best. On the way home, we stopped to see the trailer at his dad's property. The 36-foot trailer had been parked in a field for a few months, he told me. He assured me that everything worked well. From the outside, it looked like it had been sitting for more than a few months. It also looked older than he had said it was when he described it to me. However, I was feeling more and more desperate. We had spent almost three weeks in the hotel by now. Something needed to change. We couldn't stay forever.

Chapter Thirty-Six

After work on the farm with Jim two days later, I went to see the trailer spot. Driving slowly up the long gravel drive, I became immediately excited at the potential opportunity. It was almost dark. Dennis had said he was a farmer; he wouldn't be home from the field until after 8. When we arrived, it was 8:15. The sun was setting over the grass field behind the house. The sight was breathtaking. The whole yard looked well-kept. The driveway was lined with recently planted fir seedlings, which had been landscaped with fresh bark dust. The driveway had new gravel.

There was a large swimming pool next to the house in the perfectly manicured front yard grass. A shop stood to the west, with the concrete pad directly between the house and the shop. I wondered if this was where he wanted us to park the trailer. It didn't look as though there was enough room for a trailer here.

Dennis had said we could look around until he got there, so the kids got out, heading straight for the pool. Retrieving Carroll before she made it to the top the ladder, I told both children that swimming wasn't permitted. We would need to ask first. Dennis pulled in then, driving a new work truck with a gas tank mounted in the bed.

As he got out, I noticed that he dressed like a farmer. He wore blue overalls, which barely fit over his rounded belly, and a plaid shirt. He was in his late fifties. He was mostly bald and his hands looked calloused from work on the farm. He walked up to me, offering me a hand. He wasn't worried about COVID apparently. He led me toward the concrete pad. This would be where I would park the trailer, he explained, just as I had guessed. He then told the kids they could jump on the trampoline. I sighed with relief, slightly nervous that they were going to try to swim again without permission.

The worry that my kids might break something or mess up something that didn't belong to them followed me everywhere. I felt it constantly at Dex's. I was constantly on guard at the hotel. It would be the same here. It had been so long since we had anything that was ours. I sighed, turning my attention back to the potential landlord. He was asking me about my divorce. I explained that it had been a struggle and my ex-husband hadn't been the nicest to me, so we were looking for a new place to live. He said that he too, had gone through a divorce. He said he was in court again, accused of stealing from his ex-wife this time.

I was beginning to feel uncomfortable and doubt this situation. Not only was there not enough room to truly have our own space, but something was off about this Dennis guy. I didn't listen to the worries, though. We needed to get out of the hotel and leave Dex's. Mac wouldn't know where we were if we moved here. There would be no way for him to find out and we would finally be safe.

I thanked Dennis for the tour and told him we had found a trailer. We could probably move in by next weekend. The next morning before work, I called the bank. They agreed to loan me money for the trailer, if I put cash down as well. When I asked Jim that day at work, he agreed to drive with me and pick up the trailer, since he had a pickup capable of towing. Everything was falling into place. I called Shirley, updating her. She was thrilled.

Throughout dealing with logistics, a busy work week, and my normal lifting routine, my connection with Austin had become more heated. He had messaged me constantly, even calling me after work the day before. He had Facetimed me once already as well. He talked constantly of meeting me in-person. He asked if he could drive the two hours to see me the following weekend.

I told him I was in the process of buying a trailer. He offered to come help me get situated. I told him about having my kid's full time. He didn't mind. He wanted to meet them. His sister had kids and he had already mentioned that he was pretty sure my kids would get along well with his niece and nephew. Maybe I would come up to his family farm and meet them sometime, he had suggested. He lived in a trailer on his parents' property so that he could save money. He was rarely home anyway, he explained, with work taking up most of his time. He had already told his dad about me. I was looking forward to meeting him.

I left work early that Friday. I met Jim at a gas station. I loaded both kids into his truck and we headed towards the spot where the trailer was parked. Everything was moving fast. We would pick up the trailer and get it all ready to move in, hopefully by later tonight. The drive to pick up the trailer was long and the kids got bored. After an hour and a half, the GPS still said we had 30 miles to go. I hadn't realized it was so far south of us. Finally, we arrived. George and his dad were both there, waiting for us in the field.

At Jim's suggestion, I would pay the father and son $500 of the agreed total at pickup. When I got the trailer plugged in and made sure everything worked, I would give them the check from the bank for the full amount. Because there was no way to test its functionality where it had been parked in the field, this would ensure that we were getting a fair deal. I handed over the cash.

Immediately, we noticed that the trailer lights didn't work; Jim was concerned. Finally, we made some adjustments and they flickered on. We were ready to go. I thanked George and his father. I didn't plan to see George again. After our date last weekend, I had become less interested. However, I was thankful that meeting him had led us to finding a trailer.

Slowly, the trailer began to roll. We inched across the bumpy field, turning cautiously onto the pavement. As the truck gained speed, I noticed that the siding on the trailer was flapping in the wind. That couldn't be good. Thankfully this wasn't essential to the functioning of the trailer. It had been sitting for a while, so outer wear and tear was normal. I told myself to stop stressing, concentrating instead on what Jim was telling me about an experience he had had as a child. I was thankful for this unlikely friend I had made. I could act like a kid around Jim and not feel dumb. Not only that, but I could tell him things and he never judged me. He always said he was proud of me, no matter how insignificant my accomplishment. I felt safe around him in a way that I didn't even feel around my own father anymore.

Before I knew it, the drive was finished. It was almost dark as Jim backed the trailer onto the concrete pad. After about 15 minutes, he had maneuvered it successfully into place. Dennis had come home and was outside now, watching. After another fifteen minutes, we had put stops behind the wheels, hooked up the water and run an extension cord through the garage to the power hookup on the trailer. We would spend one more night at the hotel, checking out in the morning. Everything had aligned perfectly.

The next morning, we left the hotel, ready to begin a new chapter. Today would be spent hooking up the electric and getting settled in at the new trailer. The power hadn't worked last night when we had plugged in the trailer, so I assumed we would need a new extension cord. Austin planned to come today as well. This would be an opportunity to see how well he could solve problems.

We were at the trailer site by 8, hoping to avoid the heat of the day. It was July first; the temperature had been over 90 degrees every day this week. I hoped we could get the power running quickly so that we could get the AC working, then spend the remainder of the day doing something fun with Austin. After checking the length of cord needed, I drove to the hardware store. Austin had agreed to meet me here. I saw him pull up, parking a few yards from where my Pickup was parked. I bit my lower lip in excitement. His white pickup, complete with a light bar, tinted windows, and a 6-inch lift, added to his allure. I would probably never get over country boys who drove lifted trucks. When he got out, I got a better look at him. He was short, only a little taller than

I was. His blonde hair, mostly hidden under a baseball cap, was cut short. He wore his Pit Vipers again, adding to the charm. He wore cowboy boots and Wranglers, just like in his picture. He grinned as he walked towards me. When he spoke, he had a cute accent, sounding almost southern. I caught my breath. This guy was hot. We walked into the hardware store together. He showed me which items to get and soon we were headed back to the trailer. An hour later, everything was hooked up. There was only one problem.

After attempting to turn on lights, the power didn't work at all. We tried re-wiring the plug and then tried a different outlet. We tested it with the power tester. We reset all the circuits in the trailer and tried a couple of other things that Austin suggested; he had some knowledge of power systems in trailers since he also lived in one. He suggested we take a break after this. We all loaded into his lifted truck and drove to the yurt. I wanted to get some things for tonight anyway. The kids headed straight to the yard where Alana and Dex were soaking up the late morning sun. For once, Alana didn't leave. She stayed and looked genuinely happy to see me. I knew the happiness was due to the fact that we had found a place and would be gone soon, but it was nice to not feel the tension, regardless. I showed Austin the yurt. He waited until we were inside alone to kiss me. It was nice. I could get used to this.

After grabbing my slow cooker and some plastic bowls and plates for the kids, we headed back up to his truck. The kids were sitting with Dunagen, rubbing his black and white nose. His tail was wagging contentedly. I gathered up Carroll, who had left her shoes in Austin's truck. Strapping her into her car seat, and helping Luke into his booster, we left Dex's place. I wanted to show Austin the mountain roads where I often drove around solo when I wanted to think. Who could turn down a drive on back roads, riding shotgun with a cute country boy driving? Not me. This was my dream life. I smiled. This had part of why I had stayed so long with Mac. As hard as it had been, we had our good times. I wanted something like *that* again.

I spent the rest of the day with Austin. He ordered pizza and we took it back to the new trailer. Getting out paper plates, we sat at the little table and ate together. It was 8 pm before he grudgingly left, after making out with me in Dennis' shop when no one was looking. I was quickly becoming obsessed with him. I felt this went both ways. When Austin left, he asked if I wanted to come up to his family's property the following weekend. I told him I would think about it. I didn't want to seem too eager. After he had gone, I went back into the trailer.

As I turned on the tap in the kitchen, water instantly began to shoot out of the base of the sink, soaking the counter. I quickly turned the tap off. I would need to caulk the base of the sink, although it wasn't a project I had done before. During my marriage, I had become quite handy. I had learned to fix almost anything that broke, including mechanical issues with my truck, the lawnmower, and most of the other things that seemed to often break. I hadn't become a plumber yet though. Time to learn something new. Sighing, I went into the bathroom. The bathroom tap leaked also. Turning on the shower, I found that at least this worked. Since the electric still wasn't working, I would have to take a cold shower. At least there was running water. The trailer was hot from the day, so a cold shower would be refreshing. It wouldn't be the worst thing in the world.

After a quick two minutes, I stepped out of the shower, shivering. I was clean. For that I was thankful. Walking into the bedroom, I noticed the gap in the curtains. I felt uncomfortable instantly. Being right next to the house, I knew that Dennis could probably see in if he was looking. This was why I had felt we wouldn't have privacy here. I dressed quickly, helping the kids get ready for bed. Tucking Carroll in next to me, I tried to sleep. It was almost dark. Once it got completely dark, sleeping would be easier. I rolled over, listening to the crickets outside the window. It was almost relaxing, but something felt off.

A while later, I heard Dennis' truck pull in. I heard a door shut. I lay for a while longer. By now, it was completely dark. I rolled over again, this time hearing noise outside the trailer. After a minute, I heard Dennis' voice. "Are you guys still up? I brought you some flashlights." I sighed and climbed out of bed, reaching for a hoodie since I was in only a T-shirt and underwear.

It made me uncomfortable that he knocked on the bedroom door, not the door at the front of the trailer. I had wanted to leave the door open with only the screen shut, but I had felt weird. I didn't know this guy. I wanted to be able to lock the door. I tiptoed towards the door, opening it just a crack. Dennis held out two flashlights. I thanked him. I wanted to go back to bed. He wanted to talk. He asked about Austin. I said he was a friend who was helping me move. He said he hoped he was a good guy. Dennis was angrier than I was about the electric not working. I appreciated his concern, but felt increasingly uncomfortable about the situation and deciding to move here. I didn't like the idea of having him feel like he could come knock on our door at any hour.

I was irritated, but he wasn't done talking. By this point, Carroll was awake and standing next to me. He suggested that we take showers in his house until we got the power working. I thanked him and told him the kids needed their rest; it was time to sleep. By this point it was past 12. I locked both doors firmly and went back to bed. I reached up, trying to get the curtain to close more fully. I tucked Carroll in again, hoping that this time I could get to sleep. Luke was still awake and came in then, telling me he was scared. I tucked him in on my other side, telling him it would be okay.

At five, I heard Dennis' work truck start. Rolling over, I checked my phone. Today was July 4th! My first one without my ex-husband. I had a video message from Austin. He was showing me the sunset from last night. He told me how much fun he had with me. He had already let his dad know I was coming, so I couldn't back out now, he told me. I smiled. Living here, I would be especially excited to leave for a whole weekend.

I got dressed, washing my face with the cold water that came out of the bathroom shower. If we could figure out the electric, and fix the sink, this might not be so bad. At least Dennis didn't have a jealous girlfriend that hated me. I wished I could call my dad and ask him to help me fix the electric. Sighing, I brushed aside a tear. I was a woman now and I could do this on my own. I didn't need more negativity in my life. Negativity was all that my parents would add right now.

I spent the morning googling electric help for trailers. I didn't come up with anything I hadn't tried. I called Jim, who didn't know either. I had nothing to do but wait. Dennis came back at 10 that morning, saying that he had the day off. He looked at the electric again for another two hours, trying to do what he could to help me. Even he gave up after that. I had talked to George, who didn't have any ideas. He was sorry but he hoped I could figure it out. His father was an electrician and offered to come up, but it wouldn't be until next weekend. I was trying to be patient with everyone.

That night, we went to bed early again, after another cold shower. Again, Luke couldn't settle, so he ended up next to me. At 10, Dennis knocked on the door. Again, he talked for an hour. He was clearly lonely. I just wanted to sleep.

I was up by 5 the next day, getting ready for work. At least at work there was AC. The kids would be taken care of at daycare too. Because we didn't have a working fridge, we had been eating peanut butter sandwiches for the last few days. I had packed the cooler full of ice and was able to keep a gallon of milk and some jelly cold that way. I fed the kids cold cereal and milk. I washed the plastic bowls in the bathroom shower, cleaning up the little trailer in the best way I could.

Twelve hours later, after work, the gym, and picking up the kids, we got home. I helped both kids change into swimsuits and we headed to the river. The trailer was still too hot to spend any time in. When we finally got home, at 8:30, Dennis was waiting for us. He was pissed at George. "What is his number? I'm calling him," he told me.

I didn't hear the whole conversation, but I heard him say "This poor girl has been stuck here without hot water or AC or even a fridge for almost a week! How can you call yourself a man and just let her suffer like this? You need to get your ass up here and get your trailer! Now!" I didn't protest. I didn't know what else to do. I was thankful I hadn't given George the check from my bank yet. He agreed to come the next night and give me my money back and take the trailer.

Chapter Thirty-Seven

When I got home from work the next day, around 6, I packed the dishes, clothing, and the slow cooker in my truck. I unhooked the water. I walked through the trailer one last time, making sure nothing of ours was left. George pulled up in his lifted red truck. "None of the ATMs were open," he said, looking embarrassed. I wanted my money back. "There is one in downtown. I'll take you and show you." Awkwardly, I drove him to the ATM. The withdrawal limit was $300. Oh well. At least I would get some of it back. I blinked back tears.

It could have been worse. I helped him hook up the trailer and watched him drive away, towing it. What a week it had been. It was almost dark by now. Dennis wanted to talk again. He was frustrated for me. I didn't have any words. I told him that the kids were really tired; we needed to head back to the yurt. I would call him tomorrow. We headed towards the yurt. The tears came freely as soon as I was in the truck and the kids had fallen asleep.

I had been trying so hard. All I wanted was to make a good life for my kids. It wasn't fair that I had to flee from my ex just to be physically safe, while he stayed in our home, with all the luxuries that most people took for granted, like power, running water, and a fridge. It wasn't fair that his whole life hadn't been uprooted like mine had. It wasn't fair that the one I had spent so many years loving, caring for, and being loyal to, was okay with abusing me and taking from me and leaving us struggling just to keep a roof over our heads.

It wasn't fair that Dex's girlfriend was jealous of me and couldn't see the truth about me. Or that I would have to go back to the yurt again and beg them just for a place to live. It wasn't fair that my family wouldn't support me through any of this and that they found it so easy to judge me. I hadn't done half of what Mac had done, and yet, they saw no fault in him and all the fault in me, shunning me.

None of it was fair. I wiped tears with the back of my hand, trying to sob silently so my kids didn't wake up. I had kept it together so well for the past few weeks, but that didn't mean it had been easy. Why did all this have to happen to me? My ego was hurt by the fact that I would be back in the yurt; having to admit to Dex that my plan had fallen through wouldn't be easy.

I didn't feel welcome there. I didn't feel welcome anywhere. I was an unwanted outcast, drifting at the will of those who would show me kindness. I felt like Haggar from the Bible. She had been kicked out of Abraham's house after he had impregnated her. She hadn't had the choice to say no even if she wanted to. Because of the jealousy of her handmaid, Haggar was cast out, with her child, left for dead in the wilderness.

Then there was Ruth. Her husband had died and she had chosen to travel to a new land, being loyal to her husband's family. She had worked hard to make a life for herself, slaving in the fields only to pick up the leftover grain from everyone who was entitled to the crops. She was allowed only to gather what others had dropped. Both of these women had been outcasts in a way, told that they were less than, simply because of how life had played out for them, through circumstances out of their control.

God had provided for both of these women though. Ruth had ended up in a beautiful union with the man God had intended for her. Together, they had born the great grandfather of King David, who was a direct line to Jesus. Haggar had been given a well of water in a dry wilderness. God had made a great plan for both of their lives, but it hadn't felt like this during their season of struggle. Surely, he would provide for me in the same way that he had provided for these Biblical women. I wiped away more tears. I still felt defeated, but life had to go on. I needed to try to see the positive, because it was all I had now. I still needed to be up at five am the next day for work.

Pulling into Dex's driveway, I reached back and grabbed the kids backpacks. Slinging them over my shoulder, I unbuckled Carroll. I carefully carried her to the yurt, rolling back the blankets and laying her in the bed. It was cold. There was a pile of mouse poop on the comforter. I angrily brushed it aside, feeling more helpless than ever. It had been a month since we had stayed here. I would have at least washed the bedding if I had known we would be back. But I hadn't even been able to do that. I tucked Carroll in and went back up to carry Luke. Tucking him into the bed atop the cement blocks, I sighed. His bed, too, was covered in mouse poop. The counters were covered as well. There was no food in the yurt.

Sighing, I reached into my backpack and pulled out my toothbrush. Everything felt dirty. I was worried about getting sick from the lack of cleanness. I ran cold water onto my hands, scrubbing them with dish soap. I picked up the toothbrush again, taking it out of the plastic bag. Running cold water onto it, I stepped onto the back porch to brush my teeth. On the one hand, the crickets chirping, combined with the creek running directly below me, calmed me. On the other, the dark scared me. I peered into the blackness, on edge.

What if Mac knew I had come back? What if he had been waiting for this day to finally know where I was and finish me off? Would he kill the kids too, out of resentment for me trying to hide from him? Would he do it only to me, leaving them to find my body here the next day? I shivered.

Finished brushing, I walked back inside. Sliding three bins of clothing against the door, I pushed the rocking chair against the opposite door. I looked around for anything that could add additional protection. This would have to do. At least I would hear it if he tried breaking in, before he successfully made it. It might give me time to reach for a make-shift weapon. By now, it was past 11. I was exhausted from the ups and downs of the last few days. I crawled onto the side of the bed, trying to move quietly and not wake Carroll. I drifted into a shallow sleep, jumping and waking at every sound for the remainder of the night.

Farmer Dennis continued to reach out to me throughout the summer, until one day, he invited me over to give me a boxing lesson, insisting on paying *me* afterwards. During the boxing session, he attempted to physically teach me the moves by getting close behind me and hugging my body from the back. We were alone in his home and I felt uncomfortable. I had been taught to be polite, not to say no or tell anyone when their actions crossed a boundary, so I didn't know how to handle this.

I finished my lesson and left, never to return. As time went on, I began to feel thankful that I hadn't been taken advantage of in any way by this man. As I look back, I feel strongly that my angels were looking out for me during this encounter, both by helping me to get most of my money back from the trailer situation, and by making sure that farmer Dennis didn't lay a hand on me or my children.

Chapter Thirty-Eight

The morning after coming back to the yurt, I went to work at Jim's. He needed to put new bedding in the stalls in the barn and then build an addition to the chicken coop. I was exhausted, but the morning had been going well until I saw a sheriff driving slowly up the drive towards Jims's barn. At first, I didn't think much of it, but after a moment, I saw him knock on the door. A minute later, I saw Patty coming across the yard towards me, with the sheriff in tow. "Are you Sharon Trammell?" He said, as soon as he had walked up to me. I nodded, wondering how he had found me at work. "I'm going to need your concealed carry permit please," he said.

He handed me a sheaf of papers. "This is a restraining order. Is Mac your husband?" I nodded, in shock. "What are the grounds for this? He's the one that's been stalking me. I haven't once gone to his house or done anything to hurt him ever!" The sheriff flipped some pages. "It says here that you jumped on him one day. He mentions that you weigh a lot more than he does and he is worried if he had to fight you, you would win. He says that you gained a lot of muscle and he felt you may have done that to be able to hurt him". I thought back to the day the kids had gone there last, when he had changed his mind about having them. The night he had given me the ring and I hadn't wanted it. I had pulled him off Carroll. The neighbor had witnessed it and seen that I wasn't trying to hurt him, surely. How could this be happening? How could he have taken this action against me, when he was the one who had been threatening me for the last several weeks?

I walked to my car and gave him the permit. The officer was friendly, but doing his job. He said that if my lawyer could get it removed by proving that it was unfounded, I could have the permit back. In the meantime, he would take it. There was nothing more to be said. I headed back to the barn, still in shocked silence.

When I met Jim in the barn after the sheriff had gone, he had more unsettling news for me. He had talked to Mac's father, who bragged to him that he had followed me into the woods the week before, undetected. He had seen me with a man and decided to find out what we were doing, he told Jim. Mac and his father would never forget what I had done to humiliate their family. They would make sure I felt unsafe for as long as possible because of it. Because the temporary order for our divorce had recently become effective, I would now need to take the children to spend weekends with their father, every other weekend.

Mac had suggested his parents' house as the meetup place. I had no choice but to agree. Not only did his entire family hate me, but now they would get a chance to prove it when I brought the kids for the exchanges. The silver lining to the court order being in place was that Mac would now be forced to pay child support. As long as he was working, the court would garnish his wages and I would get some much-needed support that would help me pay for a rental when I found one. I was determined to see the positives among the many struggles.

When I arrived at the yurt several hours later, after going to the gym and then picking up both kids, Dex was out in the yard. I explained the situation with the trailer. He told me that it was fine for us to stay as long as we needed, since the homeless shelters were full and there wasn't another option. I would try to keep the kids out of his space more and do my best to avoid him so that Alana could feel more at ease. I knew he was risking himself in more ways than one to allow us to be there. Mac had threatened him for supporting us. Alana was angry with him for allowing us to live here. He was a hero in more ways than one, standing for justice in the face of threats and jealousy. For that, I was thankful.

Shirley called a few days later to say that she was closing out our case; she was unworried about the kid's safety. She didn't ask how things had turned out with the trailer and I didn't elaborate. She told me good luck with everything and we hung up. There was nothing more that anyone could do until I found a rental.

Chapter Thirty-Nine

On Saturday night, we packed backpacks and headed towards Austin's house. I had agreed to work that day, helping harvest hay that would be used at Jim's farm. Although I didn't work most Saturdays, it was extra money and the work had needed to be done immediately. Bucking hay was fun, but I was exhausted. The drive to Austin's family's farm would take two and a half hours. I needed to drive through rush hour traffic in the city, and then drive over a mountain pass to arrive at his family's home. We would stay that night and the next, coming home on Monday morning early, in time for work. This would be a much-needed getaway. I was excited to explore his home and see new places.

As I turned off the pavement onto a gravel road, only a mile from Austin's now, excitement built. It was dusk. The sun was setting, the air beginning to cool, and the commercial sprayers were watering the fields as I drove by. Many had some sort of grain crop, while others were full of cows, who had begun to huddle with their calves in preparation for sleep. The air smelled of freshly harvested fields. I passed a peach orchard. In the distance, a mountain peak showed itself, snowcapped still, and complete with a pink skyline where the sun had just disappeared.

After another moment, I spotted the driveway, just as he had described it. There was a gate with an arch over the top, and a sign that read *Reed Family Ranch*. The gate was open and a long gravel driveway stretched out before me, with a farmhouse and a barn at the end. As I drove slowly down the driveway, I noted that there was a second barn; it looked like it was full of hay. Next to this barn was where Austin's fifth-wheel was parked. I saw his truck then; he was standing next to it, pointing me to where I should park. Pulling in behind his truck, I got out. Austin walked up, putting his arms around my neck and leaning down to kiss me as I stepped out of my truck. He was so attractive, even more so in his work jeans and a reflective shirt. I sighed, leaning into his kiss.

Austin showed me his trailer and where the kids would sleep. He had gotten the TV set up and they would get electronics so that we could have some time together. I tried to get them settled as fast as possible. He was anxious for alone time with me. A little too anxious, I observed, brushing off the worry quickly. This meant something, that he was inviting me here and making such a big effort. I needed to trust people more.

That night wasn't about romance. I hardly knew him. Things had gone faster than I had wanted, but then again, I had agreed to spend two nights with him. What had I expected? Still, when we awoke the next morning, I was excited for the day together. He turned on country music and made us coffee as the sun rose across the field to the east. The kids woke as soon as they heard sounds in the other end of the camper. I sat on the couch, facing the small kitchen area, where Austin was frying bacon and eggs. He was making us breakfast. Watching him cook was cute. My heart melted instantly. Clearly this man cared about me and my kids. The trailer door was open and a cool morning breeze blew in, bringing with it the scent of the hay field and a faint whiff of horses. I sighed. This was the good life. All I had ever wanted was something like this. Simple moments, peace, calmness, time to enjoy life without getting yelled at or told that I wasn't enough.

After breakfast, he introduced me to his father, who I instantly liked. I felt immediately that his dad and I would get along. It was easy for me to get along with people as long as they showed me human decency. Within ten minutes his father was telling me stories of hunting elk in the mountains to the east. I liked him even more after this.

Austin had planned a day at the lake, so we got ready. He had brought snacks and drinks for the kids and beer for himself. I got both kids situated in the back of his double cab truck and stepped up into his passenger seat. He turned on country music again. My favorite. I smiled to myself.

Looking at my phone, I saw the date. July 21st. It was my brother's birthday. I sighed inwardly. I normally would call him, but this year I wouldn't. All of my family had been so judgmental. I was too afraid to even send a message, let alone call them. It would likely spark another lecture, another conversation that ended with me in tears. They didn't even know the half of it. They didn't even know that I was spending the day with another man; this would only add more fuel to their fire of judgment. I didn't need it today.

When we got to the lake, there wasn't much to do. I wasn't accustomed to relaxing. The kids instantly went swimming. I sat on a blanket and watched. Several people were paddle-boarding across the lake and more were fishing from a small aluminum boat on the opposite side. The mountain was visible from where I sat, making the entire view look like a painting. Austin waded in the water, looking for rocks. He had invited some friends to join; when they arrived, he introduced us. "This is Sharon," he said simply. Another good sign. He wanted me to meet his friends!

We got back to the trailer at midday. By this time, the sun was fully in the sky. It was hot, probably at least 85 outside. The trailer was hot inside. Austin turned on the generator and got the AC running quickly. We settled the kids in the back room with Their favorite show. They wouldn't complain. Any opportunity to have electronics was precious for them. Austin was clearly hoping for another cuddle session. His end of the fifth wheel was completely dark, due to black out curtains. It was cool now, thanks to the AC. After another extended make out session, he immediately went to sleep. I tried to nap, but I couldn't. There was too much running through my mind and I was bored. I got up, looking in on the kids. They were still watching the TV in the other room.

I peeked out the window of the trailer. Austin's dad was outside, moving hay from the field to the barn. I rummaged through my backpack, finding a pair of bootcut work jeans and the belt I wore at work on the farm. I grabbed a flannel shirt from my bag and headed out to the barn. After about an hour, we had completed the task and the hay was nicely stacked in the barn. I felt good about being able to help and get to know Austin's father. He seemed mildly disgusted that I was the one helping, while Austin slept.

Later, after shooting my bow with Austin, his dad, and his brother, Austin offered to give the kids quad rides. He spent a half an hour giving my kids and his nephews rides. His dad had started the grill; pretty soon, he let us know that the steaks were almost done. I offered to help in the kitchen. Someone put on a big pot of water for corn on the cob. I set the dining room table, smiling at the taxidermy mount of a four-point buck on the wall. I looked out the window, seeing the mountain again. What a view from the dining room. This family was lucky to live in such a beautiful place.

Everyone sat around the table and we ate steak, corn on the cob, watermelon, and potato salad. Austin's dad told more stories about hunting. I was captivated, both by the stories and the environment of family and welcome. After dinner, I used the shower in the main house. As I got kids settled for the night, I felt at peace. This had been a good weekend.

Early the next morning, Austin's alarm went off. He kissed me and got up. He told me I could stay and sleep in as long as I wanted to, since it was 3 am. I didn't need to leave till four, so I went back to sleep. When I awoke, there was a message from him. "I made you coffee, it's on preset and should be done by 4!" He was so thoughtful. I smiled, getting dressed for another day at work. We pulled out of his driveway just as light was starting to brighten the starry sky in the eastern horizon. It was beautiful. Driving along the farm roads, I watched the sun rise. Driving along the river twenty minutes later, I watched the sun begin to hit the water.

As we passed mile after mile of river, fishing boats would appear, clustered to whatever area the schools of summer chinook or walleye were currently residing. I thought wistfully about how my parents' home was so close to here, yet so far. Only about thirty minutes if I crossed the river. If it had been before, I would have gone to visit them. I would have spent a night with them, too, waking up in the uncomfortable bed in the guest room, to sounds of my mom unloading the dishwasher and my sister talking quietly to her about some boy. But that was a past life. This was a completely different time and I was thankful for everything new that was happening in life. When I got close to home again, Austin had already messaged me, saying he hoped I made it safely. "Have a good day babe!" he had said. Arriving at work, I silently thanked God for my job.

Chapter Forty

The talk that day with the client's family centered around the upcoming school year. The mom let me know that they had a new provider training this week. The family had been approved to get an ABA provider to support their child in school that year. ABA, or applied behavior analysis, was a style of therapy that worked with those on the autism spectrum, helping them to develop lagging skill sets.

Because I had been working with her since April, the family hoped I could help to train the new provider how to work with the child. I would meet the provider on Wednesday. An idea was brewing within me. I was curious what the requirements for the ABA position were. "How much education does one need in order to be an ABA provider?" I asked the parent. She didn't think it required any. She gave me the name of the company and told me what the supervisor's name was. I was afraid to ask, but I did anyway. "Do you think they would hire me? That way I could fill in hours for the other provider and still be able to support you guys when your daughter goes to school this fall?"

The idea of working in a school appealed to me. Two days later, I met the provider for the ABA services, as well as the BCBA supervisor. She had been informed of my interest and told me they could likely move forward with hiring me part-time. I was excited.

A few nights later, while lifting in the gym, I got a message from Austin. He was wondering if I would come to stay again next weekend.

Instantly, I told him yes. I was falling hopelessly for this man. When a friend asked to hang out that weekend, I told her I would be spending the weekend with Austin. She was excited for me. She asked if this meant we were dating. I wasn't sure. I had been afraid to ask that question. Things were going well and I didn't want to ruin what we had or scare him by asking for a commitment too soon. He would let me know when he wanted to take things to the next level. I had been too pushy with Mac, always asking for too much. I didn't want to do this with my new opportunity.

The question weighed on my mind, though. After another day, I worked up the courage to ask him. "So, I don't want to make you feel pressured at all, but I was wondering what your intentions with what we have going are?" There. I had asked. I was sure this would bring our relationship to the next level. I would have a boyfriend. He would tell me how he felt and we would be official. I would feel more secure, knowing I wasn't single anymore. I lay on my bed, staring up through the skylight, daydreaming about our next weekend together. He was so amazing and I loved spending time with his family. He had told me that his dad instantly liked me after I had offered to help with harvesting the hay. His dad had advised him not to mess this up, telling him that I was a good one, a keeper.

I smiled, thinking about this. After five minutes, I worked up the courage to check my messages. New chat from Austin, my Chat-app said. I opened it shakily. "I'm just having fun babe, I'm not ready for anything serious, I just got out of a relationship and I'm not trying to rush into anything else." My breath caught in my throat. How could this be? How could he invite me to spend time with his parents, on his family farm, spend an entire weekend with me, text me constantly throughout every day, call me every night for three weeks, and just be *having fun*? How was that not serious? I messaged my friend instantly. She advised me not to spend any more time with him.

He's using you, she explained. She had more dating experience than I did, and had this happen to her in the past. I couldn't hold back the tears. I felt abandoned. I never replied to him that day. The next morning, I texted him that I wasn't coming. We weren't on the same page. He tried to convince me to change my mind. I told him that if he wanted to see me, he could drive down here. I wasn't spending any more money on gas to see him. He replied with offering to pay for my gas. For what? For a free hoe? It wasn't going to be me. I was angry and sad all at once. I had never meant to sleep with him if we weren't going to be official. I had no dating experience, but I did know that I didn't want to do any more hookups.

I wanted a connection that was based on more than a physical relationship. I wanted an adventure partner, someone to hunt with, someone whose family would accept me and someone who valued me. Oh well, time to get more focused in the gym, I told myself. I had been getting too distracted with Austin; it was taking away from my powerlifting. Time to get back on track.

Chapter Forty-One

The next few days were hard. I was feeling not only the pain from being used, but also the pain that had built up from being rejected by my family. While I was enjoying the newness of dating, I could easily forget that I had been cut completely out of my parents' lives, that they were talking bad about me behind my back, and that my ex-husband hated me. I could focus on the excitement and keep my head in the clouds when I had been seeing Austin. I had gotten used to having someone text me good morning and good night regularly; suddenly having that taken away was hard for me. Although this had been a short-term thing, the pain and heartbreak was catching up to me.

I had developed a habit of avoiding the pain by staying busy, always having something else to entertain my mind. Now that I didn't have anyone to talk to, the loneliness set in again. My only savior was the gym. Because that weekend was the first weekend with the new order, the kids went to Mac's on Friday night. After dropping them off with Bryan, at our designated meeting spot, I drove straight to the gym.

The few of us who competed were religious lifters. Most had given up their routine due to COVID and lockdown, but some of us were crazy. Probably much like me, they had broken hearts and broken homes. For many of us, the gym was a welcome reprieve from the sadness. It was a way to work on ourselves, to prove what we could do, and to find community, even if it was social distanced community. Now that I didn't have anyone to talk to, and I had committed to not drinking or partying, I had nothing better to do with my Friday night than to pump iron.

The mid-summer heat made the gym like a sauna; it didn't have any AC and even after the sun had gone down, it was probably at least 85 inside. A sports bra and shorts were all I needed. Sweat running over my six pack and well-defined abs, I pushed myself hard to hit all my reps and all my sets. I was getting excited to compete again. October was only 12 weeks away; I had just signed up for another competition!

Sunday, I went to church. I wanted to show God that I was serious about a relationship with him. I wasn't perfect, but I did want to be connected to him. The service that day was outside. I stood next to a metal fold-up chair, singing along to *Promises* from Maverick City Music.

I thought about the last time I had come to church. Even that had hurt. This was why I hadn't come for the last two months. I had come the week after I had left Mac. I had wanted to find the support that people always say comes with organized religion. Surely, people would understand that I needed help as a single parent, I had thought. Surely, people would understand and step up as a church family to be there for me. I had taken a seat in the upper seating area above the main auditorium. This way, I would be farther away from the front. We wouldn't make a scene if the kids were loud.

They only needed to stay in the auditorium during the singing. After that, they would go to their classes so I could hear the sermon. Halfway through the second song, it had become apparent that Luke wouldn't stay in his seat. After fighting to get him to come back up the stairs, I held him in place on my lap, whispering to him that we would have to leave if he wasn't quiet. It did no well. There was still one more song to go and he was back to the stairs. A well-meaning older woman came up to me. "He is being too loud. Your child is interrupting the whole service! What are you going to do?" I walked out then, taking both kids with me and leaving right then. I couldn't take it. I had already been on the edge, feeling the guilt of disappointing my parents and Mac. Being told that we were disrupting the service, when I had hoped to be accepted, had been all I could take.

I had tried again the next week, feeling less sensitive. A similar situation had occurred. This time, we had been asked to leave by a different, well-meaning church goer. I hadn't come back until today. The kids weren't here, so it would be fine. Still, I wondered if a church where I could only be there if I was alone, when my kids were such a big part of my life, was the right fit for me. Oh well. I looked at my phone then. Maybe Austin would change his mind. I hadn't deleted or blocked him. We still talked occasionally. I hoped maybe he would realize his error and ask to see me. There was no message. I sighed again, trying to focus on the sermon. The pastor was talking about how trials made us stronger. I hoped it was true, because I had been going through my fair share lately.

When I arrived at Mac's parents that evening to pick up the kids, I felt an instant energy of tension come over me. Ever since my conversation with Amanda, the energy had been different between us.

225

She hadn't been friendly, instead acting cold and professional with me. This evening was no different. Since I knew they had seen me pull into their driveway, I waited by the truck, leaving it running. After a moment, Amanda came out with Luke, carrying his backpack. Mac's truck was there. I hoped he wouldn't come out. He didn't. Amanda handed me the backpack and I thanked her.

Bryan came out, carrying Carroll. When Carroll saw me, her face lit up. Her chubby cheeks turned upwards and she smiled, saying "mama!" and reaching for me. I gently took her from Bryan, tucking her head against my chin and kissing her blonde curls. I had missed my children. I had nothing to say to either Bryan or Amanda. Thanking them for bringing the kids to the truck, I loaded both children into the running vehicle.

On the drive home, both kids seemed tired. "How did it go seeing Dad again?" I asked. "We snuggled Kitten!" Luke said. They had missed their dog. I was happy for that reunion. "What did you guys do this weekend?" I looked at Carroll in the rearview as I turned right towards the yurt and Dex's property. "We got to have a sleepover with Papa and Grandma!"

They both began to tell me about it. They told me how their dad had let them spend the weekend with their grandparents. I was shocked. He hadn't seen them in two months and he chose to leave them with his parents for the weekend? When I had dropped them off on Friday, he hadn't even been there. My heart filled with sorrow again, this time for my children. It wasn't fair. They had done nothing to deserve this. Even

226

with the pending divorce and the hurt that had become a part of my life since marrying Mac and then leaving him, I wanted the children to have a relationship with him. The fact that they were being let down by him, brought a deep anger from the depths of my soul. I fought back tears, trying to be positive for my children. It was out of my hands.

Chapter Forty-Two

The next day at work, I got confirmation. The ABA company had a job offer for me. The onboarding would involve a week-long training in the city, starting the following Monday. At work that day, my clients parent pulled me aside. "After seeing the new hire with our child, I'm going to advocate for you to have the position full time. That way you could be the only one to support him in school. How do you feel about that?" I felt bad instantly. I hadn't meant to take anyone's position. However, this was something I was extremely excited about. I did want to do this full time.

It felt like a step up in the world and I was ready to take it. What had started as the only job that would hire me immediately was turning into a career path. I could feel the beginnings of something taking shape in my life, although I didn't know what yet. I was ready to ride the waves of change that were pushing me to step out into the world.

My excitement over the new job was short lived, however. At work that day, I got an unexpected email. The lawyer wanted to talk with me about a statement of character that he had received through Mac's lawyer, regarding me. I couldn't imagine who would write that, until he said the name of the person who had written it: my father's name. I was in shock. I didn't want to believe it. I didn't want to read it or see what he had said about me. How could he do this? I had never done anything to make him take such radical steps against me. Why was he supporting

Mac above his own child? The familiar dread began to wash over me. What if I lost custody of my children because of my father's carefully written jab? When I got done at work that afternoon, I opened the document, still afraid to see what he had written. The letter read as follows:

I am Sharon Trammell's father. I write this to share my perspective on Mac and Sharon's divorce case. Myself and my wife, her mother, used to respect her. Recently, though, she has begun acting strange. She has cut us out of her life for no reason. I have taken no sides at all, always supporting her. I even told Mac he should continue to try to be a good husband even though she left him. He shouldn't give up on her, I told him. I stand for this marriage, not against it.

A few months ago, Mac asked me to take the kids so he and Sharon could work things out. This was before she ran away from him, after claiming he had physically abused her. I happily took the grandchildren, telling her she could get them whenever she wanted. When she came to get them a couple of days later, she was so rude that my wife got very ill and stayed sick for two days after this.

Sharon has been known to be dramatic. I do not believe her allegations of Mac being abusive to be true. She has always stretched the truth. She is very emotional and always has been. However, as I stated previously, I am not taking a side at all.

I hope this can be straightened out and she will return to him.

Dated July 23, 2020.

Sharon's father

I was shocked that he had gone this far. I felt the negative energy through the letter. The fact that he had blamed me for my mom's sickness hurt. My mom's anxiety had been bad for several years now, often causing physical sickness. This had never been at any fault of mine. It had been going on since my teenage years. Out of everyone in the family, I was the one who constantly asked her to seek medical attention for this ailment. Each time, she would refuse, saying my dad couldn't afford it. "I'll be fine," she would sigh. Her famous words. She would smile and change the subject, ever the one to put herself last. The fact that my dad could testify as to this sickness being my fault, when he refused to pay for a doctor for her, made me sick to my stomach. He wondered why I didn't want a relationship with him, but it felt obvious to me. I saw now, more than ever, exactly why I hadn't wanted to contact them or return calls during the last few months. Emotions began to well up in me then. A deep anger that had been repressed for many years began to surface. Doubt had been growing too; now I began to see it more clearly.

I had always believed that my dad was unconditionally correct. His word had been law as far back as I could remember, not just in our household, but in my interpretation of the world. I had believed every word he spoke, every interpretation of the Bible and the ways in which Jesus had asked us, as Christians, to live our lives. I had believed his ideology that women were meant to be homemakers and to submit to their husbands. I had, like him, judged divorced people fiercely for breaking God's laws. But now, the rules didn't add up. What choice had I had? What other option had there been? Was I really to live my life in regret, stuck in a past that didn't exist? Was I really to go around believing that the only correct way was to make up with Mac? I sighed, wiping away tears. Time for a heavy deadlift session at the gym. I turned on NF *Change* and headed towards the gym.

Chapter Forty-Three

The rest of the week went by quickly. Since it was the beginning of a new month, I had another bill from my lawyer to pay. I always dreaded the first of the month. How many charges had been incurred by my lawyer in the last month? Even updating the lawyer by email cost me money; every word of his time cost me. It made me feel even smaller, less significant, and less in control of my situation. I was tired. This month, it had been $900. Responding to Mac's lawyer about my dad's testimony would cost too.

Then there was the update that Mac had filed a restraining order against me. I had told my lawyer about this restraining order, to which he replied that we would find proof to drop the restraining order, but it would have to happen as a lump processing with the divorce being finalized. Because the courts were backed up due to COVID and the whole world being backed up, this could take additional time. We would need to complete mediation first; mediation was the process by which the court asked both parties, myself and Mac, to meet and try to talk our way to an agreement. In theory, this would save us having to fight a battle in the court room. Mediation wouldn't begin for several weeks. My lawyer had urged me to find someone who would speak up about the abuse or the threats or the stalking, to give me a character witness and also to validate what I had said about Mac's recent actions.

The only problem with this, was that anyone who spoke up against Mac would surely pay. He had made this clear on more than one occasion. He had threatened Dex for allowing me to live there. He had even threatened pastor Gordon, who had given us marriage counseling, because he had advised a temporary separation when the abuse had gotten physical. He had called, threatening Gordon's wife, warning them to stay out of our situation. He had defamed my name throughout our small town, telling people things I couldn't even imagine. No one dared to even reach out to me.

No, no one dared speak up against him. Mac and his dad both were known in the small town for getting retaliation when things didn't go their way, when people spoke out against them. If people did speak up, they did so in fear, coming to me in secrecy, begging that I didn't share their names or use their testimony against him. I knew this was a battle I would need to fight on my own. After all, I was the first one who had ever stood up to this man, or this family.

Monday was the first day of my training for the new job. I was awake early, preparing for the long week. Because I had known I would be driving a lot and in training most of the week, I had meal prepped as much as possible the day before. I had cooked chicken breast and a pot of rice, gotten packaged salad, and made sure I had an abundance of protein powder to keep my nutrition on point. Training would be more exhausting this week, after almost two hours each way in the truck for commuting to the big city. As I prepared for the day, the excitement hit me again. I wanted this new position. I wanted to learn and be mentally

233

stimulated. I wanted a job that would make a difference in the world. I knew I had been called to something more than what life had given me thus far. I knew there was a purpose and it was waiting for me.

I hadn't ever seen myself as a career woman, but here I was, beginning to understand my purpose. A career was part of it. I needed to provide for my children either way. Mac hadn't paid any child support, in spite of the court order. I wondered if he had lost his job. I knew his work drug-tested him, and if he didn't pass, he would lose his position as foreman of the arborist crew. He had worked hard to get there. I had pushed him, even encouraging him to apply for a position with a better company when it had become available. I had believed in him. I had seen what he could be, even as he doubted his abilities.

He hadn't taken action when the position had been posted, but when a general foreman for the same company had turned up at our neighbor's barbeque, I had brought up my husband's name. After a half an hour of chatting with the guy, he had told me they would hire Mac if he applied. I suggested he bring it up to Mac himself, since I knew that Mac didn't want to hear it from me. He didn't like change. That night, Mac had gushed to me that the general foreman had offered him a position, and he would be doing the formal application the next day. I had smiled silently, thankful my help had paid off for him. I was proud of him. This opportunity had brought Mac a pay raise and the opportunity to advance past what his last job could have given him. Within 6 months, he had been promoted to foreman and crew lead. I had seen the vision from day one, knowing where he could go if he chose to. Now it was my turn to advance. For so long I had thought my place was supporter, wife, encourager. Now, it was my turn to step out of the shadows and be noticed, on my own. I would step into this role and let it carry me to where I was meant to be.

As the week progressed, new ideas began to brim within me. The first day, the training had involved many modules of writing and some videos. I was training to get my registered behavior analysis interventionalist (RBAI) licensure. This was the required credential for a behavior technician in my state. I hadn't ever worked to earn a credential before. It was exciting. The trainer, Kim, was brimming with positive energy. During our breaks, she asked me about myself.

Throughout the week, I shared bits and pieces of my story up to this point. She had been listening, in shock. She said she saw a bright future for me, and she hoped this new job was a turning point towards a new chapter in my life. Somehow, this conversation gave me hope. Not only that, but my conversation from the month before with my friend had been coming back up.

What if I *did* go back to school? What if I was capable of achieving a degree and moving up in the world? What if that was the path I was meant to take? Could I do it? How would it work with my living situation? I wasn't sure. I was still concerned with money. My parents had always warned against incurring any debt. As much as I didn't see eye to eye anymore with my family, I agreed that debt was something I wanted to avoid. A couple of people had told me that I may qualify for financial aid to cover tuition costs. I wondered how much I could get. I determined to look.

When I got home the next night, I asked Dex about getting Wi-Fi in the yurt. He told me there was a cable from his modem to the yurt, but the last occupants had tried, unsuccessfully, to set it up. He wasn't sure it could be done. I tried it myself, getting the correct modem to pick up a signal and transmute it to internet. It didn't work. I was disappointed, but it wasn't my focus anyway. The new job was. At the end of the week, I successfully passed all tests and submitted my application for an RBAI license with the state. I would be receiving it in the mail in a few weeks and I would start officially with the company the next week.

Chapter Forty-Four

The next couple of weeks went by alarmingly fast. My routine was set and it made each day pass quickly. One day, my supervisor pulled me aside. She confirmed that the company wanted to give *me* the position of ABA therapist full time, taking the position of the therapist who was supposed to work with me. Everything was worked out for me. I could work up to thirty hours a week if I wanted. It would be regular school hours and I would be in the school for the majority of my work going forward.

Later that week, I received my RBAI license in the mail. I cried, holding it in my hands. It was the first step in this new chapter, with this new me. I would always treasure the memories of working hard to achieve this first credential, this new position and job title. I hadn't seen any of it coming, but here I was. I was making something of myself.

For several weeks, I had been thinking about something else. I wanted to look for a commuter car. I was driving 70 miles round trip daily and the old Pickup hadn't been faring too well. The week before, the check engine light had come on, stressing me out. My mechanic friend had kindly read the code for me, stating that I needed a new alternator. I had replaced that, but the check engine light had come on again.

This time, it was a filter for something that was all the way at the back of the engine. It had taken three hours just to get it out and another $50 for the filter itself. Besides the wear and tear from driving on an engine that already had over 400,000 miles on it, the gas was expensive. I had been saving every penny I earned, both from helping Jim, and by not spending any money I didn't absolutely need to spend. I had $500 set aside. I had been checking online listings daily. Finally, I found a car I wanted. It was a 2005 coupe, with not too many miles on it. The current owner stated that he got 35 miles to the gallon and had kept up his maintenance. To me, it was a no brainer. I asked him when I could get it.

I met up with him the next day. The car was in decent shape. The outside was grey and the interior was black. I told him I would take it and we wrote up a bill of sale. My mechanic friend went with me and approved it, after looking over the engine for a couple of moments and test driving it. I was proud of myself. I would save money this way and have the truck as a backup for now.

Chapter Forty-Five

I began to get excited, the week after, for a different reason. Our state was one week away from opening weekend for archery elk hunting season. My huntress friend, Bethany, and I had planned where we would be on opening weekend. I was excited for a change of pace from the busy work weeks. Hunting had always been important to me, the outdoor life the one thing that brought me the most peace. I felt that an integral part of my identity was my connection to nature.

The stillness that I felt while alone in the woods brought a sort of centering to my life and helped me calm myself throughout the turbulence of life. While killing animals had always been the hardest part of hunting for me, I always thanked them for their sacrifice, understanding the natural flow of life and the place that humanity inhabited in that chain of life. Much as the Native Americans had always believed, I felt that harvesting fish or big game was sacred, a blessing given to people by God, something not to take for granted.

I had been looking forward to the month of September all year. It would be different not hunting with Mac, but it would be better. I wouldn't be required to perform sexually for him while camping in the back of the pickup. I wouldn't be subjected to his anger and we wouldn't scare the elk when he raised his voice into an angry hiss after I had a difference of opinion than he did. I was free to do this my way. Maybe I would kill a bull and my dad would be finally proud of me. Maybe he would show the picture to our family friends and tell everyone how I had done this on my own. Maybe he would talk of me with pride, the way he always did with Naomi when she killed a deer on her own. Maybe he would finally believe that I was enough.

The day before the season came, I headed to the supermarket, ready to stalk up on essential food items I would need for three days of camping. I bought protein bars, canned soup, and ramen packets. I needed a mini camp stove but I didn't want to spend money on it. Instead, I bought canned coffee. I couldn't start a day without coffee, regardless of where I was spending that day. I packed the few camping supplies I had, and the food, into the back of my truck.

It was Mac's weekend with the children again. Even if he was leaving them with his parents, it would give me a break. Regardless if they were rude to me, Bryan and Amanda would keep the children safe. Knowing the kids had spent their last dad-designated weekend at their grandparents gave me some confidence. As much as I was sad that their dad didn't appear to care about spending time with them, simultaneously, I felt at ease knowing they weren't involved in the parties or the drugs he had been doing.

After dropping off the children that night, I put a pin dropped location from Bethany into my hunting app. This app allowed us to share coordinates, download maps even with no cell service, and see which land was private and what was public hunting access. We had no special rights to private property to hunt, but there was plenty of public land to be covered. When I arrived at the spot Bethany and I had found on the map, I had one bar of cell service. She texted me that she would be there soon. It was dusk. I opened my tailgate and set up my sleeping bag and the sleeping mat I had brought, in the bed of the truck. This was my first time being alone in the woods in a long time. I breathed deeply, enjoying the scent of fir trees, late summer, and evening. I was at peace. The air was beginning to cool down and the crickets were starting to chirp. Being on this hillside, the mosquitos were almost non-existent. One more reason we had chosen to camp up here.

Since Mac had gotten the restraining order, I hadn't had access to any of my handguns. I had asked a friend to keep them safe and locked up for me until the order was dropped. Normally, I would feel some fear at being alone and unarmed in the wilderness; tonight, I felt only peace. Sitting there alone on my tailgate, I felt close to God. I felt like life was going in a direction I wanted it to, finally. It was far from perfect, but I was making progress. I was beginning to see that God was truly on my side. This helped tremendously. I prayed a quick prayer for safety this weekend.

As I opened my eyes, I saw Bethany's white pickup below me on the gravel road. When she parked, we talked for a few minutes, her black hair and brown eyes glistening in the last of the light from the day. She told me that her friend Josiah was going to stop by later. We might hunt with them for a while the next day, she suggested. By the time Josiah arrived, with two other guys, the sky had turned dark. The last of the sun had dropped below the western horizon, towards the ocean. Gradually, stars had emerged as the darkness enveloped the land. In the darkness, we all got acquainted. Josiah, whose silhouette in the darkness was small but muscular, from many solo hikes in this rainforest, told me he wanted to bugle a couple of times, for practice.

He stood above the clear cut, bugling out into the night. I didn't expect a response, but it was exciting to hear the first bugle of the season. Anticipation welled within me. On the second bugle, he got a response! A giant bugle coming from directly below us. We could all hear the herd of elk now, probably within 60 yards of our camp! Again, the bull bugled back at Josiah. It started as a deep rumbling sound from the pit of his stomach; it echoed to the other side of the clear cut and the trees below. I could hardly contain my excitement! It wasn't even the season yet and we had found a herd already. After another half hour of Josiah bugling back and forth with the herd bull, we settled into our trucks, ready to rest for the next morning. I could hardly sleep, so full of excitement for the next day.

Eventually, I drifted into a dreamless sleep. I awakened once, at midnight, listening to the sounds of the forest at night. I heard coyotes howl in the distance. I fell back asleep quicky, smiling as I remembered where I was. My alarm went off at four and I rolled out of my sleeping bag, shivering. It was still summer, but nighttime reminded me that fall was fast approaching. The cool night air met me as I quietly opened the top of the canopy and then let the tailgate down. I grabbed toilet paper, peeing at the edge of camp, not wanting to stray too far into the forest in the dark. My one fear was mountain lions. Of all the creatures of our forests, mountain lions were the only ones that made the hair stand up on the back of my neck. I had heard too many stories of their stealth and how they followed unsuspecting hunters for miles through the forest before suddenly springing into action and attacking someone unexpectedly. The sounds of their screams could pierce the night sky, sending shivers down the backs of many fierce hunters. I had heard a story last fall, of a man who had been followed and eventually attacked and killed by one, while elk hunting. These cats were as big as I was, but much faster and stealthier than humans. I wished I had my 38-special on my hip now. I finished peeing and quickly went back to my truck, where Bethany was now awake and had turned her truck on to warm up. Josiah was awake now too and after I was dressed and had put on a coat, we huddled together to talk about the day.

At first light, Josiah bugled again. The herd bull responded as they had before, this time further down, likely at the bottom of the clear cut. After thirty minutes, the wind changed. The herd disappeared into the forest below us. We made a plan and began dropping into the trees at the edge of the clearcut. Because Bethany had injured her leg while in the military, she was a little slower than the rest of us.

By mid-morning, we had lost the trail of that herd. There were so many elk in the area that no one was concerned. This had been more action than anyone had anticipated for opening morning. At mid-day, we all went back to camp, exhausted. The elk were likely bedded down too, resting with the heat of the day having set in by now. We would rest and head back out for an afternoon hunt. We all took naps in our truck, planning to regroup at 3. When we had eaten and rested in the shade for a while, we all followed Josiah's lifted truck until he parked by a white gate. Josiah said this next hike was a good two miles, and that we would need to start soon, in order to get to the spot before dark. All of my exhaustion from the mornings hike melted away as I thought about another chance to find the elk.

Putting on a clean camo t-shirt, I strapped my pack on. I put a bottle of electrolytes and a protein bar into the top of my pack. Stuffing my headlamp into the side compartment, I was ready to go. If we killed a bull tonight, we would be packing it out far into the night and would need flashlights for sure.

We began hiking in. The first mile was a rolling incline, switch-backing up out of the valley we were in. It wasn't too steep and we were able to hike fast. We talked quietly among ourselves, always ready in case we spotted elk. I kept my eyes open for chanterelle mushrooms, knowing it was still early in the season. It had been too dry for mushrooms, but I could hope anyway. Picking chanterelles had been a part of elk hunting, and fall season, since I had moved here.

When we got close to the clear cut, Josiah told everyone to slow down and walk more quietly. No one spoke a word. We chose our steps carefully, keeping our eyes on the forest and the road ahead. The wind blew at us, and I smelled the distinct scent of elk. I smiled, turning to Bethany. We had all smelled it. Anticipation grew. As we crested the hill, the forest opened into a three-year-old clear cut. The newly harvested field was covered in tansy, creating a beautiful yellow blanket that stretched a half mile towards the next patch of forest. I smiled to myself.

It was breathtaking. Moments like this made the long hikes worth it. *This* was why this state was home. This would always be my happy place.

As we continued on, we could see that the sun would set soon. We had about an hour and a half of daylight left. Although we couldn't see the elk, we knew they were close. We all sat down in the ditch, out of plain sight, in case the herd was headed this direction. Josiah pulled out his wind checker, a little container of baking soda like power that he squeezed out to see which direction the wind would carry it. It blew directly at us. Perfect. The wind was blocking our scent from the elk. I pulled out one of my water bottles, taking a big drink.

After we had finished getting drinks, Josiah wanted to bugle. He opted for his calf call this time. If the herd bull thought we were a calf and a cow, he might want to gather us to join his herd. Josiah began calling. Pretty soon, we could hear the elk. Peeking up from where we sat, we could see the herd. They were slowly headed in our direction. Josiah continued calling. By this time, it was dusk. Soon, we could see the herd bull. He was within a hundred and twenty yards of us and still headed in our direction, moving slowly, shaking his head from left to right, stopping to sniff the wind.

At one point, I thought I heard crackling in the tansy field on the other side of the gravel road, but I ignored it. By this time, the bull was only about 80 yards from me, his huge chest puffed up in pride as he stood majestically, silhouetted against the sky where the sun had just disappeared. I had an arrow knocked. My release was hooked into the bow string and I was ready to draw at any point. Again, I heard a branch break across from us. It might have been a deer. Still, I was focused on the bull as it approached. There was a good chance I would get to kill a bull tonight. The only problem was, it was getting darker by the moment. By now, I could hardly see my peeps. If I couldn't see the peeps, I couldn't line up the arrow. I would have to give up soon. The bull had stopped at 80 yards, watching us, looking for the other herd, not seeing any cows or calves.

It was a stalemate. I was losing daylight and the bull was waiting until he could see us before coming closer. After another minute, I turned around and shook my head at Josiah. It was too dark to see. I walked back towards where he was hidden in the ditch, ready to put away my bow and start hiking back out. Darren and Bethany had been waiting there, Bethany filming me. We all sat in the middle of the road, changing out batteries on our headlamps. It was mostly dark now, the sky in the west only a faint glow of orange where the sun had disappeared. Again, we heard rustling in the tansy next to us. This time, it was close. Too close. Josiah stood up, looking towards the tansy patch. Suddenly, he drew his small hunting knife. We all saw it then.

Fifteen yards from us was a mountain lion, crouched and ready to pounce! She had been stalking us all this time! As soon as we saw her, she turned and retreated a few yards back into the tansy patch. Although we couldn't see her now, we knew she was still close. By this point, everyone had their weapons drawn, facing the tansy patch. It was pitch black by now. Not even the stars had come out yet. I wished I had my 38 again, instead having knocked an arrow. Bethany was the only one with a handgun and she had loaded a bullet into the chamber, ready for whatever might happen next.

After a long moment, we all took a shaky breath, realizing no one had breathed at all since we had seen the cat. Slowly, we reached for our backpacks, retreating back down the road in the direction we had come. I turned my headlamp around, facing it back into the blackness behind us. We talked loudly, wanting to scare away the cat. I wondered if she was following us again. We picked up the pace, suddenly energized although we had hiked over 11 miles that day. It didn't matter.

No one wanted to get attacked by a cougar tonight. The entire hike out was one I won't ever forget. We kept checking our backs, sure that at any moment she would spring onto one of us. I didn't calm down completely until I was safely in the back of my truck with the tailgate and canopy door shut. Getting so close to killing a bull, followed by being stalked by a mountain lion, had been an action-packed opening day and one to remember.

The next day, I hunted in the morning with Josiah and then my time in the elk woods was up. I needed to get ready for another week of work. On my way home, I went to the gym. It was deadlift day and there was a powerlifting meet to train for. I had 6 weeks left to train. Just because I had hiked 15 miles that weekend didn't mean I would slack under the bar.

When I picked up the kids that night, they reported spending a night at Mac's. However, they had been forced to share their rooms with other people because dad was drinking beer with people who stayed until the next day. There was nothing I could do. I was thankful they had made it home safely. When I drove towards the yurt, I noticed the faint smell of wood smoke in the air. I wondered if there was a forest fire somewhere close. The last few years, the forest fires had been especially bad. In 2017, when I had been eight months pregnant with Carroll, September and October had yielded many fires that charred acres of forest land as well as the homes of many people that were in the path of these infernos. I hoped this fire season wouldn't be that bad.

Chapter Forty-Six

When I got to the yurt that night, it didn't smell too bad. I reasoned that the smell must be smoke from one of the fires south of us. After all, it had been windy today. The scent of smoke carried a long way in the wind.

I took a shower, thankful for clean water after two days in the elk woods. As much as I loved being in the forest, camping, and hunting, I didn't enjoy not being clean, especially in the summer. I took my time washing my hair, letting the warm water cleanse my scalp and shoulders. I was thankful for this oasis of Dex's house and the yurt. I was thankful for this place to come home to after work and adventures. Although I was still searching for other housing, I would be sad to leave the wilderness when the day came. Living in the forest was where my heart was. I smiled as I thought of the dream I had once had.

Mac and I used to drive back roads together, talking of buying property and putting a yurt on it. We would go home and search the internet for used yurts, planning the whole thing out. We wanted to buy acreage, away from everyone, and live primitively while building our perfect home. We would make a yurt home together, roughing it for a while. I sighed, realizing that part of my dream had come true. I was lucky to live out here in the sticks, although it hadn't happened how I envisioned it. A sudden wave of anger rushed over me then as I thought about how Mac had ruined our family. I sighed, turning off the water.

When I got out of the bathroom, my children were sitting at Dex's computer, watching an episode of their favorite show. Jonathan, the older guy who lived in the spare room for free, was standing in the kitchen watching them, arguing with Luke. He liked to argue with Luke, and then give me parenting tips when I came into the room. I'm not sure where he got the wisdom, as he had never had children of his own. He hadn't ever had a lasting relationship either, from what I knew. The longest one he had ever had, was a girl he had dated in high school, over 30 years ago. Still, he had advice for me about dating as well.

He had even coached me on my new job, though where he got that knowledge remains a mystery as well. He had worked part time, enough to buy weed and video games, as a caregiver, for as long as I had known him. That is, until he got upset with his client and got fired one day. Still, he had advice and wisdom to give me daily, without my even having to ask.

As I stood by the bathroom door, brushing my wet hair, I listened to Jonathan explain how people would like Luke more if he would follow directions the first time. "You really should know this by now, with how many times I've told you!" He was shaking his head in disapproval. I told the kids it was time to head down to the yurt and start getting ready for bed. Tomorrow was the first day of school for my client, which meant it was my first day in the school! I was nervous and excited. The teacher, whom I had met a couple of weeks before, was amazing. The school was a private Catholic one, so they had stayed open in spite of the COVID lockdown that most of the public schools were experiencing. When I went to bed that night, it was hot and dry, even in the yurt. Although it was usually cooler close to the creek and shaded by all the maple trees, it didn't block out the warm wind that was blowing, becoming stronger as the darkness fell. In spite of the heat, I was afraid to leave any of the plastic coverings for the windows open. I knew that, if Mac wanted to, he could still get in, but leaving a window open would make it easier for him to do it silently. I didn't know if that fear would ever leave. I tucked both children in and climbed into bed next to Carroll. I slept quickly, waking twice throughout the night to the sounds of the maple branches brushing the top and sides of the yurt. The wind had increased. When I awakened at 5, smoke was in the air, heavier than it had been the night before. When I stepped outside to go to the house that morning, I was met with a gust of smoky air. Bits of ash were falling around me.

When I came into the house, Dex was already up, sitting with a cup of hot coffee, reading a news article about the fires. "They're saying the fire to the east of us has spread," he told me. "They have issued a level one evacuation for all of the valley around us." He wasn't planning to leave, but he wanted me to be aware.

I couldn't do much regardless. I brushed my teeth, braided my hair in double French braids, and headed back to the yurt to get the children ready. I was struggling slightly to breathe, my asthma flaring up. I had my inhaler and I knew it would be fine. Today was a new start for me!

When I dropped off the children at daycare, the air was a little better in this town. The sky was cloudy from the fires and there was no evidence of the blue sky that had been there yesterday. However, breathing was more manageable. I got to the school a little before 8, meeting my client and her mother in the parking lot.

The environment inside the school was warm and welcoming. The teacher, Mrs. Littleton, was warm and bubbly. She was short, with a round face and round body, and a grey bun pulled back in a loose knot at the base of her neck. The stereotypical grandma and teacher figure, I thought, as I smiled to myself. She greeted me with a hug, welcoming my client and showing me where her supplies were. She told me again how she was thankful that I would be here this year to support. She said to let her know if I did things differently than she did so that she could support whatever I needed to do with her pupil, my client.

I let her know that my supervisor would be spending the day with us, to which she responded that she was happy to oblige. She showed me which desk my client was to use and gave me an adult sized chair, for which I was extremely thankful. She explained that this first week would be mostly about helping the kids get used to the schedule of being in school full time. We would all be learning about one another and how to do this together.

At 9, my supervisor arrived. At 10:45, it was time for all the kindergartners to walk to the gymnasium for lunch. I walked beside my client, who stayed in line with her classmates. When I got into the gym, I went to find the bathroom. Opening my phone, I saw a missed call from Dex. He had left a message. This was out of the ordinary for sure. Listening to the message, my anxiety began to grow. He was letting me know that there was a level two evacuation notice for his area. Dex and

Alana were packing their things now. The fire east of them had doubled in size overnight and was rapidly heading towards his property. It was less than five miles away. He advised me to come get whatever I wanted to salvage of my stuff. He said he hoped I had a place to stay.

I filled in my supervisor. She said she would be more than okay staying with the client so I could take the rest of the day to gather my stuff. Within ten minutes, I was headed towards the yurt. The air quality had worsened drastically since I had left that morning. When I turned on the road towards the yurt, I had to have my headlights on just to see the road in front of me. The sky on the horizon glowed red. The day, which should have been bright, was almost dark. I would have thought it was evening, if not for looking at the clock, which read 11:11 am.

Even with the windows up in the little car, I could smell the strong scent of the smoke and I was struggling to breathe freely. My windshield wipers were on, as ash swirled in the air around me, threatening to block out my view of the road ahead. The closer I got to the yurt, the darker it was. I didn't see anyone going the same direction as I was. They were all leaving, heading away from the blaze.

An eerie feeling began to creep over me, as though I was driving straight into a furnace. I didn't know how fast the fire would travel, but I was thankful that my children weren't with me. Two friends had already offered to let me stay with them. I simply needed to make sure I salvaged my stuff and then leave again, as fast as possible. The closer I got, the worse the air quality became. When I pulled in, Dex was still there, carrying totes of stuff to his van. When I got out of the grey car, the air quality was even worse than it had been on the drive there. I could hardly breathe. I put on a mask, musing how handy it was that we were required to wear them at work and they would now come in handy to protect my already fragile lungs from filling with smoke. Dex let me know that he was about to leave to go towards the ocean, where the air quality was improved. If I wanted, he could help me move my truck to safety before he left. He told me everyone was parking their cars in an empty grass field that had been recently plowed and was just dirt now. If the fire made it that far, it would jump over the field and our extra vehicles would be saved.

 When I walked down to the yurt, there was a visible layer of ash on the bushes lining the pathway. As I opened the door, I could see the thick, smoke-filled air had permeated the walls of the yurt. I wiped a layer of dust and ash off my sewing machine, picking it up and grabbing the serger in the other hand. Carrying both to my truck, I came back for some clothing for both children. I smiled to myself, thinking about the fact that Mac hadn't given me most of my stuff. Because of this, it would be easy to decide which items to rescue from a potential fire. Next, I grabbed my bow case in one hand and Carroll's balance bike in the other. I didn't need much. Everything of value was at daycare right now.

  After packing both children's bikes in the back of the truck, I started the little grey car once more. Dex followed me in his van.

   When I got to the field, neighbors had already parked their cars and some were leaving in spare vehicles or with friends. Someone had parked their tractor there; yet another, their lifted 80's pickup, still perfectly detailed. It probably hadn't left the garage in a few years before today. People were doing what they could to protect their valuables, but the feeling was overall one of surrender. All of us were at the mercy of the elements. The wind, which spread the fire and could change its direction at any point, the fire itself, and the possibility of rain which could stop the fire. We would pray for rain, pray for miracles, and then get ourselves to safety. I felt lucky suddenly. Some would lose their homes, others their land and their homes, and a few, their livestock. I had nothing to lose. The beauty of starting from scratch was that it was teaching me the value of releasing, of not staying stuck on material items.

Dex drove me back to the yurt so I could get the truck. I prayed a quick prayer of safety for his property, thanked him for the help moving the car, and headed back towards the daycare. When I arrived at my friend's house, she graciously showed me the spare room. She had blown up an air mattress and even given me a sound machine to use in the room while we stayed with her. I was thankful beyond words.

The next day, I went back to work, thankful that we were safe. There was nothing else that could be done. We would wait and see. There was a live, interactive map of the fire's progress; I checked it multiple times throughout that day. So far, the fire had burned to the north and south of the yurt, but hadn't moved any closer than it had been the day before. The air quality was so poor that it wasn't recommended for children to be outside, so my friend and I, along with all of the children, set up a bike riding course in the basement for the kids. We spent hours down there each afternoon, mediating while the children rode laps around the large garage space. After the first couple of days, I began to feel bad for the inconvenience I was placing on my friend, but there was not much that any of us could do to change the circumstances.

The fire continued to burn for another week. Another fire had ignited to the south, adding to the smokey conditions. At the end of three weeks, the evacuation order had finally been lifted. It was still smoky and there was a layer of ash on everything, but the fires were burning back on themselves. They had been over 50% contained by this point. We could go home finally, assuming there was a home to go back to. I was more than ready for our own little yurt again. Even with the challenges that we faced daily at the yurt, it was home. As far as I knew, the fire hadn't made it to the yurt, but I wouldn't believe it until I saw it. As I got close, driving back for the first time in two weeks, the road was untouched. There were no smoldering trees and there were no signs of fire.

I pulled into the driveway, thankful to be back. Dex was still staying at the coast. When I walked into his house, it was silent. It was that weird and eerie silence that comes from no one being in a place for several days. Everything felt changed. I took Carroll's hand and we headed towards the yurt, unsure of what we would find. What if Mac had come back and destroyed it? What if he was there waiting for us, ready to finally finish me good? I sighed, trying to not let the fear overwhelm me. As I approached the door, everything looked the same. I pushed on it, and although it was slightly warped, it pushed in. Everything was as I had left it, save for another layer of dust and ash on every surface.

I reached for a towel and began wiping the surfaces down. The place smelled of mouse urine. The mice hadn't evacuated, apparently. I would wash the sheets and the comforter today. I was thankful to be back. The next day Dex arrived home, bringing with him Alana and Jonathan. I was thankful to see all of them. This had been a weird three weeks.

Chapter Forty-Seven

The next morning when I awoke, the yurt was cold. My nose was tingling from the temperature and I realized we hadn't made a fire the night before. We hadn't needed to when we had left for evacuations; however, throughout the time we were gone, summer had ended, bringing instead, the crisp cold nights of autumn. It was October first today. The warm days of summer were completely gone away. When I looked up to the dome skylight, I saw big pattery drops of rain beginning to fall. At last!

The dry streak was over. I got out of bed and stepped onto the back porch. Breathing deeply, I inhaled the scent of dry earth, and smoke, mixing with fresh rain. It was beginning to come down harder now, mixing with the ash for a messy, mud like covering on all of the yurt deck and railings. I stood there, absorbing every drop, for about five minutes. Eyes closed, I smiled. I felt it cover my arms, my face, even my hair. I licked it off my lips, thankful for this blessing. The yurt and Dex's house had survived fire season.

I stepped back inside, watching it pour onto the skylight of the yurt. Today was Sunday. There was no work, only a need to clean and get used to life here again.

I did, however, need to split some firewood and stock the wood shelf for the week ahead. I stepped out the front door and picked up a round fir log that had been sitting there since the spring. The ax was where I had left it. Picking it up, I placed the round of wood onto the splitting block, a bigger and thicker piece of fir. Bringing the ax down onto it, I split the round in half with a loud "crack". Picking up one half, I split that in half again. I had missed this. Splitting firewood reminded me of the life I had once had. When Mac and I were together, I had harvested three cords of firewood every spring, preparing for the winter months. Never once had we needed to buy firewood. Instead, we bought a $10 wood cutting permit. Every spring, we headed to the private timber land and harvested it ourselves. I had learned to use a chain saw, cutting it myself, then splitting it and stacking it to cure throughout the summer.

I often felt I should have been a Native American, living in flow with the land, hunting for wild game to preserve for the winter months, harvesting firewood, picking berries and drying them to keep my family fed through the winter, always doing the work to stay prepared for the seasons. Splitting wood outside my own little yurt gave me this feeling again. I smiled. This was the life I had dreamed up for so long. It had come about differently than I had planned, but the universe had heard the cry of my soul. I hadn't had much time to reflect on any of that lately, being so busy with work and surviving in a modern world. It was still an integral part of who I was though, and it always would be.

I wiped rain drops from my face, finishing splitting one log. I quickly carried it into the yurt, setting it onto the shelf. Filling the shelf would last me about three days, if I only made one fire per day. The stove was only big enough to keep a fire going for about 6 hours, at the most. If it went out in the night, I had to start from scratch the next day. This wasn't always easy, as I would sometimes run out of paper or have kindling that wasn't the right kind of wood to catch fire easily. So far, it hadn't been too bad. I hadn't made a fire since May. Now, it would be a daily requirement again.

Chapter Forty-Eight

The next few weeks passed in a blur. Fall had arrived, and with it many feelings. This season had always been my favorite, but this year I was celebrating for new reasons. On the 12th, I was reminded that it would have been my seventh wedding anniversary. Instead of feeling sadness over the end of the union, I felt joy and freedom. I was proving to the world that I could do this on my own. I had successfully made it without Mac, just as he had indirectly dared me to do.

He had always told me that I couldn't support myself and raise the children at the same time without his help. And yet, here I was. It wasn't easy most days, but I was doing it. He still hadn't paid me anything. I was financially successful and with no help from anyone, not even my parents. I had always been a good budgeter, but Mac's constant down talking to me had convinced me to lose faith in myself for a time. Emerging from the shadow of his doubts for me, I was finally seeing my capabilities and finding my strength once again.

I was beginning to learn who I was as an individual. The process was slow but I was making leaps and bounds to achieve what I had set out to achieve. My new job had promised me a bonus after two months. I would earn my first bonus after another week of not cancelling any sessions. I was making progress in the gym. I had competed during the first week of October, nearly setting a state record. I had signed up to compete again in December. The fires of winning were burning in my veins. I wanted to achieve all there was to achieve and raise myself to the very top of what was possible for me.

I wanted to show everyone how wrong they had been to not place their bet on me. I would succeed. The haters could watch. My ex would regret losing me. My parents would see that I was making a life for myself, that I was doing a good job for my children. They would respect me again. Everyone I talked to was impressed by my resilience. During a conversation with my supervisor, she had talked to me about her position, as a board-certified behavior analyst. She had gotten her master's degree in applied behavior analysis to get to where she was.

This conversation had brought up, again, what multiple conversations over the past months had highlighted for me. I wanted to move up in my career. I had made up my mind. I would go to school.

As soon as I had told people about my decision, I was told that it would be nearly impossible with two kids, and as a single parent. One of my coworkers had told me how she had tried, too, and had quit because it was hard to be a good parent, while going to school and working. This had scared me. However, I knew that providing better for my children *was* being a good parent. The only way that I could make a life worth anything for them, was to make better money and raise to a higher status in life. Education was the obvious answer.

I had applied to the local community college, stating that I wanted to start at the beginning of winter term. This gave me two months to get my routine more secure and get situated. Upon applying for financial aid, I had found that I could get all of my classes covered through grants, at least while at the community college. I would take this one step at a time. I had always wanted to stay out of debt, so I focused on that intention, believing that the answers would fall into place as I went. I had been searching for housing again, with little success. It seemed that every open rental filled immediately.

If one stayed available, it was only because the rental agency was charging more than I could pay. I had been rejected twice in the last month, being told the places had been given to others who had more adequate incomes. I was resigned to the fact that there would be no instant escape from my situation. Still, I knew that the library offered free Wi-Fi and a quiet place to study. Since all college classes were being held remotely, I could go to the library and join the online classrooms in this manner. Things would fall into place whether or not I found a more suitable living environment.

One Saturday in mid-October, I stayed home all day to clean the yurt, a sort of season changing deep-clean. I hadn't gone through any of my bins of stuff since my mother had hastily dumped them there several months prior. I needed to sort items. I knew the mice had gotten into some of the stuff. I had been avoiding the task, pretending I wasn't fighting a battle against mice daily, ignoring the fact that certain areas of the yurt reeked like mouse urine. There was nothing I could do about it, so ignoring it seemed to be the only logical solution.

As I began digging through bins, I knew immediately that a lot had been permanently damaged by the mice. My piano books, which I had stored since the age of 18 when I had stopped playing, had been chewed through. This made me sad, as I relived the memories of playing piano, starting at the age of 8, with my grandma as my teacher. I thought then about playing the violin, and how my violin lessons had been the highlight of my week for four years. I wiped away a tear, picking out a book that needed to be thrown away. The next bin, which hadn't had a lid at all, held clothing. Immediately, I realized this was where my wedding dress had been stored.

If I was honest, I hadn't known what to do with the dress. I had sewn it myself, fashioning it after an antique civil war era pattern. Our engagement pictures had been Mac and I on an antique tandem bike; we had both been bike racing at the time. I had worn an antique, little house on the prairies style dress, complete with a handsewn bonnet. The wedding dress had been similar, elaborate but simple. As I picked it up, I saw immediately that there was a large yellow stain covering the entire front of the gown. The mice had ruined it. There would be no way to get this stain out, even if I had wanted to save it.

Some part of me had thought that if I saved it, my kids would be able to have it as a memento of their father and me, and our union. This omen, the large stain, felt like a sign from the universe, though. I lifted it out of the bin and stacked it with the other items I would be burning. Carrying it up to the burn bin, I thought my wedding day. I remembered waiting alone in my parents RV while they set up the wedding venue without me. I wasn't allowed to help, as it was my wedding day. The day had started cold, just as it was today. The familiar fog of the fall had been thick at the state park the wedding was to be held at. When it was time, I had changed inside the venue's bathroom, putting on metal hoops and then a petticoat layer, to match the style of the dress. The sleeves were only half sleeves, with lace hanging from the elbows; I was shivering instantly. I had planned to wait inside the bathroom until it was time to walk down the aisle, but my dad and Mac had needed me to sign the wedding license, so they had come to find me.

I remembered coming out of the bathroom, in the dress, to sign the document, and wondering if it would truly bring me bad luck since Mac was seeing me in it before I walked down the aisle. Maybe *this* was why things had gone so wrong. When they had come to get me, later, for the ceremony, it wasn't my dad, but my younger brother. He had told me that my dad wanted *him* to walk me down the aisle. Secretly, I wondered if it was because my dad was so disgusted in me and ready to free himself of his daughter, that he couldn't even do it himself. He stood with my mom, smiling as they watched me walk to where Mac and pastor Geoff were standing.

Remembering that day sent a shiver down my spine. The union had ultimately been cold, just like the icy winds that had chilled me through the thin dress that day. Even when Mac had kissed me for the first time later, it was a kiss full of desire, not love. I had accepted by that time, though, that this was the reality of marriage.

When I got to the burn bin, I gently laid the dress in the grass, igniting a small fire with newspaper and a lighter. When the fire was going, I added bits of cardboard, until it was blazing, flames leaping up the edges of the bin. I threw in several carboard boxes, making sure that the fire was going to do the job. I took a deep breath and dropped the dress on top of the flames. I watched as the flames licked the sides of it, as the fabric slowly lit up, as the fire consumed it. Black smoke rose as the dress burst completely into flames. Smoke that represented more than a simple dress, I thought, as I watched silently. Somehow, this felt freeing. I felt a heaviness lift as the last of the dress went up in smoke. I looked inside, satisfied that it had burned completely. There were only ashes left. This was an ending.

Chapter Forty-Nine

As October came to an end, I spent as much time as I could in the forest, picking chanterelles and soaking up the peace and quiet of nature. When the kids were at their dads, I had nothing to do on the weekends, other than wander the familiar forest paths, stopping periodically to scan for the bright yellow of a chanterelle against the green of the Oregon grape plants, moss covered logs and rocks, and soft beds of fir needles lining the forest floors. Often, I would bend down to pick a chanterelle, only to spot two or three more from the different angle of kneeling on the ground. If I hadn't brought a bag, I would take off my ball cap, filling it with mushrooms while the rain dripped onto my head, shocking me each time I felt a drop land in my hair.

I would sometimes stay on my knees, feeling the peace of the forest enveloping me, holding me, caressing me. This environment would always be home. Away from the noise, the people, the pain of rejection and loss, the isolation and hurt that had been inflicted upon me by so many people recently. This place made all of it hurt a little less. I could breathe freely, alone with my thoughts and my feelings.

In this manner, November came, and with it, late season archery deer hunting began. This was the best time of year. Every day after work, I took the kids to the forest, driving slowly, then taking my bow while we hiked through the woods watching for chanterelles. I knew that Thanksgiving was coming, but I didn't want to think about it. Holidays had always been for showing up to Macs' parents, complete with fake smiles and superficial conversations, while we all centered our attention around the children playing, and talked about how cute Mac and his brothers had been as children. Although it had been fake, it had been normal. Holidays were meant for family time.

This year, all of that would be different. The parenting plan said that Mac got to have the children for Thanksgiving, while I would have them for Christmas. During this holiday they would spend most of the week with their dad, which meant I wouldn't see them for a long time. My heart ached just thinking about it. As hard as it sometimes was to be a parent, being without children was even harder. The stress never left. The worry that they would be exposed to a drug, or that he would leave a loaded gun within reach of either child, due to inattention, always played on my mind. Every time I got a phone call, every text from Macs' parents, I held my breath, praying it wasn't notice of one of my children's deaths. I prayed for their safety, not knowing what else to do. This Thanksgiving would be hard, for so many reasons.

I dropped off the children the day before Thanksgiving, mourning as I drove home to an empty yurt afterwards. When Thanksgiving morning came, I woke up at 6. Starting a fire in the stove, I waited for the yurt to warm up. It wasn't raining outside, but the air was cold. The chill that was in the air made me shiver, as I stepped out into the darkness to grab more fire wood. Stepping back inside, I placed two bigger pieces onto the small fire I had been nurturing in the stove. I opened the dampers all the way, willing it to take off and not burn out. Leaving the stove door cracked, I went to the sink, running ice cold water onto a washcloth.

Wiping my face, I breathed deeply. Today would be a good day. I would hunt today, spending more time in the forest. As soon as I had made coffee in the French press, brushed my teeth, and finished with the fire, I headed up the hill, shining my headlamp to light the way. The fire would warm the yurt. I had put a chicken breast into the slow cooker to eat later. I would hunt for most of the day and then go to the gym after it got dark that evening. The only way to keep the sadness away, I had reasoned, was to stay busy. Hunting would do exactly that for me.

Hunting was slow that morning. After hiking for three hours, the fog finally lifted and it was easier to see around me. As the day wore on, I hiked to the bottom of the clear cut and back up around the other side. When I got back into cell service, I had a video message from my sister. It was a video of Luke feeding the goats. My heart squeezed tight at seeing this video. My breath caught in my chest. Apparently, my parents had invited Mac for Thanksgiving. I shouldn't have been surprised. I knew that they were still very close, but this blow had hit me unexpectedly. Even after everything Mac had done to me, my parents had overlooked it and invited him to their house.

This was our tradition, as a family, to spend Thanksgiving every year together. And now, he was there with them. And our children. My parents hadn't even thought to ask if I wanted to come. They had told the lawyer that I hadn't wanted to be involved with them at all, and yet, they hadn't reached out with anything other than to judge me, for so long. My heart hurt. I took a breath, steadying myself. Oh well, at least I was hunting, I thought, trying to be positive.

Late in the day, I headed back to the yurt, mentally exhausted. After stoking the fire and eating some plain chicken breasts, I headed back to the forest. I parked by a different gravel road this time, slowly walking towards the top of the hill, deeper into the forest. Jim and Patty had invited me to come for Thanksgiving dinner, but I had declined. I was far too deep in depression that day. While I was thankful that they were being kind and extending me a heartfelt invitation, I could hardly bear the pain that had been building up in my heart.

Walking up the road now, it was almost dark. I knew that many families across the US were gathered around their dining room tables, with many more meeting on Zoom due to COVID. This was a time of celebration, of harvest, a time to bring loved ones together. And yet, I was completely alone. I had never felt a pain so deep, as the pain that I felt now. I hadn't thought I could know deeper pain than the pain of being cheated on or lied to by my husband, and yet, *this* was that pain.

I set my bow down slowly and sat on the hard-packed earth next to a small stream. The fog was once again closing in around me. I began to sob. Long, deep wails that had needed to come out for a long time. My heart had been breaking as I had carried this cross for the last few months, but I had shoved down the pain. I had busied myself with work, going to the gym, and parenting, but it had been there all along. This was the loneliness of someone who had been hurt many times and yet had seen the positive each time, believing the best about everyone. The illusions were now crashing down around me. If my family truly loved me, how could they treat me like this? It made no sense.

Slowly, my pain turned to anger, welling up from deep within, until my fists were clenched in tight balls at my sides, my face pinched in an expression of pain, sorrow, and anger. I screamed then; deep soulful screams that had been buried inside. There was no one to rescue me, no one to hold me and tell me it would be okay. There was only me and my pain, and many miles of forest. My angry cries echoed against the forest and the hillside, as the fog welcomed them, settling even more thickly around me. I was completely alone, just as I had always felt I was, on a deeper level. Now, I could see clearly that I had no one.

As it got dark, I stood, picking up my bow. I brushed off my pants and walked slowly back to my truck, the anger gone for now, replaced with the depression that had been fighting to surface for a long time. At the yurt, I changed into gym clothes, stoked the fire again, and headed to the gym. Deadlifts were my savior. I would get through this.

Chapter Fifty

I found decently priced fir rounds for sale the next morning. I had recently realized that the amount of firewood I had wouldn't last me through the winter at the rate I was burning it. With temperatures dropping to freezing at night, I had no choice but to build a fire each morning; keeping it going was the only way that I could successfully keep the yurt at a livable temperature. This meant we went through over 8 pieces per day. At this rate, we would need more by the end of next week. There was no alternate means of heating the yurt. I couldn't simply turn on a heater when the fire had gone out.

Often, I found myself awake in the middle of the night, blowing slowly into the stove, tearing pieces of newspaper and blowing again, trying to feed the little spark that had been ignited through the lighter. Many times, this resulted in the yurt filling with smoke and the fire going out. This irritated my already weak lungs, making me start coughing, or more often, feel as though I would pass out. I would then search for my inhaler in the dark, trying to stay focused and not black out. Because the fire always burned out during the day, several hours before I returned home from work, the interior of the yurt was damp. This made it impossible to keep the kindling and wood completely dry, which made it less effective for lighting fires. The result was that I was spending a lot of time, especially in the middle of the night, just to keep the yurt warm. If I hadn't been balancing so many things, I would have enjoyed the adventure more; working two jobs made it less fun. Because my kids were still at their dads, I had committed to working my first shift at a new job that night. I had been approached a week before by the direct support company, who asked if I wanted a night shift with an additional client. I had thought a lot about how I would pay for a rental, if I did find one. I had calculated that working four nights per month, specifically the nights my children spent with their father, could help me to gain enough hours to stay ahead financially.

The next week went by quickly. I had decided to compete again at the beginning of December. This competition was only two days away now. Not only was I competing that weekend, but I had agreed to work Saturday night. I was the only caregiver for the new family.

Chapter Fifty-One

Friday night I stoked the stove, making sure the yurt was toasty warm before bed. The plastic thermometer on the counter read 65 degrees. I folded back the comforter on the bed, ready for a good night's sleep. I smiled as I thought about Brock, excited to see him the next day. Brock, a tall and muscular athlete with black hair and dark eyes, was a DPT student working towards his physical therapist licensure. He was also a strength and conditioning coach who owned his own gym. I had met him when I competed in October, but we had taken things slow. He had invited me to train with him once, in a fashion that felt more like a date. Since then, we had texted almost constantly every day.

He had told me that he couldn't wait until my divorce was finalized so that he could take me on a *real* date. Tomorrow, he planned to announce for the competition. I was sure he would say something quirky when it was my turn to lift, embarrassing me but also hyping me up. With this thought, I tucked myself into the sheets, which I had washed and dried that afternoon. I closed my eyes to sleep.

I never awoke to stoke the fire that night. When my alarm went off at five the next morning, my nose was ice cold and I could see my breath when I turned the lamp on. I didn't want to get out of bed. I pulled the blanket over my head, breathing under the blanket to warm myself up. My whole body was stiff. Even under the blanket, I was shivering. It did no good to stay beneath the blankets, so after a moment, I rolled them back, looking for a pair of leggings.

Pulling them on, I went through my clothing bin until I found wool socks. When I was fully dressed, I walked over to the stove, putting a hand on the top. Ice cold. The fire had been out for hours. I picked up the thermometer, looking closely at the temperature. It read 29 degrees. It was below freezing inside the yurt! I slipped into my shoes, grabbed my phone and backpack, and headed towards the door. I was too stiff to even start a fire. Even if I did, it would be out by the time I got home the next morning, so it would ultimately be a waste of wood. When I opened the yurt door, I noticed condensation on the small glass window.

The night outside was black, but I could see stars through the trees. No wonder it was so cold! The fog had cleared; this always meant the temperature would drop by several degrees. As soon as I was in the car, I turned the heat on full blast. I sat for a moment, waiting for it to warm up. I could now see the full moon above me in the trees. The first full moon of winter, although it was technically still fall according to the calendar. It was December 2nd today. This weather was what I had to look forward to for the next three months. I sighed, happy that I would be spending more nights at work. Not only was I getting paid, but it was also warm there.

When I arrived at the competition, I had a message from Brock. He was sorry to cancel because he had really wanted to watch me compete, but he was sick. He was worried it could be COVID-19. He would need to social-distance and probably rest so that he could be ready to work with clients again sooner. He promised to come to my gym and lift with me as soon as the danger of COVID was done. I was disappointed, but it was nothing new to me. I would make this a good day, regardless. I walked in and found the warm up room, still stiff and trying to shake the feeling of ice from my body. I hoped that lifting would warm me up.

When I got under the bar, everything felt off. My legs felt like jelly and then I felt like throwing up. I thought more reps would help, but I could hardly squat 275, which was light weight for me. I went up to 295; my spotter had to help me finish the lift. Something was not normal.

When I went on stage for my first lift of the morning, I missed it due to a technicality. When I went for the same number for my second attempt I got it, but missed the rack command. It didn't count again. When I attempted 315 as my final squat of the day, I failed the lift completely. Three chances and I was out. I was disqualified from the rest of the meet. I could still finish, but I wouldn't place. I was not a quitter, so I knew I could finish the next two events and prove how strong I truly was, mentally and physically. If there was anything my father had taught me, it was not to quit.

By the middle of the day, I had warmed up and was no longer feeling nauseas. I had even been able to eat a few bites of croissant sandwich between the squatting event and the bench press. When it was my turn to bench press, I finished with a 181-pound press. During deadlifts, I managed 335 for my final attempt. I had done it. I had finished the day successful. The team asked if I wanted to join them for dinner and drinks, but it was already 4 pm. I had told my work I would be there by

6. I grabbed a sandwich from the grocery store and headed to work, thankful they would allow me to use their shower. I wouldn't need to go to the yurt until after work in the morning.

After work the next day, I cleaned the yurt and spent the rest of the day hiking in the woods, checking my chanterelle spots again. The season would be almost done with all the freezing weather, but I knew I could find a few. Returning home, I grabbed grocery bags and a mask, heading to the grocery store. We needed food before we went into another work week on Monday. I had made it about halfway to the store when my check engine light came on in the car. I was concerned but there was nothing I could do. I needed the car to work. It was not to be, however. Thirty minutes later, I was still sitting by the side of the road, waiting for a tow truck. When I had called my insurance, they tried to tell me that my name wasn't on the policy and the car wasn't covered.

I had explained that it was a new policy, immediately panicking inwardly. I didn't have the money for a tow truck. They discovered that I was correct; they had initially looked me up under Mac's name. Eventually, the truck came. I told the driver where I wanted to go, my friend's shop, a half an hour from me. My mechanic friend, whom I had called while waiting for the tow truck, had told me it was likely the alternator. As soon as we had pushed the car into the shop, he confirmed. "It will likely take me two hours to fix," he had said. I needed to pick up the kids in an hour. I would show no weakness. Rather than tell Mac's mom about the broken-down car, I would show up on time and get them. The enemy couldn't know how much I was still struggling at the hands of their abuse and lack of support.

I called Daniella, who agreed to drive me to Macs' parents to pick up the kids. By the time we had picked up the children and driven back to the shop, it was past 8 pm. I was exhausted; having worked the night before, and then dealing with a broken car and long night, I felt defeated, physically and mentally. I thanked my mechanic friend and paid him, only for the cost of the parts. He had been so kind. As much as it hurt my pride to accept his help, I had no other choice.

When we walked into the yurt an hour later, I was reminded that I hadn't made a fire. It was ice cold again. I couldn't leave it this cold with the children home, though. Beyond tired, I dropped to my knees, crumpling a piece of wet newspaper and striking a match. Half an hour later, after two failed attempts, I had it going enough to shut the dampers and fall into bed, tucking both children in next to me and falling asleep instantly. Monday would be another day at work.

Chapter Fifty-Two

The next day, I knew what I needed to do. I had kept the ring given to me by Mac all this time. I hadn't known what to do with it. Part of me had wanted to keep it tucked away and someday, maybe we would work it out. Maybe I would show it to my children as a reminder of how God had miraculously brought us back together. Moving on and parting with the past wasn't easy for me. However, I saw through the illusion now. The past was dead. The time had come. The ring had never fit correctly, anyway.

I would take it to a pawn shop and trade it for money for my kids for Christmas. *They* were the priority now and they were the product of this union, the marriage that this ring had represented. After work, I walked into a small pawn shop across from the supermarket, at the end of town. Although it didn't look like a high-class place, this was the only pawn shop in town. I didn't have a lot of time. Holding out the ring to the man behind the counter, I waited hopefully.

The man held it up to another ring, comparing them. Then he held it up to the light. After a long moment, he wrote a number on a notepad. "This is what I can give you," he said. $300. I told him I had the papers to show how much it had cost originally. He wouldn't budge. I sighed, knowing that no other pawn shop would be able to offer much more. "I can pay cash," he said. I agreed. It was done. I would have money to make the children's lives just a little better for the holiday. Leaving the shop, I headed towards the tire shop. My tire pressure was low and I needed air before I could drive far. When I arrived, the man who usually filled them with air, waved at me to come over. "You see that lump on the side of the tire? We need to patch it before it blows out and leaves you stranded."

Reluctantly, I walked inside. I didn't have time for this. I waited for fifteen minutes, hoping that they would be quick. After another five minutes had gone by, a service technician in blue coveralls and a white shirt came in. "That tire is un-patchable. You can't leave without buying tires! If I were to let you leave, I couldn't live with my conscience. This could be dangerous for you!" I had no one to call and ask for a second opinion. I had no partner or dad to argue with the man or make him be honest with me. I felt small and helpless. I didn't know what to do. I didn't want to put my children in danger. I didn't really have money to spare, especially after fixing the car just the day before.

After a moment, I asked the man to price tires for me. He found a set for $500. I agreed to it, reluctantly pulling out the cash the pawn shop had paid me and then handing over my debit card for the remainder of the amount. I blinked, determined to keep the tears away. Why was there always something that went wrong? Why couldn't I go a day without one catastrophe after another? Why did life have to be so difficult? None of this was fair.

An hour later I was on my way to pick up children and drive home. It was almost dark and a heavy rain had just begun to fall, covering the road. The windshield wipers of the little car were on full blast. Even so, it was hard to see. I had another fifteen minutes' drive on the one lane highway before I reached the turn off for the daycare. After that, I had a thirty-five-minute drive back to the yurt. I was exhausted. I reached for the radio, hoping to turn on some Christian music. I needed something to help me stay positive. In that split second, the line of cars ahead of me all braked unexpectedly.

The third car in the line had stopped in preparation to turn off, without using a turn signal. In the next second, my attempts to break were deflected by the road, which was slippery and wet from the recent rainfall. The car ahead of me hit the car in front of her and I smashed into the car directly ahead of me, jolting me to a sudden stop. I had already slowed some, so the impact wasn't great. I sat for a second, in stunned silence. What had happened? I felt fine, other than the fact that I was shaking all over. After a moment, I opened my door. The woman in the car ahead of me was out of her car, inspecting her bumper. She looked carefully. When I offered her my insurance card, she said she didn't even see a dent or scratch. Her car was fine. Mine, however, was not.

The hood was dented and there was smoke coming from underneath. I tried to start it, unsuccessfully. The engine wouldn't even roll over. I didn't know what to do. By now, the tears were flowing freely. I was wiping my eyes, trying to stay composed, but I was losing it. I called my insurance, who sent a tow truck. While I sat in silence, I texted Brock, who said that, if he wasn't so sick still, he would have come to help me. This hurt. I felt like he was all talk and no action.

Then again, I was a strong woman. I didn't need anyone to help me. I just sat there, wiping tears away, then crying more, for the next hour. It was a busy time of year for the tow company. When they finally arrived, it was after 7. I called a friend who lived close by. She met me at the tow yard, where the tow truck driver said I could park the car until we figured out what was wrong with it. Picking me up, she then went to the daycare. I explained the situation and we picked up the children. We didn't get back to the yurt until after 8. Walking in, the structure was ice cold. The stove was cold to the touch when I laid a hand on it. The fire had been out for hours. I lit a fire and then checked the fridge. We had milk and I found cereal in the cupboard. This would have to do for dinner. Another day was done. $500 down the drain and I didn't know what to do about the car. Either way, I would need to be at work tomorrow.

The car was parked at the tow truck companies' lot, just outside of town. The driver had told me that I had a week to make a decision. My mechanic friend looked at it, telling me disappointedly that it would cost more to fix it than I had paid for it originally. Not only was the hood bent so far out of shape that it would need to be replaced, the front bumper was also dented. The bigger problem was that significant engine damage had taken place. My best option would be to sell it.

Reluctantly, I accepted the first offer that I got after listing it on all the car sale pages. For $200 and a fly-fishing rod, a man came and towed it away a week later. I had spent more on the tires than I had even gotten for the entire car. I was thankful to be done with the experience. In future, I would do my own research regarding when tires needed to be replaced. Life was harsh. These were hard times. All I could do was learn and press on to the future.

Chapter Fifty-Three

As December wore on, I began to feel sadness for a different reason. Christmas was coming and it would be the first Christmas without Mac. I was happy that I was free from him, but doing the holidays as a single parent for the first time would be hard. I wasn't sure what I would do for the kids this year, but I wanted to make it memorable. Growing up, we had never received Christmas presents. Christmas at my parents' home had never been a big deal. As children, we wanted to participate in holidays, but the answer was always the same. "Celebrating Christmas takes the focus off Jesus and puts it on you guys. We don't even know if Jesus was born in December anyway," my dad would say, rolling his eyes.

Sometimes, we would have a special meal on Christmas day. More often, though, my dad would use it as a day to catch up on work projects. He never quit, often working half the night. When we tried to tell him how detrimental this was to his health, he always responded with "Somebody has to provide for the family and if I don't do it, no one will!" He never exercised and rarely ate healthy food. Instead, he tried binge diets where he would cut out an entire food group for a month, drop 20 pounds, and gain it back as soon as he ate normally and got stressed about his work again.

Often, it would be juice only fasts, or worse yet, water fasts. If he was on one of these during the holiday season, the entire family had to tip toe around him to make sure it wasn't too uncomfortable for him. Everyone felt bad having festive food when he was choosing to starve. Looking back, I saw the lack of self-care of my dad and even the way in which his habits dictated the behavior of the entire family. Now that I was on my own, I wanted to make sure Christmas would be different for my own children.

A week before Christmas, I received good news. I had applied to another rental and my application had been accepted! I would be able to move into a small two-bedroom unit that was within 10 minutes of my work and the kid daycare. The lease would be effective on January first! Our time in the yurt had finally come to a close. To celebrate this, and to make Christmas memorable, I booked one night at a hotel on the beach for Christmas Eve. Instead of giving gifts this year, I would give my children a special experience. Working nights had paid off, and, even after the fiasco with the car, I had enough cash to celebrate and make this day special. Although my old truck wasn't the most reliable, I was back to driving it full time; it would get us where we wanted to go, until I could buy a newer car.

We arrived at the hotel on Christmas Eve, after spending some time walking along the beach, enjoying the quietness of the holiday and the calmness of the ocean. Although we had lived in a hotel that summer, the kids didn't have much experience aside from this. They were excited for a weekend staying in one again.

As soon as we had checked in, finding our room number and unlocking the door, Luke noticed the TV and squealed in excitement.

"Can we pleaseee watch a show, mom?" Both children asked in unison. I didn't need to think hard. This was a special treat and they would be allowed some electronics. I found the remote and settled them onto the queen-sized bed with the latest episode of their favorite show.

The room we had chosen overlooked the ocean. Although it was beautiful, I was excited for a different reason. Walking into the bathroom, I smiled. The pool and hot tub had been closed due to COVID restrictions, but this room had a bathtub. This was the entire reason I had chosen this hotel. I turned on the water, sighing as I watched it cascade in little bubbles into the white porcelain tub. I couldn't remember the last time I had taken a bath.

Having three roommates and a shared bathroom at Dex's meant taking a bath would have been out of the question, even if I had felt it was clean enough to share that many germs with others. Before this, during the last two months at Mac's, life had been far too stressful to relax in this way. Now, I could think of nothing else. I set a freshly starched white towel directly next to the tub, within reach, and dipped my toe in. The temperature was perfect. A slow smile came across my lips as I put my entire foot in, slowly easing my whole body into the hot water. Nothing had ever felt this good. I sank into the depths of the hot water, letting the tap continue to run.

My kids were settled, this room had a lock, and we were safe and protected. I had no lingering fears, no urge to hurry, and no stress that my kids would get into Dex's stuff while I was in the bathroom. It was only me and this glorious hot water in a clean bathroom. I left the main light off, sinking deeper into the hot water. I dipped my head under, holding my breath for a long second as I allowed the water to permeate every hair on my head. After a moment, I resurfaced, leaning back against the tub. I sighed, breathing in the steam as it made me begin to sweat. I was so thankful for this.

If the last year had taught me anything, it was to appreciate each small blessing. The simple pleasures of life, like hot water in a clean tub, after nine months of yurt life, were what made the hard parts manageable. As I lay there in the hot water, I thought about life. It had been exactly one year since that fateful day that had started all of this. One year ago, right before Christmas, when Mac had finally shown me, by dragging me across the room by the hair, that I needed to make a change. He had finally pushed me just a little too far and I had called the police and left for the night. It had been the beginning of such a painful time, but it had been the necessary catalyst for all the change.

Now here we were today, as a family of three. A family that was both healing, and still experiencing trauma, in the form of a tough living situation, living in daily fear of an abuser, and struggling on many levels. But we were on the right path. We were walking the path to freedom, to moving up in life. We were building a new foundation, one that was changing the trajectory of the rest of our lives. We had accomplished so much in this year. It was only going to get better from here.

That night, I decided to send my mother a happy birthday email. As much as my parents had hurt me, I still loved them. I still craved the conversations with my mother, just as I always had. Our relationship had never been close. She had always kept me at arm's length, too awkward to talk about anything of value, too blinded by religion to open to me on a woman-to-woman level. It was always teaching and reprimands. I still wanted to be accepted by her. I missed our somewhat awkward phone conversations. I missed telling her about the children's latest accomplishments, explaining how homeschooling had been going or what funny thing Luke had said that day.

Now, I had even less to tell her than in the past, but I still missed her. I sent a quick note, hoping she could see I still loved her, even if she didn't reply. She replied an hour later, with an unexpected response. "Father said to invite you here for Christmas dinner, if you want to come." I didn't know what this meant, but I accepted the invitation. I missed my family, even with the hurt. Maybe the past could be the past. Maybe we could truly move into a future of forgiveness. I could hope.

Twenty-four hours later, I lay in bed in the yurt, processing the events of the day. I had driven straight from the beach to my parents' home that morning. After four hours in the car, the kids were excited to get out and run around when we arrived. I hadn't been there since the day they had taken my children against my will. Driving up the driveway, I had noted changes: the new tractor my dad had bought and the pig pen that had been expanded below the old garden area. This had always been home in spite of the mixed emotions I felt. I parked my car next to my brother's lifted pickup truck.

Although the two oldest brothers were working full time, one as a logger and one as a carpenter, my dad felt it was his responsibility to support them with free rent until they married and bought homes of their own; this was why they all still lived with my parents. He even planned to try to help them buy land at some point. I sighed, wishing he would have seen how I could have used help during the last year too. Surely, he saw that I had no one and no choice about where I was at now. I didn't understand how he felt that staying with an abuser, a man who had cheated on me and lied to me for so long, was right. Still, maybe today would be different. Maybe he would see how hard I was working and finally respect me.

When we walked in, my mom gave me a hug, wiping away tears. She was happy to see me. Naomi simply gave me the look she always had, sizing me up, with one hand on her hip. She had never approved of me. After the incident with Mac two years before, she had reminded me that I was in the place I was because I had put myself there. I had chosen this life when I married Mac; I was now paying for the consequences of my actions. I knew the thought process. Today, she gave me a side hug, then turned to Carroll. "She has gotten so big!" she said, picking her up. I smiled; I was happy we could agree on one thing.

My mom said she had a home-cured ham in the oven and they had made pie. I had picked up our favorite holiday drink, sparkling cider, to share. We talked small talk for a while. Eventually we heard my dad's heavy footsteps coming down the stairs. He eyed me somewhat suspiciously, then gave me a side hug. I wanted so badly for him to see me, to truly see me. Still, seeing him brought back years' worth of memories that made me shiver and feel small. I suddenly remembered being 12, experiencing puberty and breaking out all over my face with terrible acne. I remembered how he used to call me over, looking over my face in anticipation and then finding a zit to squeeze.

One after the next, he would pop them all, leaving deep indentations on my face. I had felt so helpless, knowing I couldn't say no. He would get angry and guilt trip me, saying I was being disrespectful. It was my job to submit, after all. I remembered all the times we had company over and even then, in front of friends, he would call us over to pop our facial zits. I had felt so vulnerable. I would go upstairs and cry afterwards, looking at how the marks on my face were even bigger and less desirable to look at after he had finished. I had felt so disempowered.

The day at my parents had been uneventful other than bringing up past memories. We had all tiptoed around one another, not sure what the dynamic of the relationship was. My parents didn't know how to accept that I was no longer married. They played with the children and talked about the weather. My dad bragged about Naomi and her latest archery competition. They reprimanded Luke when he hit his sister, saying that he would grow up to be in jail if he kept that up.

After we had eaten, sitting around the large wooden table and passing bowls of mashed potatoes, green beans, sweet potato casserole, and ham, my mother offered us hot herbal tea. I drank raspberry tea, slowly savoring each sip, listening to the dialect between my brothers and my father, while my mother and sister cleaned up after the meal. I offered to do dishes. After this, we had thanked my mom for the meal, said our goodbyes, and driven home to the cold yurt. I had built a fire. It was 25 degrees and clear that day, so the fire took a while to warm the yurt. One more week in this yurt, I told myself that night as I rolled over to go to sleep.

Chapter Fifty-Four

A week later, on January second, I was given the code to the key box for the new house. I hadn't gotten to view it prior to signing the lease, due to COVID. As I parked on the street, I looked around. The neighborhood wasn't nice, by any means. All the houses lined up next to this unit looked dumpy. It was a block away from a gas station and the main highway that went through town. Across the fence from the backyard was a dispensary. On the street next to us stood a tall brown building, an in-patient mental health facility. Still, it was ours and we didn't have to share it with anyone.

As I turned the key in the lock, a wave of pride washed over me. I had done this, alone. I had been the one to apply for a beginner credit card the previous summer, building my credit in every way I could to qualify. I was the one who was working three jobs to make this happen. No one had given me money or helped me out. Yet here I was, providing for my children.

I pushed the door open and the children excitedly rushed in, exploring the tiny house. As I shut the door behind me, I noticed a two-inch gap below the front door. There was a rolled-up towel that had been placed there to keep the wind out. I shoved it against the door. Stepping into the smaller room, I noticed washer and dryer hookups. No more sharing a washer with Dex. Stepping up into the larger bedroom, I felt happy. I would have my own room. The door even had a lock! I hadn't had privacy in a year. As I walked into the bathroom, a slight surge of disappointment hit me.

I had hoped for a unit with a bathtub. This one had only a shower and a small sink with no counter. Still, it was *our* shower. We wouldn't have to share it with anyone. And we had our own toilet. When I turned on the sink tap, hot water came out. I smiled, thankful. The kitchen was just outside the tiny bathroom. There was even a dishwasher! I turned around, seeing the stove, feeling thankful for an oven. I could bake for my children again! There was also a microwave. This was a luxury life, for sure. This was ours!

The rest of the day was filled with moving. Jim had been kind enough to not only offer me a trailer, but also help me move. I collected our few belongings from the yurt, knowing I would need to come back the following week and clean. I shivered as I shut the door. It was an ending, so we could have a new beginning. Back at the new home, I arranged what little we had. I had bought a mattress that day, so I placed that in my room. Thanks to the kindness of a friend who had technical skills, a bunkbed that had been donated had already been set up in the kids' room.

I had found a free table online. Because I was now driving my truck again, I had been able to pick it up, complete with three chairs. The next day, I would find a $25 gray faux-leather couch from a second-hand store. This was all we needed. We were set. That night, I ordered a pizza. Baking it in the new oven, we sat around our new table, in our new home, to eat together. That night, I locked the door, sighing at how much safer I felt. I wiped away tears of gratitude, thankful for this upgrade.

The next day, I faced another new beginning. The first day of my first term of college. I had been told that textbooks were to be ordered through the website and picked up in the parking lot of the college. There was a campus within a mile of our new home, so I arrived to pick up the books after work that day. Again, the emotions hit me. I was doing this. I was changing my life. I was starting college. Me, the one who Mac said would never make it alone. Me, the one who had almost become homeless. Me, the one who was supposed to be a homemaker, as a woman. Me, the one who had overcome so much, the one who had been building her life from the ground up, the one who was digging herself out of the ground one day at a time, creating a life she could be proud of. Tears fell onto the yellow pages of the math textbook. I didn't try to wipe them away. I was proud of where I was going and how hard I was working.

As I began the work for the week, though, other emotions hit me. I was thankful that I was doing this online. When everyone was asked to introduce themselves in the first week's forum, I left out the part about being 25. I felt embarrassed that I was starting school so late. Everyone else had done this when they were 18, I told myself. While I was getting married and being pregnant with my son, most were doing college parties and experiencing dorm life. Now, here I was, doing it from my home while my children were at daycare, while I balanced multiple adult responsibilities. I knew the only way to get to where I wanted to be was to start, but it still hurt my pride.

On the weekend, I found the local laundromat. Although there was a hookup for a washer and dryer at the new rental, I couldn't afford to buy one yet. The tires, combined with the deposit fee for the rental, had taken all of my extra money. I had just enough to pay all my new bills that month. Arriving at the laundromat, I grabbed a cart. Carrying in two bags and a basket of laundry, I started them in a large washer. I left to go buy groceries, coming back an hour later to find that someone had switched my clothing to the dryer for me.

I smiled in thankfulness. When I shouted the stranger out on the local community group page, I was informed that many people had had clothing stolen from that laundromat. I had gotten lucky! People never left their laundry unattended. After that day, I would bring my heavy, second-hand laptop, sitting in the corner of the laundromat to complete assignments while my clothing washed. I was a multi-tasker. It felt as though there was never enough time to complete all my daily tasks.

With these things settled, time began to pass again. We had begun mediation appointments to try to agree on the divorce settlings. Each week we would meet and Mac would guilt trip me, beg to have me back, and then bash me for going to school and make fun of me for working. He would tell me that if we just worked it out, we wouldn't even need to be here.

I would say that I just wanted to get on with the process, not backing down on my demands to have full custody of the children. I continued to go to the appointments with my head high, knowing that there was no way he could hurt me while we were there. He wouldn't dare.

Meanwhile, my connection with Brock was progressing. I had gone to his gym multiple times to spend time with him. He told me he would come to my house soon, but had cancelled twice. One time, he had disappeared for two days, saying he had lost his phone. Although this distressed me, I told myself that I was being too needy. I should stop assuming he had bad intentions based on this. It had been four months that we had been talking, but I knew he didn't want to take me on a real date until my divorce was final. At least, this was what he had told me multiple times.

Chapter Fifty-Five

One day after work, I arrived home to find a police car and an official state car parked on the street outside the little blue house. Getting out of the car, I unlocked the house uneasily. I wondered if they were here for me; after a moment, my concerns were recognized. There was a knock at the door. I opened it a few inches, peeking my head out to see who was there. I was exhausted and had come home to study before picking up my kids. The last thing I needed was visitors, especially ones who would bring me more stress. "Are you Sharon Trammell?" the state worker asked. I nodded, waiting for them to explain. "We received a message that your daughter has a scratch on her arm. We need to see her and ask you some questions."

This was nothing new. After working with Shirley, the woman who had helped us get into the hotel last summer, I knew that state workers and child protective service agents weren't all bad. I invited them into the house; they explained. They told me that someone, who I realized must have been my ex-parents in law, had called in the children due to a scratch. I explained that this was one that Carroll had gotten due to her brother's rough playing. They accepted my explanation, saying they would need to follow up with seeing the children later in the week.

I told them when I would be home and they left. They met with the children the next day. I heard nothing from the worker, whose name was Sarah, until two weeks had gone by. She called me with news! She was closing the case. Bryan had tried to convince her I was abusing the children. He had even called her to come to their house on a Saturday night to inspect Carroll, who had developed a rash from wearing pullups at night. Sarah had explained to Mac's father that this was a diaper rash; he must not have much experience with children if he couldn't see this. She had told him she met with me and didn't see any signs of neglect. His response had been to threaten her. Bryan had told her he would report her to her supervisor for this; she should be afraid of losing her job. I wasn't surprised, only sad.

I found it slightly amusing that Bryan was using the same tactics that Mac had to try to force an outcome. Because the fear hadn't worked on me, he had tried it with the case worker. Regardless of their attempts, I had been spared. A week later, the next wave would hit.

After work on a Friday, I got a message from a mom whose children attended the same childcare mine did. She wanted to give me a heads up: the childcare was struggling and there was a good chance it would shut down. Because the woman who ran it was also a full-time mother, and ran her own business full-time, she was struggling to balance all of her roles. The suspicion was confirmed the next day; the center would be closing in a week.

The provider gave me the phone number for another woman who offered childcare services in my area. I called her immediately. She had two openings and could meet with me the next day so I could see her childcare. When I knocked on the door, I had an uneasy feeling. As she led me into her kitchen to talk, the feeling intensified. I didn't like her.

Intuitively, something felt off. The house smelled bad and the carpet was stained. She didn't look put together or neat. Still, she had passed the background checks. She was licensed. Beyond that, she was the only provider accepting children in my area. I had to go to work. It wasn't like I had a choice.

The next day, I knew what I needed to do. Because the last daycare had offered to homeschool Luke, I hadn't needed to worry about school. However, the new provider only offered after-school care. I would need to enroll him into public school. I completed the enrollment packet. He could start on Monday. This wasn't everything that needed to be done, however. I took a deep breath and called the school, asking to speak to the kindergarten teacher.

I introduced myself and thanked her for meeting with me. I told her that my six-year-old would be starting in her class next week and there were things she should know. He had exhibited some aggressive behaviors toward his sister. More than this, he had hyper impulsive symptoms and I wasn't sure if he could focus for an entire day at school. I wanted her to have a heads up, so that the transition could go more easily. She began telling me how she had complete control of her class and never allowed behaviors such as I was describing inside *her* classroom.

She then reminded me that school had resumed in-person classes in November and it was now February. Why hadn't I enrolled him sooner, she questioned? Did I not care about his education? Did I not understand that putting him in school would help him to have structure that would help these behaviors be unlearned? I thanked her and hung up, feeling even less confident in my choice than I had before.

I enrolled Carroll in an early aged preschool. This, while it was good for her, did mean that I would need to pick her up and deliver her to the new daycare myself in the middle of the day. Luke could ride the bus to the daycare after school. My life had just gotten a lot busier.

During the first week of February, I decided to start yet another job. Work had been steady, but after a couple of sessions that the client had cancelled due to being sick, I began to stress about money again. Not only this, but I was exhausted from working with clients who were children all day, coming home to my children at night and taking care of an older child at night, on my weekends without my children.

My friend was working part-time at a ski resort in the mountains. I asked her if she could get me in. They were always looking for more people and work there meant access to free lift tickets and snowboard rentals. I had never snowboarded, but this experience in itself would be fun. Immediately upon inquiring, I had been informed I could start that weekend. All I needed was to show up Saturday morning. It was all settled.

Chapter Fifty-Six

From that weekend on, I settled into a schedule that included working my regular job as an ABA tech, Monday through Friday, then, on my weekends where the kids were with their dad, I would work Friday night as a caregiver, drive to the ski resort Saturday morning, drive back Saturday night if the weather was good enough, work Saturday night, spend Sunday studying and lifting weights in the gym, and then return home Monday to do it all again. Because I was also taking 8 college credits, I needed to optimize my time. On weekdays, I spent most of my lunch breaks' studying.

One Sunday, we decided to try the local Baptist church. When we walked in, we were greeted by friendly volunteers who made us feel at home. They handed me a welcome packet and told me that the kids care was upstairs. Normally, parents checked their children in but took them back downstairs to participate in the singing portion before the actual sermon ended, they explained. After registering my children, I walked nervously into the large auditorium, which was dimly lit with lights on the wall and a large skylight above. I found a spot at the back, looking around to see who was near me.

I didn't see any other parents who weren't paired with a spouse. Not one. Each couple stood together, commanding respect from their children as they focused on the hymns that were about to start playing. Instantly, I felt out of place. I blinked, determined that I wouldn't cry today. This was a place to worship God and I would be thankful for this fellowship. I had done a lot of thinking recently and realized that my relationship with God was even more important to me now than it had been before.

God didn't require me to stay in abuse and God wasn't judging or disapproving of me for being a single mom. I could stand on that truth. I hoped people here would be understanding and see things that way, or at least try not to hurt me with their words.

Before the singing began, the worship team wanted to say a few words to start the morning. They introduced themselves and then the one who was leading the group stepped forward. "There was a verse that came to mind as I began driving here," he explained. "I just felt that there would be someone here who needed this," He began playing chords on the guitar, as he sung words from the book of Isaiah "When thou passest through the waters, I will be with thee; and through the rivers, they shall not overflow thee: when thou walkest through the fire, thou shalt not be burned; neither shall the flame kindle upon thee. — Isaiah 43:2, KJV.

A lump appeared in my throat. I swallowed hard. Blinking, I tried to avoid tears as I thought of all the struggles that I had faced during the last few weeks. The issues with my ex-parents in law and CPS, the struggle with the new childcare, which was already proving to be somewhat of a negative choice. The fact that Luke fought me every single day to walk into school, needing to be dragged into the classroom by a teachers aid. The fact that he was required to wear a mask, which he fought the teacher about, every single day. She had called twice. All of the stress I had been carrying was resurfacing.

I was reminded of every single battle as I listened, knowing full well that this verse, this message, had been for me. I knew the fire this verse was referring to; it was the fire I was in the middle of. I knew that God was close to me in this moment, reminding me that he *would* in fact walk with me through these waters. Determined not to cry, I blinked again, looking at Luke. He had been calm until this moment, but just as the song ended, he reached over and pinched his sister, who responded by screaming out and then biting her own arm.

She often responded in this way when she was frustrated, although I had tried to intervene with positive replacement behaviors. I put a finger to my lips, reminding both children to be quiet. Everyone had turned and was watching me. My face began to get red and I picked Carroll up, taking her out of the room, while Luke followed behind us. I went into the lady's bathroom, not sure where else to go. "You guys WILL be quiet while we finish this!" I told them. It didn't get better. I spent the rest of the singing in the bathroom. When it was time for the kids to transition to the kids' classes upstairs, Carroll went obediently.

Luke, however, fought the teacher when I tried to walk away. He cried and punched at him, begging to be able to go with me. I felt the tears coming again, trying hard to blink them back. I wanted so badly to make church a part of my children's upbringing. I wanted to make the right choices for them. I wanted them to learn morals and values and have a childhood grounded in faith. Why did everything have to be so challenging? If I took Luke with me to the main service, he would be loud and distract everyone. If I left him, he would cry and beg to see me. Eventually, the teacher was able to block the door and I was able to sneak away, slipping quietly down the stairs and then into a seat in the back row of the church auditorium.

The sermon was about trusting God in hard times and knowing that he had a plan for our lives. Again, the tears tried to come. Was I doing the right thing? Was I even on the right path? If God was here for me, then why did it feel like I was fighting this battle alone? Why did it feel like there was no one to support me? How could a God who loved me, allow me to fight these battles by myself? And yet, I wanted to believe. I wanted so badly to believe that He was good, that he was making beauty out of my ashes. I was clinging to a hope that things would get better.

Chapter Fifty-Seven

A week later was Valentine's Day, on a Sunday. I had agreed to work Friday night, spend Saturday studying, and then work again Saturday night. Brock had asked if I wanted to come lift at his gym for a lifting date on Sunday. I was excited, although I felt more nervous and unsettled than anything as the date approached. It was Saturday afternoon and I hadn't heard anything from him since the night before. Had he forgotten about our date? If I confirmed, would I look desperate? I hated this feeling. Why was it so hard to communicate with him? If he didn't want to be seeing me, why would he even suggest my coming to lift with him? If he never followed up, I would just go home Sunday instead of going straight from work to his gym, as I had planned.

My whole body felt tense and I felt ignored and devalued, but I didn't want to come across wrong. Finally, Saturday night, when I had just gotten to work, I texted a mutual friend about him. She said that everything was fine, she didn't know why he hadn't texted, but I should follow up. Maybe he had forgotten. How could a man forget he had planned a date with a girl? I didn't understand. Still, I sent a follow-up text. He replied immediately, telling me he still planned on it and was looking forward to it. He had been busy with clients but hadn't been ignoring me. I believed him.

When I pulled in at his new gym the next morning, I was nervous. I hadn't had a valentine's date for a long time. The last one I had celebrated, had been with Mac. Naomi had come to watch the kids and I had felt uncomfortable, knowing the way the two of them had been involved. I had felt out of place going on a date with my husband after he had flirted with my sister when she had arrived. Why was he even taking me on a date? He might as well have taken my sister.

With this thought and the thought that I was more invested than Brock, in what we had going, I parked my truck. He met me then, as I stepped out of my truck, hugging me and unexpectedly giving me an awkward kiss. We had never kissed before and he told me later he had known he should do it when I arrived or he would lose his courage to do it at all.

When I walked inside the gym, it was empty. He had just upgraded to this building and had wanted to show me everything new. Holding the door open for me, he reached behind him and handed me a dozen red roses. I smiled. No one had ever done this for me before. Mac had picked me bouquets, back in the very beginning when we were still in love. However, no one had ever bought me flowers before. The rest of the afternoon turned into a squat session intertwined with make out sessions. If there was a lack of communication and honesty, Brock made up for it in chemistry and charm. I hadn't ever been kissed like *that* before and my head was swimming with the feelings of new love.

I really hoped this worked out. I didn't want another hookup. Having done it once, I had felt so empty. When Austin had turned into more of a hookup than an actual relationship, I had felt alone and betrayed. I wanted the real thing. Brock and I could be something good if he could be more reliable. I would continue to take the physical part slow. Making out was all he would get until he showed more effort.

When I said I needed to go home and study a couple of hours later, Brock told me he was waiting for his niece to get back with his car. He had loaned it to her and he was stuck at the gym until she returned. I offered to drive him to his mom's house, where he had said he was going to spend the rest of the day. *Aww, he wants to see his mom*, I thought. *That's sweet.* When I pulled up outside his mother's home, he kissed me again and got out, telling me that next time he wanted me to come in and meet his mother. Why not today? I wondered. He always put off everything to the future. Oh well. We could take this slowly. He had offered to come to my house next weekend. It had been four months. It was time.

This day, Valentines Day, would be the last time I ever saw him. The following week when I texted him to ask if he was still coming over, I never got a response. I didn't bother to follow up again. I had *that* feeling and it was usually right. Something was different now and although I didn't know what, I knew that he was done. I was heart-broken. I had agreed to take the weekend off from work due to his coming over, so I was home alone. I went to church that weekend, sitting in the back pew alone, blinking back tears again.

Rejection hurt and this one had hurt more than the others. I had wanted this to work so badly. He had made so many good promises. He had told me so many things and made me truly believe that he was interested. I must have done something to cause this, I thought, blaming myself as usual. I would spend the next two months dwelling on it, missing him and questioning why I hadn't been enough for this man. It was but one more wound on top of the many that Mac had inflicted, but it felt intensified because I had always had the fear of being abandoned. I felt like a little girl again, all alone, and helpless. Would anyone ever love me? Maybe I was unlovable. I didn't know anymore.

Chapter Fifty-Eight

After this experience, I threw myself at work and school, becoming even more dedicated than I had been before. I finished out the term with two A+ grades. I upgraded to a newer car, getting my first car loan with the intent of building more credit. I sold the truck. I contacted a powerlifting coach who was well known online. Although he was located in the big city a couple of hours away, he could coach me virtually. I drove to his gym once to meet him in person.

Since things weren't getting better with my son, I took him to the doctor, asking for him to be tested for ADHD. The first time, they refused me, saying that he seemed fine. The second time, a month later, I filled out all the forms that were used for diagnosing ADHD and similar mental health conditions. He proved to have all the characteristics of a child with ADHD and PTSD, so the answer this time was, that he should try a stimulant medication. The battle at school and church continued. Although I had thought his struggle with separating from me would end after he got used to school, it never did.

He had been going for over three months and still fought to go in every single day, holding up the drop-off line as he did so. This often resulted in my being late to work. At church, things continued in a similar fashion. He refused to stand calmly for worship time, then fought me when I tried to drop him off at the kids' classes. Often, I ended up sitting out the service with him in the lobby, watching on the big screen TV, trying to get him to either participate or sit quietly so that I could focus.

It was now April. I had attended the required sessions of mediation with Mac. He asked for fifty-fifty custody of the children. I still refused. This man had never been able to do much with them and I knew it was in their best interest to make sure they were able to live with me full-time. In addition to this, I had recently learned he had lost his job over refusal to take a drug test. My fears were confirmed. He was, in fact, using illegal drugs. Why else would he refuse to test? We had had everything as a family. He had thrown it all away. Oh well, it was no longer my concern. I wanted it to be done. In late April, I was given a date. In June, our divorce and custody battle would go before the judge.

Whatever happened, it would be done. I would be done with the expenses, the stress of a temporary parenting plan, and the exhaustion of having to continue to fight Mac in court. Two more months. My lawyer had already cost me $8000 and I knew that just an hour of his time in court, combined with finalizing the divorce papers, would cost around $3000 more. This was money I had only from working three jobs, buying only essentials and never eating out or doing anything fun if it cost money. I still had the same bras that Mac had bought me when Luke was a baby; I couldn't afford to spend any money on myself. I was thankful there was an end in sight.

Over Mother's Day weekend, I found a washer and dryer combo on craigslist. It was the stackable kind that would fit in my little house, so finding one used, for cheaper, was rare. When I met the guy at his storage unit, he told me he also was a single parent. He understood the struggle and was glad he could help another single parent. When I got the washer home, eager to wash the first load, I found I had the wrong cord. After two trips to the hardware store, I had the right plug. I wired it myself, feeling like a true electrician. I was so proud of my work. However, when I plugged it in, I found the dryer wouldn't even start. I was disappointed.

I had spent $400 on it. $400 that I had saved from working nights, and driving in icy conditions to work at the ski resort. When I started the washer for the first time, I found that it could complete a load mostly, but that it didn't drain correctly. Upon closer inspection, I found that a pipe underneath the washer was cracked. However, to replace it would be impossible, as this part wasn't sold anywhere. Because I had no money to buy a brand new one, I would have to use this or continue my trips to the laundromat. I opted for using the washer, although it leaked and took over two hours to drain.

Often, I would pull the clothing out, wring it out, and hang it in the backyard. I would put towels onto the floor to dry up the water that ran out from underneath it afterwards. Drying all my clothing on the clothes line saved me about $20 per week in coins, so it wasn't all bad. It also saved me time. It would have to do for now. It made me sad that I had wasted money on it, but more than that, I felt sad that people couldn't be trusted. Surely, this man had known about the errors, and yet, he had capitalized on me being a single mom, making money off of me.

On a quiet Sunday in May, while my children were playing in the backyard, I sat with my Bible at the end of the kitchen table. I had finally come to peace with how life was. I was finally healing from being ghosted and was ready to make my way back into the world. My friend had bought me Jon Kim's *Single on Purpose*. Although at first, I had been hesitant to read it, I eventually devoured the material, realizing that choosing myself wasn't that bad. I had been so afraid of being alone, but I was growing from it. As I sat in silence, contemplating the plans for the day, my phone lit up, with a text from a number I didn't recognize.

Instantly, I knew it was Brock. "Hey Sharon, I wanted to reach out and tell you that I am very sorry for disappearing like I did. I have been going through a lot and I needed space, but I shouldn't have ended things like that. I hope you are well and that you don't hate me". I had been waiting for this text for so long, unsure if I would ever get it. I truly had cared about him and had been sad with the way things had ended. Maybe we could have another chance. I replied after a few moments, with shaking hands. I told him that I forgave him. He asked if he could call me. I told him yes. After an hour on the phone, I learned that he had ghosted because he had a serious alcohol problem. He was working through it now, but he had needed time. He asked if we could talk again. I said yes. After all, my parents had taught me that this was what love was. Forgiving, accepting an apology, realizing that no one was perfect, and giving chance after chance. This guy was trying. This meant something.

Things didn't go as I had hoped. We talked for a week, but when I asked if he wanted to spend a day together, and he cancelled last minute, saying he wanted to spend time with his niece, I was done. I had finally had enough. My heart had been broken one time too many by this man. I had told myself all along that, if I showed him how much I cared, he would eventually commit and clean his life up, for me. On a subconscious level, maybe I knew.

Maybe I understood that I didn't have to try harder, but there was some part of me that had always felt that working harder would get me what I wanted. If I put in more effort, the relationship would work. The one I loved would see my value finally and choose me. No one had told me that love was an internal state, an experience that truly happened through choosing the self. No one had ever showed me that I was already enough and that, if a man truly wanted to be with me, he would get his act together. He would move heaven and earth to spend time with me, to be a part of my world. I wouldn't have to continue to beg and hope, waiting forever for a man who had so little, to finally see me.

However, I wouldn't learn these lessons fully until much later. I had more patterns to repeat before my soul was ready to move forward. As it turned out, not only was Brock an alcoholic, but he had lost his driver's license because of this. After speaking to a friend of his, I was no longer in the dark about any of it. When he had told me he was loaning his car to his niece, what he had meant was that she was giving him rides because he didn't own a car and she did.

When he had told me that he had a master's degree and was pursuing his doctoral degree in physical therapy, what he actually meant was that he had only a bachelor's degree and a vague dream of pursuing more education, if he ever became sober. He had lied to me about pretty much everything, including his age. He also lived with his mom. One lesson that this taught me, was to always do a background check on my potential dates. I learned that asking around about people wasn't mistrusting; it was covering my own back, and helping me to learn to trust the words that people said to me.

By the end of May, I was almost finished with my second term of college. I had taken 11 credits this time; again, I was finishing the term with three As. I had enrolled full time for summer courses as well. One day at the gym, I saw a distant friend. During stretches in the back room, we discussed college. She was finishing her master's degree, but she had attended the university I planned to transfer to, as an undergraduate student, and a single mom.

She told me about a scholarship that had changed her life. "Apply to this scholarship," she advised, giving me a name. "If you don't get in the first time, don't get discouraged. Apply every year and you will make it eventually". I still had the crazy goal to stay out of debt. I meant to accomplish that goal by any legal means that I could. I planned to graduate without student loans. She had told me that, if I was to be awarded this scholarship, it could pay for all of my tuition that I couldn't get financial aid for.

I knew the cost would go up when I transferred to the university in another year. I applied. I also applied to a smaller scholarship hosted by a local women's group. At first, it felt weird. I had wanted to show the entire world how I could manage alone, but I was beginning to realize that I needed all the help I could get.

Chapter Fifty-Nine

When I found out several weeks later that I didn't get awarded the full ride scholarship, I was only slightly disappointed. I understood that this was a big deal and I didn't have much history in college yet. I did find out, however, that I had been awarded a smaller scholarship.

As the season changed, I began to feel more positive about everything. For one, my birthday was at the beginning of June. I had never done much to celebrate, as my family hadn't believed birthdays to be highly important. This was still my season. This was still my time to shine and I was feeling happier, finally over the mess that Brock had put me through mentally. I was excited for the upcoming powerlifting competition I had registered for. I had hoped to qualify for nationals and my goal had been requited.

It wasn't hard, especially as a woman who was among the strongest women in my state. This was a big opportunity for me. Nationals were to take place in mid-July, in the desert. I had never flown before. I was excited for multiple reasons. I had also not taken time off for anything, since I had begun working full time the year before. This was new territory for me, but I wanted to experience the world in new ways. Before I could fully enjoy the preparation season, though, there was something else that had to be done.

During the last week of school for my client in kindergarten, I had requested the day off. This date had been looming on my calendar for a while and I was ready to face it head on. I knew I was being backed up in prayer by many people. Many knew I was going to walk into the court room that day, and walk out with a verdict that the judge came to, that would affect my future and my childrens', possibly for the rest of their lives.

As I squeezed my car into the parallel parking spot in front of the ancient courthouse, I breathed deeply. Whatever happened, I knew it would be divinely orchestrated. I knew it was in the plan of God to allow it to unfold perfectly. Closing my eyes for only a minute, I quietly sent prayer to heaven. I then reached for my purse and stepped out. I had dressed professionally for the occasion, but had also wanted to look as attractive as I could. If this was a game, and it was Mac against me, I would make him remember what he had lost.

I had worn a deep red, tightly fitted, one piece dress. It came to just above my knees and it showed every curve. My slim waist, combined with a butt that had been built with many sets of squats, made for a stunning appearance. I had worn 2-inch heels, even though I hated wearing heals. I was finally getting tanned and my legs were showing it. I had recently gotten my hair layered and trimmed, adding blonde highlights. I had pulled the front portion of my hair back, leaving the rest down. I wore the only jewelry I had; hoops that were embedded with diamonds.

As I walked up the steps to the courthouse, I looked around for my attorney. After a moment, I walked inside. He was waiting at the door to the courtroom. He quietly gave instructions as to how to enter the courtroom and what he would need of me. Basically, I was to stay silent unless asked to speak. I tucked the mask behind my ears and walked in, following my attorney. I noticed Mac was already inside, standing at the front talking to the judge. As we got closer to our seats, I overheard the conversation. "Well, this is a free country and you can't force me to wear a mask". He was arguing with the judge!

I snickered inwardly. I was so thankful the judge saw that I was the one petitioning to be done with this guy. What an idiot. After we had taken our seats and the judge asked all to rise and swear to truth, my attorney turned to me. He had just received an email from Mac's attorney, who wasn't here today. They had accepted our offer! It was finished! All we had to do was wait for the judge to finish reading the petition and we were free to go. I had won! Not only had I won full custody, but they had dropped the restraining order he had gotten almost a year before, admitting that it was unfounded as I had never truly done anything to physically harm Mac.

My attorney had also asked for a clause to be put into our final agreement, stating that I could ask Mac to take a drug test before any visit if he showed signs of being inebriated. If he tested positive to even a trace of any substance, we could press for supervision during subsequent parenting time for him. Finally, we would be able to meet to exchange the kids at a public location from now on. No more going to his parents. I had gotten everything that I had hoped to from this.

More than all of this, it was done. There would be no more bills in the mail from my attorney, no more unexpected letters from my father, no more contact with CPS as a way for Mac's family to try to hurt me. It was finished. As I walked out of the courthouse, the tears began to fall, unchecked. This time, they were happy tears. They were tears of release. They were tears of thankfulness. The battle was finally over. The pain, the stress, all of it, was done. It had taken nearly 15 months, but it was finished. As I got into my car, sitting alone in the silence, the journey flashed before me.

All of the pain I had endured to get me to this moment. The struggles at the yurt, the stalking and threatening by Mac, the pain of my family turning their back on me, the way Mac's parents had treated me, and all of the people I had lost on the journey. It was all done. Yes, Mac would still be involved, but the heaviness had cleared. I was free. I was also, officially single!

Chapter Sixty

Over the next weeks, the heaviness lifted even more. I began to feel more at peace with how things were playing out. I began summer term and work began to change for the better as sessions took place at the client's home, instead of the school. One Saturday when the children had gone to their dad's, I drove to the new gym to see my new powerlifting coach. We were only a month out from the competition now; I was excited to do a few more heavy lifts and then recover and prepare for the competition. The environment was upbeat and everyone here was muscular and fit.

As I was preparing to complete my heaviest lift, a deadlift of 365 pounds, three lifters came to watch. Afterwards, a tall, awkward looking red head with a muscular chest came forward, telling me that my pull was "clean". This was code for, "you had great form!" in powerlifting language. I talked with him for a couple of moments and then thought nothing more of the conversation. When I got home two hours later, I had a message from an Instagram account I didn't recognize. The account had requested to follow me as well. Opening the message, I recognized the picture as the tall red head. He had messaged me to introduce himself, saying that he had talked with me earlier and had been impressed.

I replied with a simple thank you, trying to find something kind to say. I became mildly curious when he messaged again immediately. The conversation began to flow and before long, an hour had gone by with us direct messaging back and forth. He introduced himself as Arthur Simmons. He was five years older than me and told me that he was a high school algebra teacher by trade. He had a theory about everything and had explained, in detail, how he planned to get stronger and compete for a state title in powerlifting. Everything would go exactly as he planned, if he stuck to his theory, he told me. I was blown away by the fact that he had ultimately kept my interest for three hours. He was so far from my type. He didn't seem to be a country boy and he was much geekier than anyone I had ever noticed before.

Still, I said yes when he asked if I wanted to go out the next weekend. What could it hurt? My type never got me anything other than a broken heart, so maybe it was time to stray from the mold. Plus, he had initiated right away. He had been upfront about wanting to take me on a real date, even calling it a date. I was impressed.

On Saturday, he messaged me that he was on his way. I had suggested going to watch a powerlifting meet near the ocean. He had agreed. It would be an all-day date. Powerlifting was something we were both passionate about. This would be a good way to get to know one another. When he arrived at my gym, the designated meeting spot, I felt a rush of change. He drove an electric car. I laughed inwardly. Me, the country girl who only dated guys with lifted trucks, going on a date with a dude in an *electric car*.

The date was fun. After watching friends compete, we ordered burgers at a local restaurant, sitting outside in the wind and sun as we waited for the waitress to bring them out. Inside seating was still not allowed, due to COVID-19, but I would have sat outside either way if it had been my choice. He asked me my zodiac sign and told me he was a Virgo. My parents had always believed that astrology was almost as bad as witchcraft, so I had never learned anything about it. However, I knew that I was a Gemini.

He told me he had researched Gemini's and Virgo's compatibility. I blushed. It seemed pretty early to admit that. After eating burgers topped with grilled mushrooms and onions, we drove to the beach. By the end of the day, I knew Arthur wanted to kiss me, but I suggested walking on the beach instead. We walked for thirty minutes, me enjoying the wind in my face, and him trying not to complain about the sand blowing in his face. After we got back to the car, we sat for a few minutes more, watching the waves crash and birds swooping down to the water, then straight up, then back down.

After a while, he drove me home. It was 7 by the time I got back to my car. I gave him a hug and he asked if we could do it again. He had an hour drive home that night. I thanked him, happy to be back to my car. I had enjoyed myself in a way I hadn't previously experienced. He was so far from my type, and yet, I could see it going somewhere. I liked the way in which he seemed invested already. This was so opposite of Brock. When he got home, he texted me again. We spent the entire evening texting.

Over the next few weeks, the relationship grew quickly. After spending a couple more full day dates together, he asked me if I would be his girlfriend. I agreed. A couple of weeks later, at the end of a long day spent together, we had sex for the first time. It wasn't romantic like in the movies, but rather the beginning of two people coming together and learning about one another. Because it was late on a Sunday night and we both had to work the next day, he left after we had cuddled for a while. The clock on my phone said 1:30 am. As he walked out, a wave of fear washed over me.

I was reminded of the night, over a year before, when Mac had watched me with the boy from the gym. I began to relive it, lying alone in my bed that night. I got up and checked the locks on the doors, shivering in fear. Was this simply a triggered response, since I hadn't been with anyone since then, or was this my intuition? I wasn't sure. I pushed the couch against the front door, piling items on top of it to add weight to it. I turned on the main light, peering out the blinds into the darkness. Was he out there, watching me, even now? Did he still want to kill me? I knew he had been with multiple women, and yet, I knew how jealous and hateful he had been. Finally, I went back into my room, locking the bedroom door behind me. I lay there in the dark, wrapped in my comforter, shivering in fear.

Every car that drove by on the highway outside, every creak of the bed as I moved, every sound, made me jump. I didn't sleep until around 3 am that morning. When I woke up at 6, I was exhausted. I would ask my new boyfriend to stay the night the next time.

When I told Arthur about the upcoming national championships, he surprised me with telling me he wanted to come along. I had secretly hoped that he would, but I wouldn't have asked. I wasn't used to being with someone who actually wanted to do things with me, who actually wanted to support me in what was important to me. It was all new. Knowing that he would be there on the flight made me happy too, since I was slightly nervous about going through customs alone.

My parents had agreed to watch my children for two days so that I could go. Of course, I couldn't tell my parents that I was dating and that my new man was going with me to this competition. They had made it clear that I would always be bound to Mac, likely refusing to help me with the children if they knew. I was making the wrong choice, each day that I woke up in my own home, without returning to my husband. They knew that he had lost his job due to drug use. He had told them himself. They also knew he had been sleeping around with many women. My dad had been impressed with Mac's honesty when he confessed all this to him, that I don't think he even saw how these actions meant I couldn't go back to him, even if I had wanted to.

I had begun to accept that my parents would never see things as I did; however, the kids still needed time with their grandparents, and I was thankful that they had agreed to watch them. I could focus on the competition this way. Three days later, I returned home from the competition, ready to pick up my children. The week had gone well, overall. Arthur had been a gentleman, protecting and caring for me, serving me throughout the trip. He had been considerate when I was cutting weight and couldn't eat or drink for a day before weigh-ins. When he had eaten, he had done so away from me. After I had successfully weighed in, he had brought me electrolyte drinks and water, then snacks. He had paid for an expensive breakfast at the resort and then spent time with the other lifters while I napped. He had bragged to everyone about how strong I was and showed me off at the pool when I wore my red bikini. On the morning of the competition, he had helped me warm up, loading the correct weights on the bar in the backroom, getting me more electrolytes and making sure everything was done for me so I didn't have to lift a finger for anything.

He had bought me food afterwards, although I had said I could pay for my own food. I had always believed that I needed to prove how independent I was; having someone insist on doing it for me was strange and new. However, I hadn't resisted. Some part of me had known this was how a man should treat the woman he cared for, although I wasn't used to it. The competition itself had been disappointing to me. I had been told the day before the competition that the price I paid for coaching didn't include the coach to fly out. If I wanted that, I would need to pay for his air-fare and hotel room. Then, on competition morning, he had gotten my opening numbers wrong, mixing me up with another lifter.

He had been no support; halfway through the competition, he had called and yelled at me, blaming me for his mistake. The day had ended with me placing 6th. I had called him back, ending our work together, and meeting another coach who had helped me through the day for free, while handling four other lifters. I had booked the return flight for the day after the competition, so the trip hadn't been too relaxing. However, this was my normal. I didn't know how to relax. I was always focused on the next thing, always moving faster than a train on its way to its next destination. I knew only how to rush through life, trying to accomplish everything. This was all I had ever known.

Chapter Sixty-One

After the competition, the days all began blending together as summer passed quickly. During the first week of August, I finally had saved enough money to buy a brand-new washer. With the help of Arthur's muscular arms and back, I carried it into the house, thankful to finally have the ability to wash laundry at home. Each step in the right direction made me feel stronger than the last. At work, I was still splitting my days between my main client, helping Jim at the farm, and caregiving nights when my children made it to their father's house. The summer parenting plan involved two weeks with each parent at a time, from June until September.

Mac had failed to appear for his first scheduled two-week portion. I was slowly learning to be more available to my children. Having a flexible mindset, I had learned, helped me go far with co-parenting. Whenever I wasn't working, I wanted to adventure with my children. We had planned many hikes, and, at first, Arthur wanted to join us. He had told me on our first date that he wanted to do my adventures with me to force himself out of his comfort zone.

The relationship was progressing fast, sometimes a little faster than I wanted. He had introduced me to his whole family, who instantly appeared to love me. We had spent every weekend together since the competition. He had met my kids, who loved him. He was by far the most physically stable man I had ever dated. He had a good job, a reliable car, a physically fit body, and he had life goals. He had recently bought his first home. While Brock had led me on without any true intentions, Arthur was the exact opposite. He had talked a lot about the future, letting me know he wanted to get married eventually. He wanted to provide and be the main bread winner for the family. He wanted to have a child of his own someday. I *should* have felt content with him. Yet, doubts were beginning to surface.

After I had met his family, he had told me how much he despised his younger brother, who was a single parent that "lived off the state" as he said. While he was teaching math to high schoolers for 60,000 a year, his brother got free groceries and stayed home with his kids. He was basically supporting his brother through the taxes he had to pay, he said. I wondered if he would despise me too, if he knew that I was also living off the state? How would he feel if he knew I needed to use food stamps to afford to feed my children? Although I was working three jobs, I still struggled financially. I wondered how I could build a life with someone who judged others, including his family, this harshly.

Then there was the fact that he had initially been dishonest about his love for nature. I had taken him to one of my favorite hikes, a beautiful spot where the trail wound in and out of the trees along a river, culminating with a large waterfall. A footbridge above the falls crossed the river, making it into a loop. I had been excited to show him my love of nature. However, after the hike, he had informed me that, in future, he needed to save his energy for using in the gym. He deemed hiking as an unnecessary expenditure of energy. According to his calculations, he would need to eat an extra 500 calories to make up for the energy he had lost on this outing. While I didn't need a partner to do everything with me, being in nature would always be part of who I was. I couldn't imagine a life where my partner refused to do these things with me. His idea of enjoying summer looked a lot different from mine.

Whenever we spent time together, after that weekend, he asked to stay home. He wanted to watch movies and then have sex. Sometimes, he wanted to take me to his favorite restaurants and spend the afternoons shopping. The repetitiveness began to feel stifling. The first time I told him I wanted to hike, instead of spending the day with him, he messaged me constantly throughout the day. He felt lonely because he had to binge watch a show all alone due to my going hiking instead of being with him.

One Sunday, when he was staying over, I asked if he would go to church with me. He refused, saying he wanted to sleep in. I was disappointed. I had always imagined that my life partner would stand beside me in church. I hoped that eventually we would kneel together in prayer, reading the Bible together before bed. This relationship was beginning to feel empty. I began questioning the purpose of dating and relationships. After the pain of my marriage, I had thought I never wanted a commitment again. But casual sex had been unfulfilling too. I didn't want to be alone. I wanted someone to do life with, but someone who checked a few boxes wasn't enough anymore. I didn't enjoy the pastimes that Arthur did, and, while the sex was acceptable, staying for that alone wasn't reason enough.

Again, that familiar feeling began to creep in. That feeling of intuition that I always shoved down. I knew, deep down, that this wasn't the one for me. Still, I wasn't going to end it yet. Maybe the gut feeling was wrong. Maybe he was the one and I needed to give it more time. Maybe I needed to try harder. I always fell back on that.

Chapter Sixty-Two

In late august, Mac failed to appear at pick up time for the children. I received a call from his mother an hour after the scheduled exchange time. She chewed me out for not allowing him to take the kids, telling me that I was a terrible mom for keeping my children from their father. I explained that I had waited the required 15 minutes after the scheduled meet up time; he had never arrived during that time. I wasn't required to wait for him, especially when he hadn't communicated anything to me. This rotation would have been the last before the schedule went back to the school year schedule.

Mac had spent only one of his two-week allotments with them, although he was supposed to have four. I didn't understand how a father could forget about time with his children; however, I felt thankful for the extra time with them. When they were with me, they were safe. There was no fear of them being neglected or exposed to drugs when I had them with me. While we had our struggles, it was better this way. I kept my routine with college, waking by four am most days and studying for two hours before taking the kids to daycare and going to work.

I finished summer term, my third term at the community college. Again, I got straight A's. While I was proud of myself, the nagging fear that I was behind in life never left me. I was embarrassed that I was already 26 and only a year into my undergraduate degree. I constantly compared myself with others, wishing I had been allowed to go to college after high school like most people. I hoped that, at some point, I could begin working less and take more credits. Maybe I could finish in three years instead of four.

As summer turned to fall, it was once again time to get out my bow. I had planned to hunt on opening weekend, but it seemed that hunting with others, while having a boyfriend, was out of the question. Arthur and I had been arguing a lot. The most recent argument had started when I told Arthur I wanted to hunt with my two male friends who I had hunted with the previous season. He knew it involved camping overnight. He didn't trust that I could camp without ending up in bed with one of my friends. I had invited him to join us, saying that he could hike and camp with us and meet my friends.

He refused; he needed to save his energy for the gym, as usual. He told me that if I wanted to hunt with these friends, he would take his female friend on a date while I was gone. He had another solution: I could hunt alone, on his schedule. I could come spend the night before the hunt, with him. In the morning, we could get breakfast, and then I could go hunt for part of a day by myself after this. It felt hopeless. How was I to explain that successful hunters didn't base their schedule on a human's schedule? If I wanted to hunt, I needed to be in the woods before the sun rose. The elk wouldn't wait to have their morning feeding mid-day, when it was convenient for Arthur to allow me to hunt. Nature didn't work like that. This conversation did, however, show me that something needed to change. At the same time, I was feeling upheaval in other areas of life. I was burnt out at work. The company I was with was showing itself to be less glamorous than I had originally thought it to be. I had been promised bonuses multiple times, always finding out that the hours I had worked to earn them hadn't been accounted for. When I questioned who I should talk to for follow up, I was always given the name of someone who worked in a different branch in a different part of the country. A generic name that worked with the entire company on a nationwide level. When I contacted them, they would always send me to someone else. It turned out the promise of a bonus was a scam, a carrot at the end of a string, just out of reach no matter how hard an employee worked to earn it. Not only that, but I had been promised a raise, which I deserved and never got.

I had been awarded therapist of the month multiple times. I never cancelled sessions. I always replied to emails and followed up with my supervisor. The client was making progress in leaps and bounds. I was likely the most reliable, and skilled, therapist in the area. And yet, the raise never came. I knew I was getting valuable experience in the field, but the pay wasn't worth it. I could flip burgers and make the same amount of money. If I did that, I wouldn't have to deal with the physical demands of this job, which included physical violence, constant stimulation from not only my client, but other children in the classroom, an expectation to attend staff meetings and communicate even when I wasn't on company time, and keeping detailed notes on every session. I had also realized something else. I had created high expectations of myself by always giving 100% to the company and the client. It had begun with wanting to prove that I was be worthy of the position. A silent protest to Mac, and my father, to show them that I was enough. Now, I felt trapped by my own impossible expectations of myself. I was exhausted. I needed something new. I began job searching, applying to companies that paid more and offered me more opportunities, in the same line of work. I now had something that many didn't have: experience. I could use this to land a better job.

In October, I asked Arthur if he would go to therapy with me. He said no. He told me that my ex had been right when he said I was the one who needed it. I decided to go by myself, as soon as I got to the top of the wait list. A few days later, Arthur told me he was done. I was heartbroken. Although I had known, at a soul level, for a while, that it wouldn't work, I didn't want to be alone. I didn't want to face the fear that I might never find someone.

Within a day of the breakup, my kids tested positive for COVID. We were now officially in quarantine. I came down with COVID, testing positive on day three. Off work, feeling sick, and fighting depression due to the breakup and my work situation, I began struggling mentally. Feeling the familiar pang of abandonment, stressed about what job I would find, and overwhelmed with trying to keep two small children entertained alone, I had a breakdown. I thought back to the last time that I had been this low. I had been in the yurt, facing homelessness and reeling in the recent sadness of having to leave my ex. I had had nothing. No job, no money, and no future. That had been a year and a half ago. So much had happened since then and I had worked so hard to get to where I was. I knew I had a good start in life. I had a year of college under my belt, two years of work experience, and my own home, even if it was a rental. I was slowly saving money again and I was free from my ex. Still, the familiar thoughts came back. Was it worth it? This struggle was so hard. What if I ended it? Could Mac do a good job raising my children? I knew I couldn't rely on him for that. I knew I had to stay to raise my children right. I knew that I was the only thing between my children turning into their father. I was the curse breaker. I was the one sent to break the generational dysfunction, not only from Mac's family, but from mine as well. I was the only person rerouting the legacy of my family to become something different from what my ancestors had become. This was a heavy weight to carry. I knew I must continue on the path, no matter how painful.

Chapter Sixty-Three

A week later, the therapist's office called me to schedule. Reluctantly, I agreed. I would heal myself even if I had to do that alone. My children were feeling better after COVID, and I was allowed to return to work by this point. Arthur had texted me again. Back and forth it had gone. He wasn't sure what he wanted. I was holding on to the little bit he was giving me, out of fear. Maybe the therapist could tell me what I was doing wrong and I could figure out how to be a better partner so that the next relationship would work. I didn't know what I was doing wrong to have guys treat me this way constantly. Other than the relationship, things began to improve after this. I was called multiple times for job interviews.

My top pick, an ABA company with great employee reviews, called me for a second interview. Within a day, they had offered me a job. I would be getting a substantial raise with this company and they would pay for additional trainings for me that would elevate my position from where I had been previously. I felt hope, knowing I had overcome another obstacle. I was moving up in the world, slowly.

My first session with my own therapist didn't go as I had expected. I walked in nervously, fidgeting with my hands, hoping I didn't see anyone I knew there. This was a place that only really messed up people went. I was thankful when a man came from the back room and called my name. When I saw he was only about ten years older than me, I was surprised. He directed me to a room with a black arm chair, which I sank in to, before perching on the edge with my back straight. He sat on a couch below the window. I squinted as I looked at him from across the room. He adjusted the blinds and the sun hit the wall above me. Now I had no excuse to not look him directly in the eye. I bit my lip. Here we go, I thought. The judge will now rule me immoral and tell me what I'm doing wrong in my life. What had I been thinking? Why was I here? The anxiety was killing me. I think he sensed it. Instead of asking me a bunch of questions, he introduced himself.

When he told me his background, I found, to my surprise, that he was also a single parent. My jaw dropped. When he told me that he had gone to college while solo parenting, I was shocked again. Weird. I had always thought therapists had their lives together. I felt instantly more comfortable. We had so much in common. He gently asked me to share my story. He said I could share as little or as much as I wanted. There was no pressure. I talked for twenty minutes, ending with how I had failed at another relationship. He looked genuinely shocked after I had finished. When he spoke, it was to tell me I was doing an amazing job. Though he was a Christian therapist, he had no words of condemnation for my being a woman who had gotten a divorce, even a woman who was dating and having sex with someone she wasn't married to. He thanked me for sharing. He told me I had inspired him with my story thus far. I smiled, sighing with relief. I liked him. I left that session feeling more hopeful than I had in months, if not years.

I decided that I would continue therapy; I began going weekly. Meanwhile, Arthur and I continued to be off and on. I hung on, even while knowing that the relationship had died. Somehow, I felt like I would fail if this relationship failed. I had tied my worth to a relationship, again. It was all I had ever known. My parents had told me that being a wife was my destiny for life. This programming was still with me, although it was slowly being chipped away.

A relationship had never brought me stability in the past. The opposite was true, when I truly thought about it. I had never felt more unsafe then when I had been married. While I was tied to a long-term commitment, I had felt unsettled, like there was more to life that I was missing out on. Mac had made me feel unsafe emotionally for as long as I could remember. Leaving was what had brought me peace. Comparing this relationship to the one with Arthur, I had a realization. Physical provision wasn't enough anymore. Arthur and Mac both had been financially stable at one time. Both offered to provide a home for me, if I gave them the chance. Both had told me they wanted the traditional marriage setting. While Arthur hadn't physically abused me, he hadn't made me feel safe either. The way he spoke about others made me feel unsafe to share with him my vulnerabilities, like being on state assistance.

I realized, slowly, that I needed emotional safety. I wasn't asking for too much. While I had thought that finding someone who wanted commitment, after my failed dating attempts with Brock and Austin, was the key, I realized that there was no magic formula. There was no list of boxes to check off that could define healthy in a partnership. I felt let down by the lies that society had fed to me, the promises that my parents had made to me. "If you be a good wife, if you stick it out, everything will work in your marriage!" They had always told me to work harder. They had told me to do more, to always look at myself to make sure I wasn't the problem. Now, I began to see that life made no promises.

After another three sessions in therapy, I had another realization. This man, this therapist, was the first male I had ever felt truly safe with. Obviously, as a professional, he was required to not hit on me, and this was part of it. However, it was more than the professional boundaries that made me feel safe. He never judged me. He told me every time I talked to him, that I was doing better than I could see. He encouraged me with college. He raved about how he was highly impressed with the fact that I was balancing all that life had handed me and still holding my head up. He never told me how to live my life, as I had assumed a therapist would. He pointed out when I was being too hard on myself, always encouraging me towards self-love.

He was in shock and horror at how my parents had treated me, validating that they had no ground for any of that behavior, *especially* as Christians. I began to open up more, sharing about the pain. He had many practical suggestions for the situation with Luke, which had gotten worse. At last, I knew it was time. After another week of Arthur going silent for several days, then begging for another chance, I told him it was completely done. I blocked him. While I believed that blocking and ghosting was childish, he hadn't respected my wishes to be left alone, when I had stated them clearly. He had called numerous times, messaged me that he missed me, and continued to do his part to allow this to drag out further and further, even against my wishes. I knew, this time, that I was ready to walk away.

Slowly, I was learning lessons. Now, it was time to choose myself. For a lot longer this time. I would take a long break from dating after this. I saw now, that choosing to be alone wasn't a sentence to loneliness. It was a beautiful "yes" to myself. A gift that I wanted to give myself, an oasis of healing after fighting many storms. I needed to focus on my children more, too. Things with Luke hadn't improved. At this point, he still fought me every day to go to school. He still begged to not go, and cried all the way into the building while being practically dragged by the teacher's assistant, so that I could get to work in time.

He couldn't sleep a lot of nights. One time, a couple of months before, I had found him in the backyard after 11 pm. He had sneaked out his window, unwilling to go to bed. I felt at loss for what to do most days, concerned for my son's safety and worried that I wouldn't hear him if he tried to do this after I was asleep. When I met with the school principal about the issues going on at school, bringing up the ones at home as well, she suggested a behavior chart, implying that if I could parent more firmly, the issues would vanish.

I was hard on myself about my parenting already. I knew about behavior charts; we used them daily at work. I had tried one with Luke already, and while it seemed to work for the first few weeks, it didn't appear to be a long-term solution. I continued trying other options, not willing to give up. Meanwhile, the after-school daycare had become a nightmare. My children had picked up multiple bad habits from the older children who lived there. When my seven-year-old came home and flipped me off, I was finished. The woman that ran it refused to discipline her children and mine were learning to talk back in the same way. While I understood that being busy made it harder to discipline, I felt that this was not the environment for my kids. When another parent reported the childcare for concerns of a different kind, the woman underwent investigation by child protective services. I hadn't been able to find a different childcare in the past, but now there was one available. This new woman didn't speak English, so that made things hard. I decided, however, to give her a chance.

Chapter Sixty-Four

As fall turned to winter, life began to settle somewhat. I was in my second year of college now. I was 26, beautiful, had a budding career, a stable home, aside from the issues with Luke, and a bright future. I was free to do as I chose. In January, I found a larger home, in a city with a community preschool that my daughter could attend for free. My son would be able to attend the community after school program, taking him out of the home daycare that had proved to be only slightly better than the last. I would be closer to both my work, and the community college. In person classes were beginning to open, so I wanted to attend one. Things were looking up.

I competed again, this time winning the award of most improved lifter, along with multiple medals, and setting a state record. I applied for the full ride scholarship again, as soon as the application opened in February. I picked up a third client with the new ABA company. I was awarded therapist of the month for my area, twice. I was making progress in personal therapy. Things continued to get worse with my son, however. He had gone to therapy, which had resulted in more trauma. The building where the therapist worked out of housed many other therapists. One therapist, who couldn't stand me or Luke, had yelled at him when he had refused to wear a mask in the waiting room. I had explained that we were here because he had mental health issues, so expecting him to behave in the same way that an adult did, was unrealistic. This was what the facility was for, was it not? The scene had ended with both myself and Luke in tears.

The psychiatrist recommended different meds after that. My therapist, the only one who actually supported me through all of this, suggested I reach out to the pastor of my church and ask if he would talk with Luke. Things at church hadn't improved much. Most Sundays, the attendants asked me to come get Luke from the kids' class, after he refused to participate. I would sit in the lobby, fighting tears, determined to stay and honor God. I wanted a God centered life. I wanted to be a part of the church, although I felt ignored by the members. It felt as though there was no room for single moms at this church. I wondered, if I had been a widow, would they have felt differently about me? Would the whole church have stepped up and offered to support me, recognizing what I was going through, instead of turning my son away due to his behaviors?

I didn't know. I wanted to believe in the power of God, but I wasn't sure it could be found in a church anymore. When I finally worked up the courage to take my therapist's suggestion and reach out to the pastor, my disappointment was only reinforced. The pastor's secretary told me that the youth pastor was away on a mission in Boston, helping the homeless population. He would reach out when he returned in a few days. He never did. I wondered why homeless people across the country were more important than single moms in the church. Why was it that I was being overlooked? Why was it that I was either met with stares of judgment from the two parent families, or ignored all together? The only one who had even acknowledged me had been another single momma who had seen me one day, bawling my eyes out in the back row. It had been a tough morning for Luke and when I got into the service, the pastor was talking about the challenges that fathers face as they protect and provide for their families, and the challenges that mothers face as they care for their children and the home. As he had talked, the sadness had welled up in me. I was doing both. I was caring for, nurturing, and loving my children, while also providing for them financially. I was paying for a roof over their heads and the food they ate, as well as protecting them in the best way I knew how. Being either a father or a mother was already a tough job, but what about being both? How much harder of a job did I have? Yet, I wasn't acknowledged. I was thrown out by my family, ignored by the church, and abandoned by my children's father, left to carry the burden alone.

As I had begun to cry, trying to not make a scene, a woman had come up and sat next to me, quietly putting an arm around me and offering me tissues. At the end of the service, she had asked how she could pray for me. She had introduced herself as Heather. Later, over coffee, she had explained that her husband of thirty years had left her for another woman, and she had been forced to take on the role of both parents while raising her teenagers. She had acknowledged my struggle, noting that she also felt there wasn't much of a place for her in an environment with only two parent families. She had been the only one, though. It seemed so backwards. The church said that they would welcome all, and yet, just as my parents had not acknowledged me, neither did the church. It made no sense and I began to question God even more.

Even with all my questions, I didn't have time to stop and dwell on anything. I was busy trying to keep up. I had agreed to work in the mountains again, so I spent every other weekend working Friday night, driving to the mountain, driving back Saturday night and working again, then going home Sunday to catch up on school work and go to the gym before picking up the kids. Things had been going well with the kids' father since Thanksgiving, when he had started dating a new girl. Clearly, she was good for him. There was no remorse or resentment on my part. She spoiled my children, and although I couldn't afford to buy them as many toys as she did, I felt thankful that someone was doing it and that they had someone like her to look after them when they went to spend weekends with Mac.

I hoped he could make things work with her. The kids loved her and talked about her regularly. Mac was even dressing nicely again; when he showed up to pick up the children, often in her car since his had broken, he would wear new designer jeans and a clean shirt. I hoped this meant he wasn't partying as much these days. More than anything, though, I was honestly thankful that he had a distraction from terrorizing me. I prayed it worked out for them.

One Sunday, I knew things had changed for the worse. Mac called me, angry that I hadn't asked him before moving. I was under no obligation to, but he felt, as the kid's dad, that he should have had a say. He yelled and cussed at me, then spoke quietly as he told me that, until

I told him exactly where the new house was, he wouldn't return the children to me. I freaked out. Calling the sheriff, I explained the situation. Unfortunately, the sheriff told me, there was nothing he could do. I would have to take this up with the court if I wanted my children back. I explained that there was drug use. He reaffirmed that he couldn't legally take action to get my children back. Still panicking, I decided to go to the pick-up spot anyway. I knew that, often, Mac would threaten me with things to try to get me to do what he wanted.

I hoped he knew better than to threaten me with taking the kids away. Still, thoughts began racing through my head. What if he took the kids and left the state? Or the country? They were at the mercy of his mood tonight. If he left the state, a different one would have no jurisdiction to remove them from him or even track them down. They were his children, legally, so no one else would see the danger that I sensed. Sitting in my car, in the dark, I began to pray. I focused on God's power, begging him to bring my children to me. I had been waiting for half an hour, when I saw my ex pull up, this time in a car I had never seen. He got out and began getting Carroll out.

Luke climbed out on his own, carrying the guitar he had been given at Christmas by Mac's girlfriend. I sighed in relief, sucking in a breath of air as I breathed out a silent prayer of thanks. I helped the children get into their seats, feeling the negative energy as it oozed out of Mac and his aura. I prayed once again, as I buckled Carroll in, begging for safety for all of us this time. Mac didn't have words for me, other than to say, "you better tell me where you live, or I'll figure it out on my own, and *then* you'll be sorry." He glared at me as he got into the car he was borrowing.

I waited for him to leave, his lights disappearing down the road in the opposite direction as me, before I started the car. Taking in another shaky breath, I looked at both kids, who were settled into the back. "How did it go, guys?" They both started talking at once. "Dad said he was going to run in front of a semi and kill himself!" Carroll blurted out. "I was scared," said Luke. "I thought he was actually going to do it and then we would have been all alone". "Dad wasn't home most of the time," Luke added. "What do you mean?" I was concerned. "Well, he slept a lot and then he left for a while," he explained. Luke continued, saying that they had eaten only cold cereal because Dad hadn't fed them.

They had looked for other food, but there was nothing in the house. This wasn't the first time I had heard this. Before he had found this girlfriend, they had told me about other times they had needed to fend for themselves. Multiple times, women had stayed the night, so Mac had been unavailable to get them ready for bed or take care of them. After receiving this information, I knew exactly what I needed to do. I wasn't excited about rocking the boat, but I knew that this was in the best interest of my children. On Monday, I sent a kind email to Mac.

Hello Mac,

I am reaching out to let you know that, as per our parenting plan, I am asking that you do a drug test before the next visit with the children. It should only take a couple of days to process, and it costs about $50.

Sincerely, Sharon

I had listed all the facilities locally that offered drug testing. I had a bad feeling; for something like this to happen, drugs must be involved. I never received a response from Mac at all. When two weeks had gone by, I showed up to the assigned meeting place, hoping that maybe he had brought the test with him and would communicate with me now. I wanted the children to see him, but at the same time, I knew their safety came first. If he didn't show this weekend, I would miss 30 hours of work. I was scheduled for two nights shifts as a caregiver, and one full day at the mountain. At the meetup spot, I waited for twenty minutes. I left then, calling my parents. They agreed to watch my children, provided I brought them to their house that night. I let my work know I wouldn't be able to start until 10 pm.

It was 6, but it would take me two hours to drive to my parents' house. I later received a call from Mac, which I didn't answer. He explained that he had never gotten my email. I knew I was under no obligation to respond, but I sent him a picture of it, just to be sure he had a copy. He never responded again. Exhausted, I arrived at work after four hours in the car that night. I was fighting not only sleep, but also tears. They would have to wait though. At least the kids were safe with my parents.

Several weeks later, I received a message from someone who had known Mac since high school. She felt it was time to let me know the truth, but she asked that I never tell Mac she had contacted me. Mac had been using heroin and meth since she had known him when he was 17, she informed me. I was in shock. I had known about the cocaine, but the meth and heroine surprised me. The mood swings suddenly made more sense. The constant need for Mac to spend money, the fact that it hadn't all reflected on our joint account, the fact that he would disappear for hours, it all added up. I had thought he was out hunting or hiking, but in reality, he had likely been getting high off a drug somewhere many of those times. The news came as a cold hard slap in the face, but also as a wake-up call. My intuition had been right all along.

I had felt deeply that drugs were involved, but he had always sworn that it was a lie. His mom had said she couldn't imagine him choosing to use a drug. Everyone had told me it was my imagination, even my parents. They had said I was looking for the bad in the situation, that he was a good man who was doing his best. And yet, here I was facing the truth. From then on, I decided, I would listen to the gut feeling more.

Chapter Sixty-Five

After that week, I didn't hear from Mac again. There was no message begging to see his children. There was no drug test, proving why it would have been fine for them to go to the scheduled visits. There was no phone call, even, asking to speak with them. I was sad that it had been that easy for him to give up time with them. Still, I felt much safer knowing they were only with me, at school, and at the after-school program. I could once again sleep at night, knowing that my babies were safe. I still had the nightmares, waking up in a cold sweat often, going to check that my doors were locked. I would peer into the darkness, praying to God I didn't see his truck outside. I could never sleep after these episodes, so I spent many nights sitting on the living room carpet, shivering in the dark. Eventually, I would put on sweatpants and turn on the laptop to study.

School helped me take my mind off it and I was thankful for that, especially during those long nights. The dreams began to change, too. One night, I dreamed my dad was trying to teach me how to have sex. I was young and unmarried, so he felt it was his duty. I had that dream multiple times after that, always waking up feeling dirty and wanting to scrub my skin with gravel. I was tormented by the ghosts of my pasts, finally in a place where I was beginning to process things.

I realized then, that I had spent the last two years in survival mode, just trying to keep a roof over my head. Now that things were stable, the past was coming back to haunt me. I had a safe home, reliable childcare, a good job, and an education in the making. I was beautiful and young, and had physically healthy children, who were safe with me. Still, these things didn't undo the trauma that I had faced, not only in an abusive marriage, but also at the hand of a father who abused me under the guise of being the mediator between myself and God. The more I thought about it, the more I saw how his reign over his family had been about control, not about leading the family spiritually. I still wanted to see him in a good light. He was my father.

Deep down, I still wanted him to be proud of me, even though I knew he would never change. I still felt like a little girl, begging for the approval of her father. On a subconscious level, I began to understand that this was why I had given men like Brock so many chances. This was why I had accepted him back in after being given less than the bare minimum, being lied to and played with, and yet still believing it was my fault when he ghosted me. I wouldn't have done that if proper love had been modeled to me as a child. I wouldn't have picked Mac when I was 18 either. However, I knew that my father had picked Mac more than I had.

As a girl who had just gotten engaged, I remembered someone asking me, *how did you know this was the one*? "Well, my dad approved," I had said. "I trust his judgment completely so I know I am marrying the right one." Now I was beginning to see the truth. My dad had picked a man like himself, only worse. He had picked a man who would lead by control. He had always taught me that blindly following was the woman's place. He was the go between when it came to God's will. When I had asked him one time, what if God told me to do something that went against my father's wishes, he had replied that God would never ask a child to disobey their parent. While this had seemed valid at the time, I had been 18. He had assumed that, as was customary thousands of years ago, women were under the leadership of their father until they came under the leadership of their husband. Even as an adult, I had no right to make my own decisions.

This mindset hadn't set me up for success. It had set me up for abuse and living in chains at the will of another. How could I truly have a relationship with God, if I was meant to only take my father or my husband's word for the voice of God? I thought back to all the times that my ex had told me how sad God would be if I left him. He had reminded me again and again, that God didn't approve of divorce. God didn't even approve of my going to the gym, he had said. But how had he known? Even the Bible said that women were to strengthen themselves physically, as part of becoming the ideal woman. And yet, I had blindly followed. Not out of devotion, but out of fear.

Out of the fear that he would leave me for another. Without a husband, according to my father, I was nothing. Without the title of wife, my life was valueless, according to my father. That was my whole identity. No wonder he had gotten so angry when I told someone that my mother was treated like a doormat. He had called me, asking me to explain why I would say something like that. When I explained that he expected her to do all the housework, to wait upon him like a servant, to bring him meals to his home office so that he didn't even have to look up from his work, and that she had no say whatsoever in their affairs, he became angry. He accused me of being rebellious, saying he was disappointed he had raised a daughter to be so ungodly. He said it was no wonder Mac was struggling, with how I was becoming. He reminded me that controlling one's wife was a hard job; Mac was doing his best.

He told me then, too, that my mom wasn't a doormat. I was completely wrong. I had hurt her feelings by saying that. I had agreed with him then, knowing the conversation would continue until he got his way and I agreed. With him, it didn't matter what the facts were. He was right, no matter what. The argument wasn't over until he was right.

The last time I had gone to see them, I had cringed as my brothers began making fun of my mom for something she had said the week before in public. They laughed, talking amongst themselves, at the dinner table, while she silently prepared the meal. I knew they had gotten this habit from their father. How many times had my dad come down from his home office, talking about my mom, in front of her, not including her? He said it was playful and he was teasing her, but making fun of her for small things, like getting someone's name mixed up, or buying the wrong brand of a health food product he had instructed her to buy, was rude. She never defended herself.

Once upon a time she had, but my dad always won the arguments by putting his foot down as a man. He would say, "it is because I said so. End of conversation." In a halfway joking manner, that really said, if you continue this conversation, I will get defensive and then upset that you disagree with me. During this same visit with my family, both of my brothers began arguing with me about how I shouldn't have left Mac. When they brought him up, they said it was sad how he had been drinking recently. Even *they* acknowledged the drug use now as well. He had admitted it to them, telling them how hard it had been since I had left. They had brought this up, telling me that he never would have turned to drugs if I had been there for him through the hard time.

They looked at each other then, shaking their heads in disappointment. "I probably would have done the same things as Mac if my wife had betrayed me," said my middle brother. The oldest nodded, reminding me of a relevant Bible verse. "You know that the Bible doesn't justify divorce, right Sharon? You are living in sin, even now. You can run from the truth, but it doesn't make it any less true. Eventually, your sin will catch up with you!" My sister had chimed in then, reminding me that I had chosen this man. "Father didn't like him even from day one!" She had added, telling me that she had a feeling about him even back then. "I never would have chosen a man like that, after seeing how he acted".

I wondered what she meant. She had been jealous of me, talking only of how unfair it was that she lived at her parents still. She was always searching for a new man who would sweep her off her feet. She had always accepted the attention from Mac, not telling me about the incidents until at least a year after they had begun. True, she may not have known the full extent of his intentions toward her, but she had texted him back all those times. She had carried on conversations, offered to spend time alone with him whenever we went to visit, and had only told me after he had finally tried taking pictures of her.

Yet, she wanted to remind me how I had been wrong for choosing him. After this lecture from my family, I had packed up the kids and left, shedding tears as soon as I was driving down the long gravel driveway. It was no use. They would never see the truth, regardless.

Chapter Sixty-Six

As spring began to emerge from the cold, rainy days of winter, life began to improve. In April, I received an email invite: I had been selected for an interview with the scholarship committee! I was overjoyed to have made it this far. When the morning came to join the meeting, I took several deep breathes, sitting at my kitchen table, fixing my hair in the zoom camera before joining. I would be transferring to the university in the fall. Now was the time, if any, to get awarded this scholarship. If I didn't, I would surely end up with student loans. As I waited to be admitted to the meeting, I prayed for calmness. I would show up as myself. If they didn't like that, then it wouldn't be any use anyway.

The interview went well. I was asked some basic questions pertaining to my education plan. I was asked to explain how this scholarship would benefit me. Knowing that it would pay for my entire degree, I explained my life long goal of staying debt free. At the end, I was asked if there was anything else I wanted to add. "I just want you guys to know, I am working hard and I will reach these goals. I am almost halfway there, and if anyone has ever pulled themselves out of a dark time, it was me. I will not disappoint the foundation if I am awarded this scholarship." I then briefly explained my year in the yurt, the abusive relationship, and the struggles with the kids. I felt embarrassed, admitting to being a victim of domestic violence. However, I knew it was the truth, and that now was the time to speak my truth. I thanked the committee and signed off. Now, it was up to the universe to make the decision. I had done my part.

Spring continued on toward summer, bringing with it hot weather, longer days, and sunburns. I spent a lot of time at work, excited as I watched the progress of multiple children I was helping. Issues with Luke continued to escalate, and I continued to try to attend church anyway. Church was now outdoors, so I hoped it would be easier. It wasn't. One Sunday, I decided to try the church that Greta was attending.

Greta, the woman who had reached out to me so long ago after her own divorce and escape from abuse, had become a dear friend. We had become close during the last two years. One day I discovered by accident that she lived two blocks from me. When I had gone through the breakup with Arthur, she had followed suit, having to walk away from a three-year relationship shortly after. What had started as a way to console each other from the pain had quickly turned into the two of us becoming soul sisters. We talked about everything, often calling each other only to begin bawling on Facetime, no words needed.

Having decided to try her church, I liked the smaller atmosphere. My kids seemed to do okay in the classroom the first time, so I went again. It was on the third visit, however, that my name was called over the speaker by the pastor, interrupting the worship songs. "Your child is acting up and you need to get him from kids care," he had said.

After that, I decided that a hiatus from church was in order. There was something more spiritual for me, and I would find it with time. Taking a break from church didn't mean that I was not spiritual. Being a single parent was hard. Doing it alone was harder. Ever since Mac had stopped taking the children, I had needed to adjust my work schedule. I was no longer able to work weekends, so my income had declined by 50 hours per month. I was stressed about money, feeling the weight of the world now more than ever. I had no clue how I would make it if I didn't get the scholarship. Still, I chose to stay positive. Something told me that I had what it took to be successful. I didn't need to stress the details. I was doing everything I could to survive and the universe was listening to my needs.

I had chosen to take summer classes and take them in person. Now that COVID was close to being done, I knew taking in-person classes would be easier. I arrived at my first day of summer term two hours early. I had worked a morning session with a client, coming straight to the college building afterwards to study in the quiet room. I had a virtual class at 10, followed by study time, and then a science class at 12.

When I walked in to the biology room, I noted the professor, who I had seen earlier in the day when he had walked in to print something in the quiet room. He had smiled at me then and he greeted me kindly now. I felt instantly at ease. He introduced himself as Instructor Peterson. He was tall, with a shaved head and a clean-cut face that wore lines from the stresses of a hard life. He was about 50 and had a booming voice that made everyone pay attention, although not in an unkind way. He wore wire rimmed glasses that perched on the end of his short nose.

As class began, he patiently helped each student get set up. He started with a short introduction about his own experience. He explained how he had been a single parent of 3 children. He had faced homelessness, job insecurity, and was the first in his family to go to school. He had worked as a stone mason, carrying heavy bricks all day, while trying to care for his children alone. One day, he had injured his back at work. This had led to a disability that made him realize something. Getting an education may be the only way for him to move up in the world without working an overly physical job that would break his body down. He had decided to pursue an education through a grant that was available to him. It had been hard, but he had eventually finished, squeaking by with C's and D's at first, to eventually graduate with his PhD as an honors student when his oldest child was 15.

He ended with saying that, if he could do it, all of us could do it, and we could do it better. I had felt inspired instantly. Halfway through the class, my son's school had called. I had needed to take the call, stepping out and excusing myself. When I was done, and at the end of the class, I waited for the others to leave. In private, I explained the situation with my son. I told him that I was also a single parent. He told me that he was working for me, not the other way around. He would do whatever it took for me to be successful in this class. He believed in me. Right then, I had a good feeling about this man. I was so thankful my angels had aligned me to be in his class.

One day in June, I received an email that changed my life. I was sitting in an unexciting virtual class, trying to stay awake, when I noticed I had an email from the scholarship foundation. The subject line read "Congrats Scholar!" I opened it, not believing what I was reading.

Dear Sharon,

We are pleased to inform you that you have been chosen to be a recipient of our class of 2022 scholarship! We are inviting you to a Zoom orientation, to take place two weeks from today at 1 pm. We hope to see you there. Congratulations on your hard work and achievement! Being selected is no small feat, and we are so extremely proud of your work thus far. We feel you will represent our organization positively as you proceed with your education!

Sincerely, the Scholarship Committee

It was all I could do to not cry. My camera was still on, so I couldn't respond. I took a sharp breath in, unable to control the emotions I was feeling. A flood was coming and I couldn't stop it. I had worked so hard to get to this point. Deep down, I had felt I would be awarded this, but to have, in writing, that they had chosen *me*, was almost too much. Me, the girl who had been afraid of my ex. Me, the girl who was supposed to be a stay-at-home wife, the one who was supposed to spend her life cleaning and cooking and building up a man. Me, the one whose family believed she had ruined her life by leaving Mac.

Me, the woman whose child was kicked out of Sunday school every week, the one whom the church couldn't bear to look at or accept because I was a single mom. Me, the one who had been ghosted, lied to, and abused. Also, the one who was an honors student, the woman who was working three jobs while raising two kids alone, the one who had overcome abuse, who had been resilient, the one who had just paid off the last of the bills from an ugly divorce, the one who had rebuilt her life. *They had chosen me.* I blinked, reading it all again, wiping away a stubborn tear that had rolled down my cheek, unbidden. Everything was truly changing for me, for the better. God had heard me! He had chosen me; he had blessed me far beyond what I could even imagine. This was a true miracle.

Chapter Sixty-Seven

Four Months Later

I stood on top of the hill, scanning the valley below, breathing heavily. I could see far out above the trees, looking to a mountain in the distance that still had snow on the very tip. Beyond this, the clouds settled at the horizon, floating like a white blanket that shrouded the world below in mist and grayness. Above me, a few clouds floated, in front of the sun, and then drifted away again, warming my back as the sun peeked out from behind them. Directly below me, the brown and dry grass of late summer grew in little tufts between the cracks in the rock I stood on. The rock dropped off steeply to the east, revealing a cliff, and below that was a long sloping hill that looked like mountain goats would have inhabited it. Small pumice rocks were scattered across the hill.

The only other growing things were late summer bushes that had begun to shed their leaves for fall. Although it wasn't officially fall yet, it was almost time. I could feel the changes deeply. As if on cue, the wind blew then, rustling the leaves of the bushes, blowing my straightened hair off my face and shoulders, cooling me off just a bit. It was warm, probably close to 80, so the wind felt good. I closed my eyes, breathing deeply. After another moment, I turned, walking back down the dusty trail towards my car. So much was about to change. Today had been my last day with clients. Because of getting the scholarship, I was able to let my supervisor know I would be resigning to focus on school. My dream, this dream that I had built for so long, was coming true. I would be able to graduate debt free. I had been awarded enough that, with the help of the scholarship, and the state assistance I was receiving, I could afford to pay my bills without a full-time job. I would be able to focus on college and my children. A week from today would be my first day at the university. I had signed up for 12 credits at the university, and an additional 8 through the community college, for a total of 20 credits for fall term. The advisor had told me I was crazy, in very professional terms. "Have you thought this through completely?" she had asked. Patiently, I had explained that I had spent the first two years of my educational career taking 11 credits per term and working three jobs, while also raising my kids almost completely on my own. Her jaw had dropped; she was speechless. I had smiled, telling her that I could always drop a course if I needed to.

While I was nervous, I believed I could maximize my education by getting it done faster. Carroll was now in a state-run preschool that offered after school care on site; having reliable care for both children helped. I knew I would manage. The kid's dad hadn't contacted me again, but I had received a call from our old landlord the night prior. He wanted to meet me the next day, at the house. Mac no longer lived there. He would explain all of it.

When I arrived the next morning, having purposely scheduled this for when the children were at school, I took in a deep breath, before slowly getting out of my car. Jeremy, the landlord, was sitting in his red truck waiting for me. When I got out, he did too. He walked over to me slowly, waving the traditional greeting that so many had adopted since the pandemic. He stood a respectable distance from me as he said, "Hi, asking how everything was going?" I didn't want to give him too much information, not knowing if he was friends with Mac still or not. However, when he began to explain, I felt more at ease.

He began by telling me that, after I had moved out, he had been disappointed to see that the lawn never got mowed and the weeds never got pulled. The yard began to look uninhabited almost instantly. He said that Mac had told him and many others how I was a terrible person who had ruined his life. There had been nothing but negative talk about me, since the day I had left. At first, he had believed it, but after seeing how things began to change visually for the property, he had gained more understanding.

This had led to him gaining more respect for me and my situation, even without talking with me directly. He then told me that he hadn't received a rent payment for over a year. Mac had apparently moved a roommate in, who paid half of the rent every month. However, when the roommate had told Jeremy about this, the truth was exposed. Mac had never given that half of the rent to the landlord, instead stealing it each month. I was then told that Mac had moved to a different city to stay with a new girl. Jeremy wanted to give me the chance to get whatever stuff I wanted, before he began taking everything to the dump. This was my chance to say goodbye, not only to the house, but also to this life I had previously lived here. He told me that he would leave, and I was to simply lock the doors when I finished. He said there wasn't much of value left inside; either Mac had pawned it all, or someone had gone through it before they had told Jeremy that it was vacated. He had one more thing to tell me. Kitten, the hound pup that my children had loved, the queen of eating from the trash bin, was dead. Mac had shot her, after neglecting to feed her or walk her for days on end, when he would leave her in the kennel. My children would be heartbroken.

With that, the landlord got into his truck and left. I stood there alone for a moment, not ready to enter. This house held so many memories. This had been my home for so long. This had been the basis of a life that no longer was. Again, I breathed deeply, thankful the children weren't here. I walked up the front step, turning the door handle slowly, pushing it open a few inches. I halfway expected to be met by an angry Mac, so intense had the emotions been the last time I had been here.

Alone inside the door, I shut it carefully, sighing quietly as I stood, taking it all in. The house opened straight into the kitchen, so I looked that way first. The counters were coated with dust. None of the appliances were there. Only a can of instant coffee sat on the outdated, brown linoleum countertop. Opening the fridge, I saw long expired milk and a half empty jar of pickles. An empty vodka bottle sat on top of the fridge. The sink was filled with beer cans. When I pulled open a drawer, I found it full of unopened condoms. Disgusted, I wished I was wearing gloves. I hoped I didn't pick up any disease and that there was no paraphernalia from the drugs left anywhere.

As I stood there, silently taking in how much my kitchen had changed, a memory came to me; painting this kitchen blue and yellow. I had spent many afternoons on this project, sanding down the outdated cupboard fronts to replace what had once been an ugly brown, with bright yellow hues. I had painted the drawer ends blue, contrasting the yellow. It had been home back then and we had been a family. Mac had come home from work, telling me how good it had looked. He probably hadn't cared, but he had made an effort back then.

Luke had been a baby, jumping up and down in his walker in the living room. Mac had picked him up, talking to him for a moment before bouncing into the kitchen and kissing me on the lips and then hugging me, dirty work clothing and all. He had loved me back then, at least I thought so. I sighed, walking into the living room. The old couch with the flower pattern was still there. The couch I had napped on during the pains of my daughter's birth. The couch I had sat on with both of my children, reading the same books again and again when Luke was two and begged for them. Also, the couch that Mac had sat on when he had tried to kiss my sister. Disgusted at the thought, I walked towards the bedroom.

What had once been *our* bedroom. I was almost afraid of what I would find, but I opened the door anyway. There was a layer of dust on the king-sized bed and a pile of Mac's old clothes on the floor. I wondered if the kids' skis were still under the bed. Opening the storage section of the bed frame, I found it to be empty. Of course. These items were worth money. I sighed, turning around. On the headstand of the bed lay Macs Bible, the one his mother had given him at our wedding. Apparently, it hadn't made the cut when it came to what he was to take with him. Picking it up, I noticed a piece of yellow sheet paper sticking out. It fell out.

I wouldn't have thought anything of it, but I saw that the writing was familiar. It was my mother's handwriting. Picking the note up, I read. It was dated February 25, 2022. This was the weekend that my parents had watched my children because Mac had refused to take the drug test. This was the weekend that I had needed to work and I had entrusted my precious children to my parents.

Dear Mac,

I am writing because we tried to contact you but your phone didn't go through. We had the children this weekend. I am sorry Sharon has kept them from you. We tried to get a hold of you so that you could come and get them before she came back. Hopefully we can catch up with you soon and give your children back to you. All my

Love, Mother

I stood, in shock. I had known my parents didn't agree with my leaving him, but to go behind my back like this? I was astounded. How could they put my children at risk in this way? They knew about the drug use! They knew about the abuse, and yet they would give my children away like this? I didn't know how to respond. A wave of grief washed over me then and I knew things would need to change between my family and me. There would be no more begging for their approval, no more being the one to drive and see them, no more putting in effort to show them how I was living a respectable life, and no more entrusting my children to them. I had had enough abuse for one lifetime. It would stop now. They had lived with the blessing of me in their lives for long enough. I would choose myself from now on, even though that meant cutting them off completely.

After finding the letter, I suddenly felt the negativity of the energy in the room. I needed to get out. As I walked past both of the kids' rooms, I noticed that at least there were clothes in there. This would help me out, if any of them still fit. I would go through those later. Walking through the living room, a memory flooded to me, unchecked in its vivid detail. This was the room in which I had delivered my daughter. The daughter we had conceived, out of love, I had thought. I realized then, as I stood recalling the details of the birth, that for him it had never been love, for he was uncapable of love. For him, it had been lust.

He couldn't know love, but only desire, needs fulfilled. *This* was the absolute truth. I had loved him in the best way that I had known how. I had *truly* loved. Yes, I had been childish at times, immature in my youth, but it had been love. As I thought of my daughter, and then my son, I felt thankful for their existence. I had born them out of love, and regardless of this painful ending, I knew that they would be cherished and loved their whole lives. I knew that I would do whatever it took; I would move mountains to protect them, to shield them from the negative forces that threatened to take away the happiness from our lives. I felt at peace suddenly. I headed towards the garage then, hoping against hope that some of my food preserving items were still there. They weren't. It seemed that Mac had sold anything that held any monetary value at all. I opened the back door, stepping from the garage into the backyard. Kittens' kennel sat on the concrete pad, empty. My heart squeezed in pain. Some things would never make sense. I looked toward the chicken pen where my hens had once roamed, digging for worms and living their best life as they created eggs for our family. It was empty, one side falling in on itself. The little garden spot, which would have been yielding heirloom tomatoes for preserving about this time of the year, had grown tufts of grass after being ignored for all this time.

There, beside the garden, was the pile of old tires I had filled with soil to make a vertical potato growing garden bed. Next, I noticed the posts from what had been my raspberry trellis. I sighed, seeing no beautiful green leaves. There were no juicy berries for my children to eat off the vine before I had a chance to pick them and bake anything with them. The bark dust I had so carefully wheeled in with the hand cart, was buried under a layer of grass and dandelions. The grape trellis was overgrown to the point that it was hard to see if it was even there. The woodpile, which had kept our family warm throughout five winters together, stood destitute.

A round of unsplit wood lay next to a metal garden post, probably abandoned because it had a knot in it that made it impenetrable by the ax. Turning to where my herb garden had been, I saw only weeds. The grass was patchy with big holes where Kitten had dug, likely out of boredom. She had never been cared for properly. I wished I had had a way to take her with us. Even if I had tried, Mac wouldn't have allowed it. He would have said that she was his dog, probably threatening me even more. A pang of guilt hit me, even though I knew that her fate hadn't been my fault. I wiped my face on my shoulder, trying to get the stubborn tears to go away. My hands were dirty and I was worried about getting an infection. Still, the tears came. I stood for a moment, allowing them to flow freely.

This had been good for me. I would bring the children, not for the sake of fun, but so that they could see the truth and move on. This was closure. In a way, this had needed to happen. A thought came to me then, like a gentle breeze. A whisper in my ear, reminding me of all the days I had spent on my knees, in this yard, in this house, begging for strength. I had asked God to make me strong. He had. Through a painful process of growth, my strength had slowly built up. I was truly *becoming strength*. I walked out of the house then, leaving behind my old life as I welcomed the new.

Epilogue

A while ago, after visiting many different churches, and getting the same result from many different religious organizations, I felt a call from my soul. I knew there was more for me, spiritually. Through a painful awakening process that followed, I came to understand spirituality differently. I came to see religion much like any other addiction. I had witnessed this in my parents, Mac's family and their church, and the churches I attended. Many had chosen to follow religion as a way to devote themselves to something that had rules. With rules, one is safe as long as they follow them. There is no need to think for oneself. Organized religion, I realized, provided the safety net of structure that justifies abuse and controlling behavior toward others. One can be a devout Christian, or Muslim, or Jew, or Mormon, or Mennonite, or any other religion, organized or not, and use this to harm and control innocent, unsuspecting victims.

If any person can claim to be in alignment with a higher force, and use this claim to get others to obey, that individual can keep hold of power. Greater than the fear of physical harm, is the fear of disobeying God, for many. This was the case for me. My fear of disobeying God kept me in abuse for a long time. On a deep level, it wasn't my fear of what my father would think if I left Mac, but the fear of what God would think, that kept me there. As long as I saw God as the head boss that only connected with me through a father or husband, I felt I must stay with Mac out of devotion to that God. When I came to see God as a powerful force of love, my life began to change. He was trying to get my attention all along. By providing financially and materially when I stood up to Mac and left, he was showing me.

Again, when He provided a hotel room to protect me from Mac. This continued to be a theme throughout. He was whispering to my soul, *I AM. There is no force more powerful than I AM, Sharon. It is I who is making a way. It is I who is delivering you from the hands of bondage and fear. It is I who is calling you to this new life.* He provided every step of the way and ultimately showed me that His will was *not* for me to live in fear. I was shown that fear, while crippling, has only the power we give it. Fear is fed by our own shadows. Fear is fed by what we imagine, what we choose to conjure in our darkest worries. When we shed light onto fear, we see that it is a lie. We see that *truth* is stronger. We see that any fear can be dissolved by the light of God.

In March of this year, I graduated with my Bachelor of Science in Human Development and Family Sciences, with a Minor in Psychology. I kept my grades high and was able to graduate Magma Cum Laude as an honors student. Instructor Peterson went on to become one of my close friends. He has helped watch my children more than once and we even began fishing together when he isn't teaching. He is a part of my soul family and I am thankful that college brought him to our family. The scholarship I got enabled me to graduate debt free. The foundation even offered to renew it for graduate school. While I plan to pursue more education, I've learned not to rush. Each event in life comes at the exact time that it is meant to, I have discovered. We are not behind. Our souls are right where they are meant to be. Time is a construct created by a society that wants everyone to fit into a mold. Our lives here on earth are such a tiny blip in the big picture.

Stressing or being hard on ourselves serves no higher purpose. With this in mind, I have learned to treat each day as a sacred blessing. I wake up with a clear vision of the mission I am here to fulfill. Currently, I homeschool Luke. After many more visits to doctors who told me to be a firmer parent, and then, that his condition was non-existent, when parenting "better" didn't work, I finally pushed for more answers. After finally being connected with doctors who actually cared, and running many tests, I realized that his case was complex; he has medical issues that make it much harder for him to manage his behaviors and even interfere with his learning. It turned out that blaming his behavior on my parenting was another lie that had been fed to me by many who didn't understand, who wanted to keep me in fear. I learned that digging deeper and not accepting answers until I knew the absolute truth, was the only way to succeed when dealing with illness and the medical system.

I was finally able to release the guilt of feeling that I should take the blame for my son's unexplainable condition. This knowledge has led us on a long journey to find the cause of his diagnosis, so that we may give my son a true healing. While we don't have all of the answers yet, I fully believe that we will get them at the correct time.

After all of my experiences with dating, I have come to understand love differently as well. It turns out that I was right when I felt that hook ups were unfulfilling. I was right when I felt that true love should be based on deep, mutual, soul level connections. It is more than meeting physical desires and checking boxes. True love also requires firm boundaries. It requires standing up for the right kind of treatment and being willing to walk away from any partner who chooses to not value both themselves and others. While I learned a lot about true love, what it's not *and* what it *is,* I didn't realize, initially, that to find love, you truly have to *become love.* However, how I learned all of that, is a different story entirely.

A Note About Abuse

While I was in the process of writing this book, I was contacted by multiple women who had gone through abuse at the hands of men like my ex-husband. Nearly all of them told me the same thing: they felt they were going crazy due to the lies and the gaslighting which ultimately had turned to physical abuse. By the time they contacted me, no one else believed their story. These women had covered the abuse for so long that, when they spoke up, no one listened. Often, their abuser had even tried reporting them to the authorities, claiming *they* had been the one to harm the abuser, even though the truth was, these women were defending themselves. If you are reading this and questioning if you are in an abusive relationship, seek help. Document *each and every* instance of physical or mental abuse. Take pictures. Call the police. TALK TO SOMEONE YOU TRUST! Do not fall victim to the fear that these abusers are desperately trying to use to control your life. Only by following this advice can one start the process to be truly free from abuse. There are many free resources where one can confidentially discuss the abuse without having to make a decision that will put them in danger or disrupt their lives. Many have waited until it is too late. Don't be the next victim.